Tom Cox lives in Devon. He is the author of, among others, the *Sunday Times* bestselling *The Good, The Bad and The Furry* and the William Hill Sports Book longlisted *Bring Me the Head of Sergio Garcia*.

21st-CENTURY YOKEL

TOM COX

This edition first published in 2017

Unbound
6th Floor Mutual House, 70 Conduit Street, London W1S 2GF

www.unbound.com

Text Design by PDQ

FSC
www.fsc.org

A CIP record for this book is available from the British Library

ISBN 978-1-78352-456-3 (trade hbk)
ISBN 978-1-78352-457-0 (ebook)
ISBN 978-1-78352-455-6 (limited edition)

Printed in Great Britain by Clays Ltd, St Ives Plc

1 3 5 7 9 8 6 4 2

For The Bear (1995–2016) and Shipley (2001–2017).
RIP, little magicians.

Take the scorn and wear the horn
it was the crest when you were born
your father's father wore it
and your father wore it too.

Hal-An-Tow (traditional)

Dear Reader,

The book you are holding came about in a rather different way to most others. It was funded directly by readers through a new website: Unbound. Unbound is the creation of three writers. We started the company because we believed there had to be a better deal for both writers and readers. On the Unbound website, authors share the ideas for the books they want to write directly with readers. If enough of you support the book by pledging for it in advance, we produce a beautifully bound special subscribers' edition and distribute a regular edition and e-book wherever books are sold, in shops and online.

This new way of publishing is actually a very old idea (Samuel Johnson funded his dictionary this way). We're just using the Internet to build each writer a network of patrons. At the back of this book you'll find the names of all the people who made it happen.

Publishing in this way means readers are no longer just passive consumers of the books they buy, and authors are free to write the books they really want. They get a much fairer return too – half the profits their books generate, rather than a tiny percentage of the cover price.

If you're not yet a subscriber, we hope that you'll want to join our publishing revolution and have your name listed in one of our books in the future. To get you started, here is a £5 discount on your first pledge. Just visit unbound.com, make your pledge and type **badger5** in the promo code box when you check out.

Thank you for your support,

Dan, Justin and John
Founders, Unbound

CONTENTS

1

WITCHES' KNICKERS

January. Haldon Hill, the border hill. Such a long, high wall in the sky as you approach it from the north-east, so thick with trees, always a tiny bit surprising that a few minutes later you can be on top of it in a car. Also surprising, perhaps, to my car itself, which lets out a harassed groan as I change gear for the final ascent. My ears pop hard as I reach the brow. It happens every time. When I've told hardy natives of the South West Peninsula the same thing, they have sometimes claimed I'm being overdramatic but I'm honestly not. Maybe it's because my sensitive eustachian tubes spent too many years living closer to sea level, in a more recumbent landscape, but the altitude is too much for them. 'Ppppop!' they go, as always, maybe even a bit louder than usual today. What that noise signifies to me is that I have entered the unofficial country that I call home, comprising Cornwall and the western two thirds of Devon.

Haldon rises, dividing the land, around six miles south-west of Exeter, which has always struck me as the most sarcastically named of small cities: a place that, when you're attempting to get out of it at rush hour, appears to have no exit at all. If you look at it another way, though, the name is apt. When you reside on the west side of Haldon Hill, as I do, Exeter feels like your exit to the rest of Britain: the beginning of that place which, when you've lived down here for any time at all, you start to think of as Everywhere Else. Draw a line directly south from Haldon's summit and you reach the exact point where the cliffs change colour – soft sandy red giving way to gnashing dark grey. Haldon seems like a barrier and must have seemed an even bigger one before it was tarmacked over with dual carriageway. Evidence of several sunken medieval lanes ascending the hill has been found on its east side, but almost none on its western slopes. Weary fourteenth-century travellers from the east would arrive at Lidwell Chapel near the eastern base of Haldon and receive offers of hot food and a bed for the night from Robert de Middlecote, the monk who lived there. Middlecote would then drug them, cut their throats and dump their bodies in the well in the chapel's garden – allegedly bottomless, like so much still water in folklore. 'Ooh, bloody hell, I'm not going over that,' you can imagine similarly weary Romans exclaiming, thirteen hundred years or so earlier, as Haldon came into view. 'We've done enough conquering, anyway. Let's just leave whoever lives over there to carry on cuddling boulders and worshipping trees, or whatever it is they do.' The

Deep South West was its own country then and remains so now. Making a home in it is still a commitment to a certain kind of life, with more potential to be a self-contained part of its own immediate surroundings. Pass over that long brow and the land begins to steepen and get more intimate with itself, employment becomes more scarce, communities become more scattered and the idea of a day trip to the middle of the country becomes more fatigue-inducing.

As often as not, you drive up to the top of Haldon in one kind of weather and descend in another. In Exeter today there's been squally showers and the lingering grey of a collective tetchy mood, but as I come down the opposite side, the sun switches on its spotlight function and illuminates the valley. Dartmoor streaks away in front of me on the right, unearthly and moody and promising and electric. They say in Devon that if you can't see the moor, it means it's raining, and if you can see it, it means it's about to rain. That's a comic exaggeration, of course, but not a huge one. Today the moor looks like a giant outdoor factory where witches make weather. There are countless small bright gaps in the sky, like holes stabbed in a tent roof to let the light in, then longer, bigger, more jagged gaps, as if the person in the tent has lost patience and gone at it with a bread knife. Some hills are enigmatically yellow in a way that doesn't seem to correspond with the cloud above them, others a dark green verging on black that's no less confusing. I can't get nonchalant about this view, and it's become even more fascinating to me as I've become more intimate with the moor. I will glance across and try to work out which shape or shade might denote a patch where I've walked. *Is that where the farm is that I walked past that time with the huge ball of wire outside with the variety of animal skulls placed in it?* I will think. *No. Perhaps that's a couple of miles further north. Maybe it's the wildflower meadow I was pursued across last April by a small, determined pig.*

I press on past Heaven and Hell Junction, Heaven being the moor and Hell staring it down from across the tarmac in the form of Trago Mills, the vast, grotesque shopping and leisure park whose toxic-waste-dumping, UKIP-supporting, wildlife-shooting owners the Robertson family once printed adverts calling for the castration of gay men. Up another big hill, past Ashburton Junction One and Ashburton Junction Two – the one which looks like my junction, that I take by mistake when I'm tired – and I'm home, or as good as, heading seawards on the smaller road where home begins in the most graspable sense: a zigzagging one, full of roller-coaster dips and climbs. To the right of the road is the River Dart and, because the road attempts to use the river as its guide, it is at the constant mercy of its indecision. All the Dartmoor rivers are capricious, but none that race down from the moor prevaricate about their route more often than the Dart. The hills here are not like those in Somerset or east Devon, which have wide valleys and plains between them; they are a community, bunching together as if nervously fearing solitude. The Dart finds the tight rare spaces between them and curls around them at flamboyant length, making its scenic way to the ocean.

Just two of the hills in this post-moor, pre-coast landscape rise up in a more noticeable, individual way. Unlike most of their less spellbinding neighbours, both of them are known locally by name. The bulkier of the two is called Hood Ball Hill, a corpulent sovereign of a hill topped with a copse somewhat resembling a mullet haircut. Its lankier neighbour, around a mile away, is called Yarner Beacon, although it was initially introduced to me as the Dragon's Hoof, a name that became even more appealing upon my failure to substantiate it using any historical or electronic source.

At Hood Ball Hill's foot, as well as the river and the bridge where the road crosses to the water's eastern bank, is the track belonging to the Buckfastleigh to Totnes tourist railway. The steam from the trains that run along this enhance the hill's mystic quality like dry ice around the ankles of a wizard. Talk to the more shamanistically inclined around here and they might tell you that Hood Ball Hill is the Atlantean Temple of the Moon, to which people have been known to travel many miles in order to face their shadow, or at least that a ley line passes directly through its centre, carrying mellow vibes down from Glastonbury, eighty miles to the north-east. In the late seventies an annual hippy fayre was held on its slopes. I met a carpenter called Brendan in the pub at Staverton, one of the two villages Hood Ball Hill overlooks, who attended the fayre regularly as a child and remembers it as an event where people often dressed in sackcloth and there were always 'lots of dogs running loose and having a go at one another'.

Nowadays Hood Ball Hill has no footpath and is strictly, even a tad angrily, sectioned off from the public. I know this because I have checked out the situation assiduously from every angle. I have, however, climbed Yarner Beacon several times, both after the advent of the new permissive path leading to its peak and prior to that as a wide-eyed trespasser. For weeks before I made my maiden ascent, the beacon would call to me. Every time I saw it I could think about nothing but getting up into the comb of trees at its peak. This hill fetish was new to me and I did not understand what it meant or what I hoped to achieve through it, but if anything that made it all the more powerful. I had moved here from one of the flattest counties in England, Norfolk, where I once had a neighbour who spoke longingly of 'living in a house on a hill'. It was quite a big deal to him since they only have about six of them there. I lived for a long spell after that on what I thought was a hill but now realise was only a tussock with ideas above its station. People visiting me from Devon said they liked the place but asked how I coped with the flatness. I didn't understand what they meant. It was merely a topographical characteristic, surely, not a malady? But as a resident of Devon's South Hams region I soon began to get it. Flat landscapes have a subtle enchantment of their own, but a landscape dense with hills makes everything more of a fascinating puzzle. Voices and revelations tend to flood the head on a good country walk, as if imparted by well-meaning unseen sprites hiding in the countryside itself. These voices and revelations are imbued with a different magic when emerging from the secret folds and crevices that hills create. Being accustomed to that magic, then visiting a place where it appears to have been steamrollered and rendered ostensibly more prosaic, must come as a shock.

I like to climb Yarner Beacon on a clear day, gaze several miles into the distance towards the sea and try to pick out the location of the footpaths I've walked, which, after three years of living here, is almost all of them. I once made the mistake of moving to an exciting new part of the British countryside and not immediately investigating every bit of it forensically on foot and I don't intend to make the same error again. From up here I'm always amazed at the way all the threads connect, their shimmies and jinks and thrusts being disguised when you're beneath hilltop level, in the thick of it. It could be compared to the moment when, having only previously travelled through London by Tube, a person explores the city at ground level on foot and realises the unexpected interconnectivity of the stations, their surprising proximity to one another. So many of the paths here in south-west Devon are of a hidden nature: sunken lanes that were already old in Saxon times, created by landowners digging ditches on the boundaries of their properties and piling earth into continuous banks on their own sides. These holloways feel impossibly solid when, as a walker, you're bracketed by their banks below the bulk of the land, in an eerily quiet semi-subterranean shale, fern, mud and moss world.

In winter this countryside is a totally different colour to Norfolk's: reddy brown and green, as opposed to grainy brown and muddy grey. Rich rain-sodden earth and leaf mulch provide the reddy brown; plentiful moss, resilient fern and lichen add back-up greens on the borders of fields and meadows that stay more emerald luminous in the cold months than any other fields and meadows I've known. There is a strong argument in favour of every season here: autumn for its crunchy lysergic coppers and golds, its sunlit spider's webs and sudden forgotten woodsmoke rush; summer because summer here is just dizzying with all the possible ways it offers to fill your time. But in winter as the land strips itself back it shows you new secrets and you feel like you're getting a glimpse into something special behind everything else: intangible, ghoulish, a necessary dark pigment on the edge of the land of the living.

Restless from driving, I arrive home and go straight out again on foot, wringing the daylight out of the day. On a steep rocky holloway leading down from the hamlet of Aish the leaf veil has fallen back to reveal a ruined barn I never knew was there. One of its broken woodworm-riddled doors creaks in the wind as I pass, which is odd, as I hadn't realised there *was* any wind. At the bottom of the hill, beside a water lane, on a fence in a stark garden belonging to an isolated cottage a well-known death figure has been made using thick black polythene draped over two crossed sticks. Hooded and faceless, he holds a lantern in one unseen hand and a scythe in the other. I step gingerly over to photograph him, and a man of baby boomer age wearing a fisherman's jumper emerges from the front door of the cottage. 'Ooh, he loikes the *reaper*,' he says to me in a strong West Country accent that leaves me unsure if it is genuine or being put on for hillbilly *Straw Dogs* effect. Something ominous hangs in the air for twenty seconds until a younger man – possibly his son – emerges from the house, chuckling. I ask the younger man if he made the reaper himself and he confirms that he did, with the help of friends, and that it was the centrepiece of a recent New Year's Eve party. There is no such levity to explain away another haunting site I see six and a half miles upriver, near Staverton: a fence post, recently denuded of nettles and bracken and draped with a blue shawl, matching floppy felt hat and

off-beige scarf to form what looks chillingly like a small, stooped woman, turned away from the footpath, crying over some crippling recent tragedy. Of these two ominous home-made figures this is undoubtedly the greater piece of art, constructed using nothing but a banal pre-existing boundary marker and three dirty pieces of clothing, yet conveying absolutely no sense that, were you to touch her and ask her if she was OK, she would not turn round with glowing crimson eyes and gnashing teeth, crunch your skull into fragments and suck fresh blood from your neck hole.

I hike these paths more often in winter, when daylight is scarce and I am reluctant to waste what there is of it on car journeys to further-flung walking destinations. South Devon is by far the most touristy place I've ever lived, but in January, February and March you can take a route across the hidden places and get a genuine sense that no other human feet have preceded yours for weeks. One of my favourite walks is a thirteen-mile loop to the village of Tuckenhay. I love the way the village looks from the top of the valley in winter, with smoke billowing from the chimneys beside the creek and the jumbled houses climbing into the narrow opposing valley as if forming an unruly queue for a magic tunnel. This most recent winter I walked down the steepest of the hills leading to the village and was reminded of the time my dad drove down the same lane in icy conditions in an old, untrustworthy car during a family holiday in 1987. With unintentional perfect timing Vivaldi's 'Winter' had been playing on the car's cassette player as he drove, and the combination of the perilous road and the hysteria of the music sent my mum, me and my auntie Mal into fits of laughter. Now, on the same hollowed-out road, I spotted a hubcap eight feet above me, lodged in the mossy, ivy-strangled bank; above it, brassy robins flitted about. How had it got all the way up there? Maybe the driver of the car it had been attached to had been listening to Vivaldi too, and got carried away. That is, if the hubcap was a hubcap and not a tiny flying saucer that had veered off course and crashed, which was what it more realistically resembled.

My preferred route back from Tuckenhay is the most arduous and impractical one, along the creek bed, where hopefully the tide will be low. The first time I was about to take this route I encountered two dishevelled, wheezing walkers coming from the opposite direction, who told me that I shouldn't try to get down there, since they'd only just made it through, and they, unlike me, had walking poles and proper anoraks with labels on them. Had they known me, they would have realised that 'I wouldn't try to go that way if I were you – it's difficult' is one of the three main motivational hiking phrases a person can say in my vicinity, along with 'There's a great pub at the apex of this route' and 'This hill is well known due to the coven which is said to have practised in the copse at its plateau during the middle of the seventeenth century.' I thanked them and pressed on in exactly the direction I'd intended, negotiating slimy pebbles and fallen trees with relatively little trouble. But this latest time along the creek was tough going. Rain had wrecked the valley for the previous five days. Vast mounds of slippy alien bubble seaweed sat on top of even slippier wet rocks, like the soggy crust of a treacherous pie. I took an hour to walk a broken studded necklace of land that I'd taken just fifteen minutes to make my way over last May. I only narrowly avoided tripping over, although in some ways it wouldn't have mattered if I had, since I was already a six-foot strip of pure mud-spatter masquerading as a human male. I had some shopping to do on the route home and thanked my lucky stars that I lived in the kind of place where the sight of a man who looked like the Creature from the Black Lagoon buying biological washing liquid and bananas would raise few eyebrows. The seaweed smelled less pleasant than usual: it gave off a salty pungent rot threat. Some of it, blasted there by the storms of recent days during high tide, had caught in the branches of the gnarly oaks which stuck out on precarious crooked noses of granite above the creek. Above it was another lonely haunted-looking barn I'd not previously spotted. A few strands of black binliner were caught in the barbed wire of the adjoining field. I'd not all that long ago learned the excellent Irish term for such a phenomenon – witches' knickers. The creek formed a thin channel through the mud, then rounded the corner to merge with the river, which, like all other rivers in Devon at this time of year, had acquired that black look it does not possess even on the coldest and most unforgiving day of autumn, summer or spring. It whispered in my ear about the bad stuff it wanted to do to me, and I climbed away, back to higher, more solid earth, relieved. Further on, in a hedge on the hill above Sharpham, near the natural burial ground, I saw another example of witches' knickers, far more elaborately and eerily crafted by nature: a curved strip of former black bag, complete with hood and slanted eyehole, which only someone in the most fierce denial about the dark side of existence would fail to admit looked like a demon – if not the Devil himself – reclining among the thin twigs, watching weary travellers struggle up the hill and idly planning their fate. If I looked closer, which I did not quite want to, I half-expected him to be casually examining his fingernails. A few weeks earlier similar nearby hedgerows had been strewn with redoubtable, undying wild clematis. Forgetting what the folklore name for it was, I asked a man emerging from a nearby garden if he knew. 'Those? They's dead men's whiskers,' he said. He was incorrect; the name I was looking for was in fact old man's beard, but I preferred his term and resolved to use it on all tenable future occasions. Now, though, the wild clematis seemed to have vanished. We had entered January, winter's peak. Time of tax return terror, bare trees, delusional gym resolutions and scheming hedge demons. Too bleak even for the strong and wiry whiskers of the deceased.

If you spend enough time out walking and witnessing this stuff you realise that there was always a predestiny to the ghosts and monsters that have, for centuries, spilled from the imagination of rurally situated British writers: if the people who invented them hadn't made them up, someone else would have, or at least ones not unlike them. The countryside – particularly the gnarly, craggy, knobbly countryside of the Deep South West – and the creaking, weather-blasted architecture of that countryside, especially when stripped back by seasonal change, is too rich with spooky imagery for it never to have happened. I am hugely inspired by this on my walks, to the point that it can send me into a minor state of witchy rapture, and I welcome its onset, but, even so, winter is not my season. It claws at me with its mucky nails and strips me back until I'm in the proper fallow state to best receive and fully appreciate my true season, which is spring.

I love spring. I feel it in every fibre of my being. This is not an unusual feeling of course for a human who wants to feel warm and sensually switched on, but there might be an extra, biological factor to it for me. I was born in May, the middle part of the month, when everything has usually fully kicked into gear, and May is when I feel most alive, most me, and never more so than here in Devon – because it's more fertile and wild than anywhere I've lived before and because that makes you feel more entrenched in May's essence.

I love May so much, I attended three Devonshire May Day festivals last year. At the most memorable of these I walked down Lustleigh Cleave – a dramatic cheese-wire slice in the wooded land on Dartmoor's softer south-eastern edge – on the first roasting hot day of the year to watch the crowning of the Lustleigh village May Queen, a tradition revived in the early 1900s but stretching back unknown centuries prior to that, and a perfect day out for anyone who tends to see the original 1970s version of *The Wicker Man* less as a horror film and more as a sweet, well-meaning documentary about agroforestry.

14

After descending the Cleave's soft wood-sorrel paths past standing stones and glistening streams, I and my five companions for the day entered the village orchard, where a maypole awaited us. To the maypole's immediate rear was a large rock with a stone seat on top of it and five decades of young female names carved into it. A person could perhaps find a scene in Britain more suggestive than this of the declaration 'We are ready for the sacrifice' but it would be difficult. Outside the village hall old black and white photos of previous Lustleigh May Queens were displayed, and out of the ingrained habit of a person who has watched *The Wicker Man* fifty-seven times I could not help but check to see whether or not the 1972 photograph was missing. 'They do love their divinity lessons,' said my friend Andy in his best Christopher Lee voice. It was always only going to be a matter of time before somebody did.

May's pay-off is felt even more acutely on the edge of the moor, the celebration of it perhaps even more necessary. Suzi and Fergus, whose hard-to-find house we have walked down the Cleave from today, have been snowed in for long periods during all but one of the twelve winters they've lived here. In that time, Suzi – a careful driver, like most people who live on or near Dartmoor – has written off three cars on these narrow lanes. Even the psychedelic moorland spring comes with its dark side: this time last year Suzi and Fergus had a weasel slaughter all but one of their thirteen chickens in two days flat. Deeply traumatised, the lone survivor had since moved next door. As I climbed back up the Cleave to my car, I was followed by a special Dartmoor sun: that sun you feel is palpably closer to you than it is elsewhere in the county, simply because you're a little nearer to the roof of the world. The air had a slow, sparkly quality, as it often does on the moor, and this seemed to follow me home then stick around for the next few days. Cherry blossom and dandelion seed heads floated through the air in my garden, adding to its psychedelic reinvention. My cat Ralph, who has fantastic sideburns and a rugged late-hippy-era look about him, walked lazily through the blossom with a beatific expression on his face, and I felt like I was watching a dream sequence from a road movie made in 1969 by cats about cats.

All around us, everything was growing frantically. The garden's copper beech hedge went from rust to dazzling green in barely more than a day. I mowed the lawn, nipped inside for a shower and a cup of tea, and it seemed that while my back was turned another twenty daisies had appeared. I mowed it again soon after, shaping two thick new border areas and leaving them free do their own thing where I'd scattered wildflower seeds, a decision that, though relieving me of part of a weekly chore, was made out of a wish to encourage more bees and butterflies into the garden rather than pure laziness. My current lawnmower had been a birthday present from my parents two years previously. Along with its assembly kit and instructions, the mower arrived with a lined pad marked 'NOTES'. In here the true mowing connoisseur was presumably intended to make observations on the quality of his mow. My dad told me not to mow any pebbles because a bloke his friend Jeff knew mowed one and the pebble shot up and sliced off one of Jeff's friend's Labrador's testicles. I don't have a Labrador, and if I did and it was male I would almost certainly have it castrated at the earliest possible opportunity, in the normal legal manner, but the advice stuck with me, and I am careful not to mow pebbles. I viewed the notes section in the mower handbook as absurd for a long time, but I adore notebooks and can't stand to see any of them empty and unloved, even – and perhaps especially – if they're plain and dull, so I began to put it to occasional use, recording my user experience as a weekly handler of the Bosch Rotak 43 Ergoflex.

MOWING NOTES: 18.5.2016

STRANGELY INVIGORATING MOW IN A 9 MPH BREEZE, INTERRUPTED AT THE 37 MINUTE MARK WHEN I MOWED AN OLD TENNIS BALL. BROKE OFF AFTER 52 MINUTES TO EAT A PACKET OF SALT 'N' VINEGAR HULA HOOPS : THE TRADITIONAL VARIETY, ALTHOUGH I SURPRISE MYSELF BY ~~PREFERRING~~ PREFERRING THE NEW LOW FAT 'PUFT' VARIETY. UPON RESUMING I LISTENED TO THE 1968 BYRDS ALBUM 'SWEETHEART OF THE RODEO', WHICH I GIVE AN 8.7/10 RATING AS MOWING MUSIC. FINISHED THE LAWN AND GAZED BACK ON MY WORK, FEELING NOT UNLIKE A KING WHO, IN HIS OWN SMALL WAY, HAD REMADE THE WORLD.

Even after the lawn had been mown short and smooth, a dark diagonal line remained visible across the largest segment of it. This line led to the place just beyond some brambles, through a hole in my garden fence, where a group of badgers had made their sett: the most direct route there from the copses on the hill above my house where they went to forage for grubs and rodents at night. I'd first noticed badgers in my garden the year before last, when one took a similar path across my lawn at dusk. It looked like an animal surprised at its own ability to run. Soon afterwards, another badger went through my recycling and separated plastic from aluminium: a needless gesture, since it all goes in the same bag in this part of Devon, as dictated by South Hams District Council. The following year, close to Summer Solstice, as I was taking a long cut across the hill overlooking my house to the post office, engrossed in a Garrison Keillor podcast on my iPod, I very nearly trod on a much younger badger, who scuttled away into the thick hedgerow. As the afternoon wore on a mixture of emotions set in: annoyance at my absent-mindedness, elation and that special remorse that only comes with almost treading on a very young creature that resembles a small snouty folk-rock bear. I read up on badgers a little when I got home and discovered that they are omnivores and not, as I first thought on a hasty misreading, 'omnivoles', which, being not a real word, does not in fact mean a vole who is in every place at once, which to me seems a shame and a missed opportunity. A couple of foods that badgers especially enjoy, I learned, are peanuts and cat biscuits, both of which I had a decent supply of in the house. At dusk that night I took some of both up to the hillside in bowls and sat in the long grass where I'd almost trod on the badger, determined to make amends. A bonus sight greeted me a few minutes after I arrived and scattered some of the peanuts and cat food: not just the reappearance of the original young badger from earlier, snuffling about on the shorter turf, but a shyer, smaller sibling, in the long grass and weeds a few feet away. Neither seemed hugely bothered by my presence, perhaps not yet being fully schooled in the lesson that human beings are massive bastards. I crouched in the grass and watched the two badgers for a quarter of an hour or so then emptied the remainder of my peanuts and cat biscuits from my bowls, which they duly chomped, the bolder one coming within about a foot of eating from my hand.

Over the ensuing days, without any special effort on my part, my life became very badger-themed. The following week I visited the annual summer Scythe Fair at Thorney Lakes in Somerset. To remind myself about the fair's imminence, I wrote 'Scythe Fair!' on the appropriate day on my calendar. 'Why does it say "Scythe Fair!" on your calendar?' my girlfriend asked, and I told her that it was because I was going to a scythe fair. The Scythe Fair featured several stalls selling scythes, old and new, while children romped in freshly scythed grass heaps and competitive unisex scything took place in the central arena, some of it (male only) topless, some of the competitors surprisingly youthful. This gave the place the slight look of a Grim Reaper Hogwarts. Jay, my companion for the day, who suffers from the most virulent hay fever known to man, had not quite allowed for the results of this in his planning, so I took refuge with him and his ever-reddening damp face in the far corner of the fair, away from the scythed grass. Here I got talking to Leslie on the Dorset for Badger and Bovine Welfare Group stall; who was raising awareness about the government-endorsed badger cull, which, based on deeply questionable scientific evidence and with a ludicrously wasteful budget, was moving further into the South West. I told her that I'd recently fed my local badgers peanuts, and she said she went a step further and made peanut butter sandwiches for her local ones every day at dusk. The badgers had come to expect this and, with time, even view it as their right, but one evening when they arrived in her garden with their typical punctuality she realised she was fresh out of peanut butter. She searched her fridge and freezer but the only slightly appropriate meal she could find was a dish of oldish ratatouille from her freezer which, if she was honest, she wasn't sure if she was ever going to get around to eating. 'They loved it,' she told me. 'But they ran off with the dish afterwards.' She paused and a wistful mood appeared to overcome her. 'I really liked that dish,' she added. At one of my spoken-word events only a couple of days after this a member of the audience told me about a close friend who'd been bitten on the bottom by a badger in the garden at a house party in Exeter, which made me wonder not just about the finer details of the attack but whether I was going to the right house parties. A couple of initial small signs of a sett appeared in my garden a week or so later. The badgers reconsidered and abandoned this but in early spring 2016 the other sett, at the end of the diagonal path in the lawn, appeared. Intrigued, I set up a trail camera not far from its entrance.

Each of the three springs I've experienced in Devon has been markedly different from the other two. When I arrived from Norfolk in March 2014 it rained relentlessly for weeks, transforming low-lying fields into lakes, then a fierce sun finally hit and the whole place exploded in fluorescence, giving me unrealistic expectations of just how many primroses and bluebells I might find squeezed into an average South West Peninsula woodland copse from here on. After a dark, dingy winter, spring 2015 brought a strange, stark heatwave. With April barely under way, the footpaths near my house were full of walkers in shorts, and the trees, still largely leafless, appeared almost harassed, like people being hurried out of the house to an engagement when they have not yet finished getting dressed. But last spring was just about perfect: mist that seemed to paint itself over all the right bits of the land then got burned away slowly by an assertive, calm sun, creating tingling days that were warm but not too warm in their middle then cool and atmospheric at their close. Days that made you realise that the chief reason people talk about the weather a lot in casual conversation is not out of dullness or awkwardness; it's because somewhere deep inside we realise that weather is our one true leader. I want to grab days like this hard and wring every bit of goodness out of them, which is why spring is a time when I am not always the working beast that I should be. I am a Morning Person, whose best creative energy comes between the hours of 6 a.m. and noon, and must, vitally, be bottled during that period, but when I sit at my desk on a bright morning in spring it's invariably with the febrile sense that there's a party going on outside and everyone but me has been invited. Oscar Wilde said, 'Only dull people are brilliant at breakfast,' which is nonsense, but sounds pithy and smart and makes you seem devastatingly hip to actual dull people if you quote it in your favour. Announcing 'I'm a night owl' is full adulthood's equivalent of a flamboyantly lit underage cigarette. It's a statement designed to impress: all people who say it naturally seem more interesting and mysterious. Perhaps they frequent jazz clubs and consort with beatniks and intellectuals? Certainly they must do something fascinating with their lives and not just, say, stay up late scrolling through Facebook. I know a penchant for waking early is going to win me few friends, but I'm not going to hide from it to try to make you like me. My love of mornings is as undeniable as two or three of my limbs. But it is not synonymous with any antipathy towards night-time or Night People. I can happily go to bed late but I'll still invariably be awake at dawn. If I choose an early night, it's out of a mixture of self-knowledge and self-preservation, and if I am doing spring in the best way – which I do not always have the self-discipline to – early nights become increasingly important.

On a Sunday in the early part of spring 2016, a couple of weeks after I'd first arranged the trail cam near the badger sett in the garden, I skipped down the lawn to retrieve the memory card from it. The sun was peeking over a row of beeches like a pastoral equivalent of the classic graffiti of Kilroy and his wall, and the owls of the valley had just handed the avian noise baton over to the Dawn Chorus. This morning the band, which was rapidly becoming one of my all-time favourite British ones, right up there with Led Zeppelin, Pentangle and the Stones, was working on a fuller sound: lots of new session players were chipping in and trying out new ideas, including a pheasant, the ensemble's answer to a notoriously unreliable bagpipe player who stumbles in, still drunk from the night before, blows a couple of off-kilter notes, then leaves. Still in my pyjamas, I walked down to the river, inhaling overpowering wild-garlic stench, and immediately saw a kingfisher zipping along above the surface, fish in beak. As I walked back along the lane, a small white van pulled up beside me and its driver wound down his window. 'Bloody hell, the things you see around here in the morning!' said the driver. 'I thought you were an escaped convict from Dartmoor prison, dressed like that.' It was Ian, my plumber. Ian is a Morning Person too, and it was his trail cam that I had borrowed to film the badgers.

'Any luck over the last couple of days?' he asked.

'Neh,' I said. 'Got a magpie yesterday. At least it was the right colour scheme.'

In a fortnight of striving to catch the badgers on film I'd so far managed to get one good clear eleven-second video of one scuffling around and another of a tail – thick and almost certainly badger-owned – wafting about in

the corner of the frame. I'd also managed to record six other moving things that were manifestly not badgers: that magpie, two field mice, my left leg, a fox and my industrious female cat Roscoe returning from a hunting expedition with a mole dangling from her mouth. The mole, although assuredly deceased, wobbled slightly from side to side, so if you counted it as a moving thing too, that made seven in total. I said, 'Good morning, Mr Magpie, and how's your wife?' to the magpie. I always say, 'Good morning, Mr Magpie, and how's your wife?' to solitary magpies, as popular superstition dictates that I must, for good luck, but doing so can become very tiring as there are a lot of magpies where I live and very few of them are in steady relationships.

I went inside and checked the results of last night's surveillance: no badgers. I got the impression that they had become wise to the trail cam. All my latest footage had turned up was another mouse, and even she had appeared a bit self-conscious. I'd woken in the night, looked down from my bedroom window and seen one of the badgers skittering across in front of the doorstep in what could easily be perceived as a cocky dance, yet, even though I'd scattered peanuts and dry cat food in the perfect place and aimed the trail cam directly down the line of their diagonal path...nothing.

Looking at that diagonal path – more multispecies A-road than badger byway – was instructive. It was a reminder that most of the paths in the British countryside were not planned by people in suits with clipboards and agendas; they were made organically, by silent, casual committee: a mixture of animals and humans deciding on the best route to suit their needs and forging defiantly ahead. Desire lines is what they call them in the transportation planning industry. I recently spoke to a woman from Maryland, on the east coast of the United States, who'd never visited rural Britain and was astounded to learn that I could walk in the countryside and get up close to cows and sheep that did not belong to me. Coming from a place where most of the greenery and all of the arable land is sectioned off from walkers, she found it an entirely alien concept. It's conversations like this that make you realise how privileged we are in the UK to have the green lanes, bridleways and footpaths that we do, allowing us to clamber over stiles nibbled by horses into farmyards filled with inquisitive guineafowl or wild meadows where we might surprise a pheasant and it might surprise us back with a loud *ch-kooick* as it explodes from the grass. Later during the morning on which my conversation with Ian the plumber had taken place I set off on foot down to the river and in what seemed like no time at all was cuddling a large, docile ewe, a sheep I'd taken for a troublemaker the first time I'd seen her, waiting for me on the path above the Dart, but who it turned out just wanted to say hello and find out whether I needed anything. I told the sheep that she was the best sheep I'd ever met, then immediately felt bad because it was something I'd told lots of other sheep, even though this time I genuinely meant it.

I believe it is my duty to get to know my immediate natural world thoroughly, to not be complacent about it, as it's the least I can do as a gesture of thanks to it for being kind enough to allow me to live within it. My need to explore my home county on foot – sometimes as much as sixty miles a week of it – also comes as a natural by-product of being one of those odd people who are excited by the design of an old kissing gate, a small pool in a depression at the top of a tor or the blotched patterns lichen makes on a boulder in a spinney. Not everyone will impulsively go 'Ooh' upon seeing moss and navelwort laying siege to an old wall – they will need some sort of violent modern stimulus to be prompted to lose control in an equivalently undignified way, and I accept that totally –

but I am someone who does. I think my time on local footpaths, and in various places just off them, is also a reaction to something I'm told repeatedly about the way I should live, almost every time I turn on any electronic device with a screen. The whole world is there on the screen, for the taking, and a hive of demanding voices encourages us to absorb as much of it as possible, and keep up with it frantically, as it moves on, and it is *always* moving on, more swiftly and forgetfully than ever. If you're someone with a thirst for knowledge, you can very easily get sucked into the excitement of this, before you realise it's a flawed, impossible pursuit, and it's not making people, en masse, any more knowledgeable. What it instead often leads to is a brand of knowledge that's thousands of miles wide and half a centimetre deep: a pond-skating mentality of misleading screenshots and thinly gleaned opinions and out-of-context sound bites and people reading hastily between the lines while forgetting the vital thing you also need to do when practising that skill is to read the lines themselves. The idea of getting to know an area of limited size extremely well works as an antidote to this, and even in a very small area there is always more to know. You can reduce your space right down – to one hedgerow or wall or flooded out-of-use tin mine – and there will never be enough time to know it all.

It could be argued that I have a particularly fertile area in which to do my local investigations, but I've done it in another very different place too: Norfolk. And when revisiting the places in the East Midlands where I grew up – rural areas, but localities defined not by hills and rivers and water lanes and creeks but by parks and chip shops and factories and railway cuttings – I've been drawn to do the same, to start looking behind the obvious in a way that never would have occurred to me in the distant past: at the thirty-mile view from the hill above your aunt's old semi and the haunting tower at its hazy edge, at the lovingly designed pattress plates on an abandoned brewery or the stag beetles beneath some bark on an eerie broken oak in a copse behind a litter-strewn lay-by not far from the motorway junction people take if they want to go to IKEA.

This part of Devon isn't perfect either. Just like other parts of the British countryside it has litter and barbed wire and and recklessly driven cars and motorbikes and horrendous fuckwads who put their dogs' shit in plastic bags then leave the bags on tree stumps and in hedges. It contains people too, contrary to popular belief: quite a lot of them (I'm not counting the horrendous fuckwads who bag up and leave the dogshit as people). Without ever really intending to do so, on the walks I take nearer my house I regularly update an internal top three of regularly spotted walking strangers. As of May 2016, this read – and had read for several weeks – as follows:

1. Lycra Santa
2. Man Who Narrates Events To His Bulldog As They Occur
3. Woman Who Never Says Hello Back To Me And Smiles Like She Has A Little Secret

May is the time when the bluebells in the woods near my house take over from the primroses. In a path on Lustleigh Cleave redolent of old faery activity – the kind without gossamer wings or wands – I ate one of the last ones of the year, on Suzi's urging, and it tasted not unpleasantly of flour and untart lemon. In Devon – less so than in the part of Norfolk where I used to live, where they are far thinner on the ground – I think of primroses as heralding spring, more than the daffodils that emerge in late January, which are often just early tester daffodils, sent out on suicide missions. In the folk song 'The Blacksmith', written at an unknown point by an unknown author, but brought into the modern age transcendentally by Planxty and the lesser-heard artistically bold initial incarnation of Steeleye Span during the early 1970s, the narrator sings of her lost metal-forger-love's 'good black billycock' hat 'crowned with primroses', and I can see how such attire might be an extra bit of salt in the wound of losing him. She also sings that, were she with the blacksmith, she'd 'live for ever'. Part of the magic of primroses is that you never see them die: in decline they are simply subsumed amid the growth spurts of lankier vegetation until one day it hits you that they're no longer there.

Near a bank of them still fighting valiantly for space beside a fish-ladder tributary that makes a no-nonsense dash down to the Dart, I ran into my gardener friend Andy.

'Oh, I was just thinking about you,' Andy said.

'Really?' I asked. 'Why was that?'

'Someone's nicked a shopping trolley and dumped it

down there on the path. I thought to myself, *If Tom's heading down here today, he's going to walk straight into that.'*

I was touched that Andy would think about my welfare in such a way. His comment was also perhaps indicative of the fact that I had now lived in this part of Devon long enough for my rampant doziness to have become fairly common local knowledge. My status as someone who is a very observant person in some ways goes hand in hand with my status as someone who is a very unobservant person in lots of others. Combine this with my short-sightedness, and if I'm walking the paths at the edge of my local town, Totnes, at the same time as someone I know, there's a high probability that they'll see me before I see them. This can present a problem. I'm always worried about being perceived to be ignoring friends or acquaintances when in fact I'm just off in my own myopic dream universe. But I can overcompensate too. When a well-dressed woman in late middle age walked down the river path towards me one day last spring with her arms stretched out in greeting I readied myself to say hello. Was she a friend's mum I had been introduced to at the pub a few weeks ago? The industrious widow I did stone-row conservation up on the moor with two winters ago? As she got within a few feet of my face I realised that the answer was an emphatic no to both questions. I had definitely never met this person before.

'Can you tell me,' she asked, arms still open, then paused, and I got my geographical head on, poised to offer succinct directions – perhaps to the castle, or the wharf, or the medieval hall a couple of miles up the river, 'whether Nietzsche was Russian or German?'

'German,' I answered.

'Well *done*!' she said and walked briskly on.

A few weeks later, buying avocados at the greengrocer's, I ran into the woman again. She didn't appear to recognise me from our previous encounter but asked me why it said 'Traffic' on the T-shirt I was wearing. I told her that they were one of my favourite bands.

'Do you go to Glastonbury to see them?' she asked.

'No, I haven't been for years,' I said. 'And they split up in 1974.'

'Is that your wife?' she asked, pointing to a woman I'd never seen before, who was standing in the doorway, minding her own business.

'No,' I said. 'I don't have one of those.'

'And if you keep wearing T-shirts like that, you never will!' she said, and walked off.

It has been claimed by some people reasonably close to me that I have a knack of attracting society's uninhibited exiles and eccentrics while going about my business. I refute this allegation, just as I did when my girlfriend made it in 2012 on a Norfolk towpath, seconds before a stranger carrying a large fish ran excitedly up to us and said, 'Please can you take a photo of me and my fish?' to me. Spring does tend to have a giddiness which brings out a certain unsuppressed behaviour in many sections of the Devonshire population though, and I often find myself close witness to it. It was in spring that a dreadlocked lady in a smock approached me in the garden of my local pub and showed me a stain on the tray she was carrying which she claimed was the representation of her previous warrior self from untold centuries past. It was also in spring – this latest one, again – when Robert introduced himself on a sunken lane a few miles from my house.

The weather was bright, though cool, the day I met Robert, and a lot of people were out. I'd already passed Lycra Santa and Man Who Narrates Events To His Bulldog As They Occur by the time I curved up a long sunken lane leading away from the south side of Totnes. 'It's cold, isn't it?' I had overheard Man Who Narrates Events To His Bulldog As They Occur saying to his bulldog. 'I bet you wish you had warm clothes. We're going to the supermarket soon, then we're going to John's house. This tree just here is weird.' But by the time I was in the long sunken lane I was very much alone, protected by its quiet green banks from the clanking of the industrial estate half a mile away and the slick gravelly zip of traffic along the Newton Abbot road. I passed a tall ivy-fringed stone trough in the hedged bank that always looked like a risky promise of an alternate dimension, then made my way over the brow of the hill down to where the walls of the holloway get more rocky and subterranean and turn a dreamlike dark green. A man walking in the opposite direction stopped in my path, grinning. Seeing that there were fewer than eleven visible buildings nearby, I said hello and he returned my greeting. In my early days as a countryside rambler I'd be tentative about saying hello to strangers – I'd try to assess them first, see if they were 'Hello!' kind of people. Now I tend to say it to everyone as it makes life simpler and less angst-ridden. Most people will say it back, and if they don't they're probably a serial killer, and you'll be dead soon anyway. The exception to this rule is if you're in an area where there are more than eleven visible buildings nearby: the time in 2011, for example, when I walked past another lone man in his thirties on a walk on the outskirts of Long Stratton in Norfolk, and the two of us couldn't quite work out if we were in a countryish enough area to say 'Hello!' so mumbled a half 'Hi!' to one another, then shambled off, saturated in an awkwardness that would probably still be with us, in some small but significant way, for the rest of our lives.

The man on the sunken lane, fiftyish and dressed in very colourful and expensive-looking branded outdoor clothing, seemed keen not only to say hello but to stop and chat. He introduced himself as Robert. 'I saw you over on the other side of the river earlier,' he told me. 'I said to myself, *He's not a walker, dressed in that duffel coat*, but…you are! Look at you.'

I followed his instructions and looked at me. I didn't wear my duffel coat all that often while out on hikes but had never viewed it as a serious impediment to getting about in the countryside on foot. To Robert the fact that someone should be able to negotiate hills, stiles and footpaths wearing such a garment was clearly a small miracle. He shook his head and gasped, like a man who'd seen a deer in a skirt. We talked a little about routes we'd enjoyed in the area and he asked me what I did for a living and I tried my best to tell him.

He explained that he had made a lot of money from property development, taken early retirement, and his expensive walking equipment was part of his way of spending the inheritance of his offspring, who no longer spoke to him and, in his words, 'didn't deserve it'. As if to compound this abrupt, unexpectedly uncomfortable turn the conversation had taken, another walker passed us – a woman in her late twenties clad in a long thick cardigan and bobble hat – and Robert immediately began shouting across to her about my 'great job', which I'd in fact just told him was my old job, which I'd emphatically and with a considerable amount of relief quit the year previously. He then instructed her: 'You need to get with this guy!' Considering the fact he'd clearly never met her before, what he was saying and the various assumptions it betrayed, her response – to smile awkwardly and step up her pace just marginally as she passed us – was an impressively restrained one. I offered her an awkward smile of my own, which I hoped communicated *I do not know this man and am very sorry about the words that keep coming out of his mouth*, then made my excuses to Robert and walked on, passing beneath a railway bridge on whose roof grew lichen that looked halfway between stalactites and loft insulation, then up a steep lane to a spot where, the previous year, I'd seen a small, pristine, black rabbit run across the tarmac in my path.

Is there a proper way to be a walker? Apart from showing the fitting amount of consideration to your environment and your fellow humans, I don't believe there is, and that's something I like about it. Walking tends to be

35

goal-free in any official sense, yet can be associated with any number of small unofficial personal goals. Some clothes are more practical for it, without doubt, but it's entirely up to you what you wear. Something that changed about my walking habits between 2015 and 2016 was that I became a bit better at watching and listening, but I don't think even this represents the 'right' way to walk; it's just something I wanted to try. I wasn't watching or listening too well the day on the hillside overlooking my house in 2015 when I almost trod on the young badger, or when I saw the back end of that pristine black rabbit disappear into the hedgerow, but I started making a bit more of an effort shortly after that. A few weeks later, I was heading through a kissing gate from a twisting path to a field when I heard a miniscule anguished squeak coming from the bushes behind me: something that, in my previous, less present-aware state, I might not have picked out of the light din in and around a wildflower meadow in midsummer. I slowed down and listened some more, and in under a minute, two furry animals, each not much bigger than one of my feet, locked together, spun onto the path behind me, at least one of them in extreme pain. One of these animals was a young rabbit and the other was a weasel. I'd watched rabbits suffer a few times in the jaws of my cats but this was another level of ruthless. Seeing the nameless dark burning in the weasel's eyes and the shrieking rabbit in its jaws, I momentarily became the rabbit and the weasel became the headlights.

What happened next astonished me further still: a larger rabbit, bouncing out of the undergrowth and hurling itself at the weasel. There was something deeply, heartbreakingly powerless about the gesture, but it was just enough to break up the original ball of weasel and rabbit. As they separated, all three creatures noticed me for the first time in my static, mesmerised position, not more than eight feet away. The adult rabbit hopped into the bushes, its offspring flopped and writhed behind it, probably mortally injured, until both were out of sight. The weasel made a fast-forward creep in the other direction, pausing and getting on its hind legs for a second to peer at me in a way that suggested it blamed me for everything and was wondering, just for a moment, if nipping over and disabling my spinal cord in punishment was a viable option. I sat quietly on the grass, and five minutes later the weasel re-emerged, scuttling across the path like a cackling villain in a Hanna-Barbera cartoon, confirming everything we know about the etymology of the word 'weasel'. I heard nothing more. I wondered about looking for the young rabbit and putting it out of its misery. I decided not to, not just because such a prospect filled me with dread but because I had no place interfering in any part of this episode. I had been in a slightly fragile state of mind on the day of the weasel's attack, and for the ensuing twenty-four hours I could not help returning repeatedly to the image of that mother rabbit flinging herself out of the bushes, doing everything in her power to save her offspring, even though what she had in her power was virtually nothing: the impossibly touching, doomed heroism of it. A small part of me wished I'd had my phone with me and filmed it but then I realised I didn't wish that at all. The Internet just conned me into wishing it, because the Internet knows that humans like to share stuff, and that sharing stuff often comes from a kind place and carries the promise of bringing us all closer, so it gets us all addicted to the process, but leaves us ultimately emptier as a result, hovering in a state of non-presentness, getting nostalgic for stuff that happened barely any time ago that we didn't even take the time to properly absorb when it did happen, skimming across everything, not quite fully experiencing any of it. But the Internet is also teeming with good intentions and seductive promises, and that is the problem.

Summer Solstice is a punctual visitor whose punctuality, though unvarying, always takes me by surprise. Midsummer's Day does not really happen in the middle of summer of course, and if it did genuinely mark the midpoint of the warm part of the British year, that would feel desperately unfair, but its arrival always elicits a slight sense of injustice in me: a *Hold on! We've only just got to the point where all the leaves are green! You can't start heading in the other direction yet!* protest. As I headed home from the site of the weasel attack, this protest rose inside me more acutely than ever. There were signs that the lush party of June in Devon had reached its crescendo: nature's equivalent of that moment on a night out when you stay out, thinking things will get wilder, and they do, but in an insalubrious way that you regret. Blood-caked bird wings and gristle lay on the path ahead of me. My bare legs had been stung by the towering bully-boy nettles of full-throttle summer, thistles that didn't have the guts to slag me off to my face. A local foraging expert named Brigit-Anna McNeill – more commonly known as just Anna – had told me recently that the stings were good for you. In which case, I was seven stings healthier than I had been at the beginning of the day.

A forager is much better than me at looking and listening as they walk through the countryside: they see beyond the wall of green that the rest of us see flanking us in midsummer and recognise individual species. My Scythe Fair companion Jay, who cooks a lot of foraged food, regularly walks the paths near my house sampling all manner of leaves and flowers like some kind of mystic ground-level giraffe. I wanted to gain the confidence to do the same so in midsummer 2015 I joined one of Anna's foraging courses in the grounds of Sharpham House, on the hill above the spot where the river reaches the spectacular peak of its congenital indecisiveness. After only a few hours in a tucked-away corner of the UK's Deep South West like this with a group of strangers, a strong sense of community sets in: a possibility in the air of being part of a new underground society. To be fair, the particular characters of the day perhaps exacerbated the effect: a towering floppy-haired mushroom expert called Louis who reminded me of the hunky rebel leader Diane Keaton falls for in the futuristic Woody Allen film *Sleeper*, for example, and a barefoot father–son team called Rainbow and River who constantly seemed to be climbing trees, even on the few occasions when they weren't. In this environment a sentence such as 'Look – Rainbow is making a spit poultice!', which might seem outlandish in most places, becomes normalised suprisingly quickly.

One of the bits of vegetation I ate for the first time on Anna's foraging course was a thistle. There is a tendency to force your mind open when you eat a thistle, to prepare yourself for it to taste very different to what you expected, but what it tasted like was a thistle. At best you might have said it had overtones of fibrous, angry cucumber, which didn't work for me as someone who's always believed cucumber to be redolent of many of the most disappointing aspects of life as a UK citizen. I preferred my first tastes of wood sorrel, mustard leaf, Anna's nettle tea – which she said had completely cured her hay fever – and hart's tongue. Ancient wisdom says that hart's tongue prevents people from having impure thoughts and, sure enough, I did not have any impure thoughts for a whole three hours after eating it, but that might just have been because I had a headache. We also found some lady's mantle – also known as alchemilla – in the garden at Sharpham, which, Anna informed us, helps to regulate the female menstrual cycle. I noticed that at this point most of the men in the group hung back slightly from the lady's mantle, as if concerned by the prospect of having their own cycles regulated. I am sure that I was far from the best student on the course – my decision to wolf down a bag of samosas straight after it had finished would seem to underline this – but I did notice that my ability to see through the green wall – whether I had the intention of eating some of it or not – improved afterwards. A huge teasel growing behind my back fence became no longer just a nondescript weed in the wallpaper of the land but a masterpiece of natural bee-friendly architecture, with leaves that curved to collect rainwater and form organic drinking bowls for blue tits. Strimming an unexplored patch at the far end of my garden and catching a familiar odour,

I stopped just in time to rescue a previously undiscovered patch of verbascum and mint then picked a few leaves of the latter and used them to make tea.

I often end up with stuff in my pockets during my local walks: the odd bit of wild food, but also shells, pebbles, a horseshoe, a lichen-coated stick with a fetching accidental sheep's wool wig. Pockets become different things here to what they are in many other counties. In Devon having a large collection of twigs or a mollusc in your pocket is regarded in pretty much the same way as having some keys in your pocket is in Kent, Berkshire or Leicestershire. I get home and empty mine, finding places in the garden for the knicknacks I've discovered. Some of them stay on a permanent basis, often becoming mildly talismanic, and the rest gradually fade into the earth. I can't help but pick up a long thin piece of seaweed with a bulbous head, noting its resemblance to a zombie snake, and it comes back home with me to live on a low granite wall for a while, guarding my back door until it withers and then one day is no longer there. A tiny bird skull found on a green lane near the village of Blackawton replaces it. In horror films an animal skull in or near a house is one of the early signifiers that you've entered the place where the Bad Folks live, but the people I've met in Devon who have them near theirs tend to be the opposite: some of the least scary people you can come across. A farmer will often affectionately hang on to the skull of a favourite ram. A friend who has campaigned against the cull keeps the skull of a badger, found beneath some gorse on a walk on the edge of Dartmoor, in her workroom. It is there for the same reason that the stone-floored mid-Norfolk farmhouse of the late artist and robot maker Bruce Lacey, which I visited in 2012, was full of taxidermy: it is a lament. It's about love.

By late summer 2016 badgers had become a regular, almost casual, presence in my garden. One morning in mid-August I was woken at four by a loud crunching sound directly below my bedroom near the living room's French windows, where my elderly cat The Bear liked to sleep. I remembered that I'd fed The Bear a chicken thigh earlier and neglected to get rid of the bone. 'Don't crunch the bone, The Bear!' I shouted, then, worrying, went downstairs to remove it. I arrived at the windows to find a small badger, its mouth full and a somewhat sheepish look on its face. The Bear sat calm but wide-eyed, two feet to the badger's left. I began to leave the

leftovers that my cats were too spoilt to eat outside for the badgers in bowls, knowing they would be empty by morning. I watched several times from the window as one of the badgers scuttled to within a foot or so of where one of my other cats, Shipley, sat on an old beanbag, a sorry-looking item long since relegated from the house, which, despite my attempts to patch it up, haemorrhaged polystyrene beads onto my lawn, but, owing to Shipley's abiding attachment to it, I couldn't bring myself to throw away. Shipley had always been a loud cat, unafraid to speak his mind, but his face as the badger went by suggested that they had reached some sort of arrangement and everything was totally mellow and tight.

A little over a month later, though, I woke again not long after having an early night, and heard gunshots ringing out from the hillside. After that I did not see any more badgers in my garden. I knew it was no coincidence. All in all, between August and October almost 11,000 badgers would be killed across the UK, yet since the beginning of the cull in 2013 there had been no evidence of it reducing the spread of bovine TB. Undoubtedly losing cows to TB must be awful and heartbreaking for farmers, but scientists and animal charities have repeatedly told us that there is nothing to say badgers are more likely to spread TB to cattle than several other animals, and the initial evidence that they spread it at all has been questioned by scientists. But – when innoculation of badgers would have been far cheaper – the government had opted for mass slaughter, in the process costing the UK taxpayer almost £7,000 for every badger killed. I'd signed petitions, tried my best to use what little influence I had to spread the word, but of course it was useless. I wish I'd been able to do more, but what? Run up the hill in my pyjamas and hurl myself between gun and badger? Over the next few months I saw just one sign of a badger in my garden: a new hole in my lawn, too big to have been made by the green woodpecker who sometimes visited and foraged for ants.

The land was beginning to rust again. You could see it best from the top of the hills. I wonder if I have become addicted to hills, or maybe just those near me. You weigh less standing on the ones here than you do on those in other parts of the country. This is due to the granite limb that makes up Devon, Cornwall, the Isles of Scilly and part of Somerset, whose low density has the power to subtly alter gravity. The name of the granite limb is the Cornubian Batholith, which, I have decided, is also what I will call my stoner rock band when I finally get around to forming it. I sometimes think I can sense that lightness – an almost floatiness – when I'm walking. There can be a unique rhythm to walking in Devon, where you frequently reward yourself with beer for walking up hills then walk up some more hills as punishment for the beer you drank. But often the intoxication has nothing to do with the fact that you've incorporated a pub stop into your route; it's about the endorphins accumulated on the clamber to a small summit, the rush of good air at the plateau. Curiously, my final walk as a Norfolk resident was to the top of one of the few proper hills in that part of the country: to Mousehold Heath in Norwich, where the angry rustics of Kett's Rebellion camped out with their scythes and pikes in the mid-1599s, and whose shepherdfolk and scrubby hillocks were painted by Cotman and Crome in the early nineteenth century, just a little before branches of Homebase and HSS Tool Hire opened on the industrial estate to the rear. There's a scrawled question in my journal from the day I walked to the top of Mousehold Hill, already deeply in love with Devon and excited about my new life there: 'Can undulation be an addiction?' Mousehold offers the best view of the best side of my favourite British city: Cow Tower in the foreground – the tower nobody wants to believe that a cow once didn't climb to the top of by accident – then the gentle staircase of land leading up to the castle mound via the cathedral and the plague pits of Tombland. But because even the few small hills you do get in Norfolk tend to be loners and hillanthropes, you don't get those glorious localised weather patches there that you get in an area of vertiginous topographical bunching like south Devon.

Looking back across the Dart Valley towards my house early on a golden morning last autumn from the tallest of the hills that circle Totnes, I wondered if this was the best season of all for light in this part of the country. In all fairness though, I sometimes wondered that in spring too, and in summer. Even in winter too, although less often. In a couple of months the reds and golds would be stripped back to reveal the ghost land behind autumn's LSD curtain: the ivy-choked quarter barns and ruined bothies, the witches' knickers. But now the foliage, moisturised and sun-kissed, was almost blinding. Haytor, up on the moor, was clear and distinguished – half a day's walk away but almost touchable. Isolated regions of mist and cloudlets hung below it over the mini-valleys. The town was a bowl of hazy light. The sky – as always on the Cornubian Batholith – looked to be planning something big, even when it wasn't. Down at the bottom of the origami fold of the jumbled land, the river looked smoky. As high as I was, I didn't feel above the wildlife of the valley; I felt within it, no more than its equal, exactly as I should. But there was something bothering me, something in addition to the knowledge that most of the badgers that had lurked in the fields and woodland below me in summer were no longer there, something about the view that wasn't quite right. On the town's margins, in the nearly three years I had lived here, several wounds had appeared in the green hillsides. Famously, graffiti artists used to self-mockingly yet proudly add TWINNED WITH NARNIA to the town sign, then later, TWINNED WITH AREA 51, but recently the sign had been defaced again to read, less playfully, TWINNED WITH LINDEN HOMES, a reflection of the strength of local feeling about the succession of executive home developments being vomited onto one of the most beautiful stretches of countryside in Britain.

There is part of me that wonders if it's greedy to complain about these estates. Most other places in Britain are full of concrete, so why shouldn't this one be too? A lot of people in the centre of the country would auction a close member of their family to be surrounded by countryside a quarter as unspoilt as this. But I know that's the wrong way to look at it. You can't evaluate a pushbike using the rules of a tank. We need some recognisable places to still be recognisable places, particularly at a time when most places no longer are. There's nothing about these developments that smacks of necessity; they're what you might call large uninspired expensive boxes if 'boxes' didn't imply something more brutalist and original. This isn't a weasel killing a rabbit or a hen to save its family from starving. One estate calls itself Origins, presumably to commemorate the origins of stoats, deer and owls losing their homes. Another far less imaginative one looked like it had reached its unsurpassable apex of blandness then decided to outdo itself by building the blandest wall known to man in a place where a wall did not need to be built. There's no excuse for a terrible wall. Walls can be great, even those erected on a budget – miniature stone or brick galaxies – but you could stare at this one for hours and gain no extra vision. It's just a wall. It will only become slightly interesting if nature kicks seven shades of shit out of it.

Devon is a little culturally isolated from the rest of the country, and there's not a lot of employment to be had here; the upside of that has always been that it's ruggedly beautiful and very green. But now it's starting to look like going down to the woods here could become like going down to the woods in most other places: you'll be in for a big surprise, which is that the woods aren't there any more and have been replaced with an identikit housing estate called The Woods. The building and naming of these places work on the same logic of a large powerful man killing a defenceless chicken then renaming himself The Chicken afterwards. I've seen the plans, the red marks scattered on a council OS map like plague pustules, and this is only the beginning. The developers are selling a rural dream while bludgeoning the dream itself – not to mention the local infrastructure – as they do so. No doubt there'll be a break at some point, maybe in a year or so. All the roadworks will be gone, and there'll be a brief period of respite until the next lot of protected land is sold off to make rich people richer and the next, and the next, until finally almost all the magic will have been sucked away, and for miles around dawn in the countryside will be signified by little more than the sound of people waking up and starting some car engines where badgers and weasels used to live.

2

WOFFAL

A few of us were sitting around having a chat in my mum and dad's living room in Nottinghamshire: me, my aunt Mal and uncle Chris, my mum and dad and my cousin Fay. My dad, who was wearing Chris's jacket, having stolen it from a coat peg in the hall when Chris wasn't looking, was telling everyone about the area's annual festive hunt, which was taking place in the fields to the rear of the house. An hour previously, accompanied by a slightly reluctant me, he'd driven three villages east to watch the hunt begin in weather that made your teeth hurt.

'COME ON! GET IN THE CAR, YOU BIG TWAZZOCK,' he'd said. 'I KNOW YOU HATE IT AND I DON'T LIKE WHAT THEY USED TO DO EITHER, BUT THEY HUNT A MAN IN A FOX SUIT NOW, NOT A FOX, AND IT'S REALLY SPECTACULAR WHEN THEY ALL COME OVER THE HILL, JUMPING THE HEDGES.'

'But it's the same people who did hunt foxes, before it was banned?' I asked.

'NO,' said my dad. 'THIS LOT ARE ALL FROM *SOCIALIST WORKER* MAGAZINE.'

My feeling about fox hunting is this: if you do it, I don't want to be anywhere near you, let alone in a situation where I might have to speak to you. Recently the prime minister, David Cameron, had been edging worryingly around the subject of re-legalising it, making noises about some kind of compromise which he described as a 'middle way'. To my mind the only acceptable middle way for fox hunting would be if the foxes were replaced with hungry wolves, hounds were banned and each hunter was forced to hunt alone with his hands tied behind his back. But I make my living from writing about the countryside, which I know means I should take an interest in all sides of it, dark and light. There was, on the surface of things, a mixture of the two here. On the one hand, a man in a furry bright-orange suit, capering around, watched by giggling children. On the other, the parents of these children, dressed in black, some in veils, all in big hats, celebrating the tradition of ripping a wild animal apart for fun. They looked like the guests at Death's wedding.

I was glad I'd gone with my dad: it took me far out of the arguably oversafe bubble of animal lovers I normally spend time with. Also, the beginning was as explosive as he had promised, a thunder of hooves that reverberated across a dozen fields or more. Even more explosive was the moment five minutes earlier when a man had shouted 'Loose 'orse!' and a chestnut mare galloped through the crowd, almost trampling us, chased by two huntsmen.

'IT WAS FOOKIN' SPECTACULAR,' my dad told everyone now, in the living room. 'WE ALMOST GOT KILLED. YOU SHOULD HAVE COME. TOM DIDN'T LIKE IT AT ALL. I THOUGHT HE WAS GOING TO THROW HIMSELF IN FRONT OF ONE OF THE HORSES AS A PROTEST FOR A MOMENT, LIKE A SUFFRAGETTE. THEY'RE COMING OVER THE BACK FIELDS BY HERE IN A MINUTE. JO! GET THE CAT IN! HE'S ORANGE. THEY MIGHT MISTAKE HIM FOR A FOX.'

The conversation moved on, somehow, to owls. I told my cousin Fay about the noisy tawnies who roosted in the trees behind my house, which reminded her of the time that, upon the birth of her son, who is named Hal, a colleague of his father had sent the family a card which said, 'Congratulations on the birth of your son, Owl!' We talked also about Granny Pam, Fay's dad's mum, who nobody ever seemed to call Pam, always Granny Pam, and who lived in a high-rise flat in an area of Nottingham later to be even better known for gun crime than many other areas of Nottingham which were known for gun crime. I remember Granny Pam as a long skinny grin in a cloud of cigarette smoke, who – despite barely knowing me – always bought me amazing, imaginative Christmas presents, but Fay explained that Pam had a less-well-known vengeful side too, especially when it came to her parking space outside the flats.

'She once got mugged and turned round and punched the mugger in the face with her keys inside her fist.'

'Wow,' I said.

'Did I tell you about her lipstick?' said Fay.

'No,' I said.

'When I was a kid, if ever anyone nicked her parking space, she'd say to me, "Right! Get my lipstick!" Then we'd go outside and, while she put a chain across the space and padlocked the car in, she'd get me to write all over the car using her lipstick.'

I was keen to find out what Fay had written on the cars in question, but she didn't get the chance to tell me, as the phone rang at this point. My dad picked it up. 'HELLO?' he said. 'FOOK OFF, YOU BASTARD.' He put the handset down and turned to us. 'IT WAS ONE OF THOSE BASTARDS YOU GET SOMETIMES.'

Nobody was particularly surprised by this, as everyone in the room had known my dad for at least twenty-six years. He was in typically high spirits this festive season, although to be fair the season itself had little bearing on this. He'd got what he saw as the most indulgent bit of Christmas out of the way with typical alacrity on the morning of the day itself, eagerly shaking a bag next to my mum and me as we opened our presents, then packing the wrapping paper into it ready to be recycled. 'RIGHT!' he'd said as my mum carefully finished unwrapping the last of the usual huge mound of gifts she'd received from her friends. 'LET'S ALL GET BACK TO WORK.' This was standard behaviour on Christmas Day, at the dawn of which he had greeted me not with 'MERRY CHRISTMAS' but the bellowed instruction from his upstairs workroom: 'THERE ARE SOME CRISPS AND

MILK IN THE FRIDGE IF YOU WANT ANY!' Boxing Day or one of the days immediately following it, such as today, was the time we reserved for getting together with the rest of the family. There's not a lot of us, and this gathering was a particularly quiet one, as my other cousins, my uncle Paul and my auntie Jayne and Chris's daughters from his first marriage were all otherwise engaged. The plan was to go on a short walk, for which my dad would be the guide, pointing out landmarks and bringing in stories from his past as a teacher in inner-city Nottingham: the one, for example, about the time he broke up a brawl in the playground and discovered that one of the youths he had separated and now held by the collar was in fact Mike, the head of English, who was not very tall. My dad nipped to the loo before we embarked on the walk. I noticed as he came back through the door that he was holding a piece of toast liberally coated with pesto and salt. I looked at him questioningly. 'DON'T WORRY,' he said. 'I ALREADY HAD IT WHEN I WENT IN THERE.'

When my dad goes on walks or days out, he likes to incorporate a rest into his itinerary, during which he will find a patch of grass on which to lie ritualistically in a starfish position with his eyes closed. Those closest to him are accustomed to this now, but it can be a troubling image for people witnessing it for the first time. This summer Chris and Mal told me about a trip they'd been on with my mum and dad to the Yorkshire Sculpture Park, during which some Japanese tourists found my dad lying in a starfish position with his eyes closed and prodded him to check he wasn't dead. He was probably more tired than usual, having earlier air-boxed with a twelve-foot-tall statue made by the sculptor Tom Price. My mum took a photo of the boxing, on my dad's request, so it could be added to our family collection of pics of my dad pretending to fight with exhibits on days out, alongside such classics as the time he pretended to wrestle a stuffed hyena at Creswell Crags Museum and Visitor Centre near Worksop. It was unlikely there would be any exhibits with which to stage quasi fights on today's walk, and, although it provided no absolute guarantee, the icy ground made a starfish sleeping break improbable.

At the back door my dad took off Chris's coat and returned it to him, enabling Chris to put it on over his sweater, which was thick, fuzzy and light green. 'YOU LOOK LIKE SOME MOSS,' my dad told Chris.

As we passed through the porch I noticed that the small African wooden head that usually lived there had fallen to the ground. I had always been nervous around the wooden head, which my mum had purchased from a car boot sale a few years previously. I picked it up and returned it to its perch in the manner of someone holding a segment of something very recently deceased.

I enjoy going to car boot sales with my mum, but because I don't have her amazing vision, my experience at them often ends up tarred by the brush of anticlimax. When I arrive at a boot sale, full of foolish hope, what I inevitably see is an impenetrable wall of 1990s computer parts and grubby children's toys. When my mum looks at the same scene, she is able to home in instantly on the one exotic and interesting artefact amid the worthless garbage. 'I got this for you,' she said a couple of summers ago, fresh from a boot sale in Lincolnshire, handing me a sharp-ended varnished stick about a foot in length. 'I don't like it, but I know you're quite into weird stuff like that so I thought you might.'

I inspected the stick more closely and realised it was a letter opener, probably made in the early-to-mid-part of the last century. On the blunt end a double-sided Devil's head had been carved. To be totally honest, I wasn't sure I liked it either, but it intrigued me all the same, and I thanked my mum and carted it back home to Devon.

Over the next few months I tried to find a comfortable place for the Devil's head letter opener, but wherever I put it never seemed quite right. I certainly didn't want it staring at me from on top of the chest of drawers in my bedroom at night as I slept, and when I placed it near my work desk it seemed to send negative messages from its screwed-up wooden eyes. Like all writers, I already have at least one invisible demon telling me that what I do is a load of crud, and I certainly didn't need a corporeal one joining in and doing the same. By the following year I'd realised that the letter opener had crossed the line separating 'occult artefact you keep purely due to historical interest' from 'seriously freaks me out and needs to leave'. Also, I could argue that its influence had not been a positive one: in the twelve months since I'd got it, I'd contracted a lengthy illness and broken up with my partner. I didn't think of myself as a particularly superstitious person but whatever move I made next with the letter opener now seemed crucial to my future. However, the process of getting rid of the letter opener wasn't as easy as you might think. I'm very careful about recycling and I certainly wasn't just going to shove it in the kitchen bin, while the idea of throwing it into the flames of the fire in my living room gave me visions of vaporous ghouls materialising out of the smoke. I could have just gone and placed it in a field, but what if the crops caught fire the following day, the flames subsequently licking their way up to the associated farmhouse and reducing it to cinders? Lives would be wrecked and I would feel responsible.

Next to my mum's wooden head though, even the Satanic letter opener seemed of a fairly frivolous and easy-going nature. The wooden head had a monobrow frown that made the countenances of its larger spiritual ancestors on Easter Island look like those of *Blue Peter* presenters pumped on a home-crafting adrenaline rush. 'Like' does not sum up my mum's initial feelings towards it; she bought it because she found it intriguing and is interested in sculpture and the different historical approaches to it around the globe. For years the head's home was a crevice between the branches of a willow in the garden, and it lived there for some time in an apparently innocuous and peace-loving way, but in late 2009 my dad fell out of a eucalyptus tree opposite the willow and broke his spine. Upon her return home from the hospital, where the future of my dad as an independently mobile person hung in the balance, my mum noticed that the head's dark gaze was directed at the exact spot from which he'd fallen.

The years 2008 and 2009 were especially energetic for my dad. In late 2007, after over two decades of doing almost no exercise of a conventionally athletic or sporting nature, he'd made the surprise announcement that he would run in the London Marathon the following spring, dressed in the costume of a superhero directly from his own imagination. He began to train hard, doing circuits around the village cricket pitch, first in a pair of gym shoes three sizes too big for him that he had bought me for school PE eighteen years earlier from the Nottingham footwear seconds shop Jonathan James, then – after a bout of cajoling from my mum and me – in proper modern running shoes that wrapped themselves snugly around his feet. For motivation, he listened to Zairean and Senegalese pop music from the 1960s and *Deliverance*, the 2003 album by the redneck rapper Bubba Sparxxx. 'DO YOU WANT TO COME AND WATCH ME RUN ROUND THE FIELD?' he asked when I visited, standing at the door to the kitchen in tracksuit bottoms and a running shirt stained with brinjal pickle. Not quite sure what I would do to show support as I watched – Clap? Cheer? Fashion a makeshift pompom from some nearby meadow grass? – and feeling a little awkward about it, I declined but later regretted it. The only times I'd seen him run or even been aware of him running since the 1980s had been on the couple of occasions he'd jogged after my car and rapped his knuckles on the window to ask if I had adequately topped up my screenwash. Now, at fifty-eight years of age, he was covering fifteen miles a day, ignoring his doctor's advice to wear a heart monitor and my mum's to pace himself more gently.

'He thinks he's twenty-six,' my mum told me. 'He won't listen to me. But you know what he's like. All or nothing. He's never done anything in moderation in his life.'

My dad's personal brand of hedonism has never manifested itself in the obvious. His vices are more humdrum than those traditionally associated with high living. In this way he's very clever. If you try to sit someone down and tell them they've got a chutney problem, you're just going to look like a lunatic. Similarly, it's unlikely that anyone has successfully staged a salt or orange juice intervention, and I doubt I'd have been the one to break the trend. The risks from excessive running were more obvious, but it seemed churlish to highlight them when he was enjoying himself so much and looking fitter than he had done in years.

My dad has always seemed a little invincible to me. He's never been subject to the head and stomach aches from which my mum and I often suffered. To my knowledge he has only had two colds in his entire life – although, to be fair, they were also the loudest two I have ever witnessed. Still, twenty-six miles over hard ground was a long way in the sixtieth year of a life that had not been characterised by regular athleticism. I reminded him about *Hitchhiker's Guide to the Galaxy* author Douglas Adams, who'd died following a heart attack on a treadmill, arguably because he'd thrust himself vigorously and heedlessly into exercise after a long hiatus. He'd been ten years younger than my dad was now. My dad waved me away. 'DON'T WORRY. I'M AS FIT AS A FLEA. I DID EIGHTEEN MILES AROUND THE FIELD TODAY. I WAS LISTENING TO SOME TANZANIAN HIP HOP. IT WAS BRILLIANT.'

Our concerns escalated when, with the marathon only a few weeks away, my dad fell off a ladder in the garden while trimming the hedge with petrol-powered clippers. It was early March and he had been dressed in shorts and a T-shirt. The blades of the clippers continued to rotate as he bumped down through the cool air and he was lucky to escape with only a few bruises and two big cuts, neither of which were quite serious enough for stitches.

My dad is a heavy sleeper but also a lively, noisy one who, without warning, in the witching hours will often make an emphatic slumberous statement or break out into shout-mumbled song. During his marathon training his dreams also took on an energetic, high-risk flavour which, with the Big Day approaching, only intensified. A diving header in the FA Cup Final resulted in him bashing his temple on the bedside table and waking up sprawled and dazed on the bedroom floorboards. 'I wonder if it might be best if I sleep somewhere else until he's got it out of his system,' my mum remarked after a high-pressure rugby union game during which she was drop-kicked from one side of the bed to the other. 'I'M SORRY. I SCORED A TRY IN THAT ONE, AS WELL AS A DROP GOAL,' he told her. 'I NEVER USED TO SCORE A TRY IN REAL RUGBY AND NOW I HAVE!' On the night of my last visit to my parents' house before the marathon, my dad – tired from a morning of heavy training – fell asleep on the living-room floor part-way through telling two experimentally conjunctive stories about the time that someone cut the elastic off his mittens at primary school and why TV weathermen are nearly all fuckpigs and bastards. I headed in the direction of bed but, upon reaching the stairs, turned back and returned to the living room to move the coffee table a couple of feet further away from his snoring head.

As I drove away from my parents' house for the final time as a son with a dad who had never run a marathon, my dad jogged after the car as if he had forgotten to give or tell me something important. I wound down the window. 'WATCH OUT FOR FOOKWITS AND LOONIES,' he said.

On the day of the marathon I decided not to join my dad for the start in Greenwich, feeling that, as an easily distracted man, he'd be better served by having as few objects and people as possible occupying his attention. Instead I met my mum on the north side of the Thames, near the Embankment, to watch the final stretch of the run. When I finally located her she admitted she was a little cross with him. Earlier, as they'd walked up the hill past Greenwich Observatory towards the place where the marathon would begin, my dad had spotted several people in bibs running across the grass, shouted, 'OH NO! THEY'RE STARTING!' and hoofed it away from her, not giving her time to hand him his water bottle, towel or banana. It later transpired that these competitors had been running towards the starting line, not away from it. Only by sheer luck did my mum manage to relocate my dad in the ever-thickening crowd of runners, ten minutes later. He was jogging on the spot and held an open can of the energy drink Red Bull.

'HI,' he said. 'I'VE NEVER HEARD OF THIS STUFF

BEFORE, BUT IT'S GREAT. THEY'RE GIVING IT AWAY FOR FREE.'

'How many of those have you had?' my mum asked.

'THIS IS MY FOURTH.'

'You know what's in it, don't you?'

'NO. WHAT?'

'Well, lots of caffeine, for starters.'

'OH.'

My dad, who operates like a permanently caffeinated person and delights in informing anyone from close family to complete strangers that he has 'BEEN UP SINCE FIVE', had experienced typically little difficulty rising on marathon morning. At just before 6 a.m. the fire alarm had gone off in the hotel where my parents were staying in north London, and my mum had opened her eyes to see him standing by the window, already fully dressed in his outfit for the day: bright orange cape, black tracksuit bottoms and grey lycra top emblazoned with the orange letters JC, the initials of Johnny Catbiscuit, the crime fighter central to a children's book he had written recently called *Johnny Catbiscuit and the Abominable Snotmen*. 'Oh God. What have you done!?' my mum asked him.

'I did feel bad about that,' she told me later, 'and I said sorry, but when I heard the alarm my first thought had been that it must have been his fault.' The hotel's guests and staff filed out into the car park. Many were still in various forms of nightwear, but my dad was the only one dressed in the uniform of a leftfield superhero.

Now he was in the thick of the action with his kind: other runners in superhero costumes, a couple of Spice

Girls, a spavined Spiderman, a man in a gorilla suit with baffling comedy breasts. My mum caught up with him again around about the halfway mark, near Millwall. 'How did he look?' I asked. 'Totally out of it,' she said. He took longer than we expected to come past the Embankment, and when he did he looked more out of it still. 'Go on, Johnny!' spectators shouted, seeing the name on his cape, and he performed for them, spreading his arms wide beneath the fabric as if flying. Judging by his facial expression, it was very possible he believed he was genuinely aloft above the brutalist buildings next to the Thames. 'Dad!' I shouted. Realising that there were lots of other dads running too, I modified this to 'Mick!' but he could not hear me. In the end I joined in with the masses. 'Go on, Johnny!' I hollered, realising that the finishing line was not much more than a mile away, and what had seemed impossible six months ago was going to happen: he was really going to do this.

While my mum and I were waiting for my dad at the Embankment, I'd heard a woman standing to my rear who'd watched a lot of marathons talking about the state competitors get into afterwards. 'You'd think they'd want to be quiet when they're that tired,' she said. 'But they usually don't. They talk and talk. They're on such a high, they can't stop.' Sure enough, my dad talked a lot when he'd completed the marathon and, almost nine years later, has still not stopped. In the months directly after his run he discussed his intention of competing again the following year but, heeding my mum's reservations, eventually decided against it. Nonetheless, he retained his fitness levels with a new zest for horticultural activity, both in his own garden and in the space that my parents' next-door neighbour Edna had allowed him to use in her garden to grow vegetables. 'TOM, CAN I HAVE A WORD?' he said to me during one of my visits to Nottinghamshire. I followed him into the garden and he pointed to a large basket of potatoes he had grown. 'SEE THESE? YOU'RE GOING TO NEED SOME OF YOUR OWN WHEN IT ALL FALLS TO BITS.'

Benefiting from a new arrangement with the local farmer that allowed him and his friend Phillip to gather wood from much of the nearby land, my dad chopped vast amounts of logs, stacking them in artful circular *Holzhaufen* formations which allowed the logs at the centre of the pile to cure and dry. Towards the end of the following year, when a eucalyptus – a tree infamous for its rapid growth spurts – began to rocket towards the clouds in can-do fashion and block out the light in the house, my mum suggested that it might be wise to employ a tree surgeon to prune or remove it. 'DON'T BE RIDICULOUS,' said my dad, fetching his bowsaw. 'I'LL DO IT.' My mum held the ladder as my dad climbed it then the tree itself in old loafers with very little grip to them. The sky filled with rain and my mum said that they should stop and seek shelter. She went back into the house but my dad stayed outside, busying himself with other tasks. 'You won't go back up the tree, will you?' she asked him.

'NO,' said my dad.

'Do you promise?'

'OF COURSE I WON'T. WHY DON'T YOU BELIEVE ME? IT'S NOT FAIR. YOU'RE ALWAYS TELLING ME OFF.'

Five minutes later my mum glanced out of the bedroom window and saw my dad back up the eucalyptus, balancing on its highest branches in the same smooth-soled loafers, saw in hand, rain streaking against his squinting, determined face. 'And then I saw him go,' she told me. 'I knew it was bad from the moment he hit the ground.'

My dad might have fallen on his front had it not been for the fact that during his descent he was trying to avoid the blade of the falling bowsaw. This caused him to flip over in the air and land hard on his spine. It was half an hour before the paramedics arrived, and during that period he and my mum made a major mistake. Due to the vast amount of pain he was in, he could not stand or crawl properly, but he tried to edge along the ground in tiny increments towards the back door, encouraged by my mum, in order to escape the rain. When you've fractured your vertebrae, as my dad had, the one thing you should not try to do is move, as this can sever the spinal column irreparably.

'I was such an idiot,' my mum told me. 'But in my defence it's very difficult to know when someone is really hurt when they're as melodramatic as he is. When I give him a haircut and his bare skin touches the back of the chair he yells like he's been stabbed.'

The paramedics ticked my parents off for their error, loaded my dad into their ambulance then attempted to reverse the vehicle out of the house's awkwardly shaped driveaway but got stuck. As the morphine the paramedics had given my dad began to kick in, he shouted instructions to the driver, who after several tense minutes got the vehicle pointing in the right direction and on the road to the hospital, several miles away, in Mansfield. Upon arriving and seeing a consultant, my dad was asked if he had any allergies. 'YEAH, JEREMY CLARKSON,' he replied.

He would walk again, the doctor said, after my dad had been properly examined, but it was of paramount importance that he stay absolutely still in his hospital bed for a week after the surgery. Strapped to the mattress, he was attended by a very camp male nurse who, every time he caught my dad attempting to move, would slap my dad's ankles and say, 'Naughty!' 'I WAS OFF MY FACE ON MORPHINE AND THOUGHT KENNETH WILLIAMS AND HATTIE JACQUES WERE GOING TO WALK IN AT ANY MINUTE,' my dad later recalled.

After the week had elapsed he was told that he would be able to go home as soon as his body brace arrived. A day later the brace had not arrived. He amused himself by asking my mum to photograph him doing an *I'm dying!* face then instructing her to send the photograph to me. Three days later the brace still had not arrived. The consultant told my dad it would be here soon. 'IS IT COMING FROM FAR AWAY?' he asked. 'LONDON? OR CASABLANCA?' The consultant said no, that it was here in Mansfield, in a cupboard downstairs, but the man who was supposed to bring it up hadn't got round to it yet. My dad asked the consultant how much it was setting back the NHS per day to keep him in this bed. The consultant put the figure at around eight hundred pounds. 'SO YOU'RE SAYING BECAUSE A BLOKE CAN'T BE ARSED TO WALK UPSTAIRS WITH A BACK BRACE IT'S COST THE HOSPITAL TWO THOUSAND FOUR HUNDRED POUNDS?' The consultant admitted that this was more or less the case. My dad asked for the phone number of the man who was supposed to bring the brace up and called him and said that if the brace didn't arrive soon he would call the local newspaper and tell them about this fiasco. Four minutes later the man arrived in the room with the brace.

Back home, wearing the brace and severely limited in his movements, my dad admitted that his injury had served as a wake-up call: he'd been trying to do too much for a man of his age. 'So you're going to stop chopping logs?' I asked, when I visited. 'YEP. NONE OF THAT ANY MORE,' he replied. 'CAN YOU GET ME A DRINK? I'M SIXTY. I USED TO DO EVERYTHING FOR MY DAD WHEN HE WAS SIXTY.' My mum, meanwhile, moved the wooden head from the willow tree to the porch, directing its gaze away from the house and the offending tree, towards the garden hedge. 'I can't bring myself to get rid of it,' she said. 'I feel like something bad will happen if I do, either to me or somebody else. It's all nonsense of course. I know I'm being silly.'

My parents' house is in a shallow, bright valley, and Sunnydale is what it says on the front door. My mum chose the name after talking my dad out of his first choice, Alien Sex Pit. They purchased the place in the uneasy final days of the last century, when people thought computers would set fire to the world. The house's former owner had died in it on her hundredth birthday: a feat of very specific hanging-on and letting-go that, even though numbers are just numbers, seems a beautiful demonstration of personal willpower, even more so for the fact that it happened only a few weeks before the final curtain of an entire millennium. When my parents first viewed the house no object in it appeared to date from beyond 1958. The building is made from the small red Cafferata bricks synonymous with villages around Newark-on-Trent. The covered, open-sided oak porch is a much later addition by them, along with a third bedroom and the airy downstairs room where my mum paints, sews, prints and sketches. For the five years after my dad's accident the head remained apparently content in its new home on the wall in the porch. On a wooden rack below it, toads moved in and out of my dad's old loafers and running shoes, but the head never seemed swayed by their itinerant spirit. For me these five years passed more quickly than any before them: years of final fully entrenched adulthood, unshockable years of muddling along, caring a hell of a lot less about a few things I once did care about and a fair bit more about a lot of things I once didn't. I imagine they passed more swiftly still for the wooden head, as years probably do when you're a wooden head carved at an undetermined point in history and of a potentially haunted nature who has lived enough to be surprised by very little. In early 2014 my parents had to have a large part of the house rebuilt on their insurance after discovering that the long-term leaking of a shoddily fitted shower had caused serious structural damage and the roof was in danger of collapsing. This was the latest in a long series of water-based mishaps in the house, including a cracked pipe in 2011 which resulted in a large stain on the living-room ceiling resembling a short but bulbous penis.

'Do you think this looks rude?' asked my mum.

'Not at all,' I replied.

None of these events affected the wooden head. It continued to stare implacably away from them towards distant fields containing cattle, none of which were struck down during the same period with any significant or mysterious cases of murrain or cowpox. But after its fall from the porch during Christmas 2014 – the Christmas when I accompanied my dad to watch hunters set off to hunt a man dressed as a fox – the head began to get restless and embarked on several other excursions. None of these were very ambitious, usually ending with the head on the flagstones below and never straying beyond the porch's threshold, but as 2014 became 2015 and 2015 wore on, the head's tiny holidays became more frequent. My parents would replace it on its perch – always looking away from the house and the now-pollarded eucalyptus – but sometimes by the end of the day it would be back on the ground. A couple of times they found it inside the footwear on the rack below where it lived, including in one of the fateful loafers, which my dad still refused to throw away and continued to wear for lighter gardening tasks. More and more puzzled each time, my parents replaced the head again and again. Its tumbles to the ground were never witnessed by human eyes and occurred not just in high winds but in weather so still that the leaves on the trees in the garden barely vibrated.

My dad's exercise regime had slowed down by now, marginally. A month after coming out of his back brace he dusted down his axe and began to chop wood again. Then, after going to see the consultant at the hospital and being told that the condition of his fracture had regressed due to his chopping, he stopped. Then, a few weeks after that, he started again and never stopped. He did cease running around the village cricket field but began swimming at the local public pool, making new friends from eclectic walks of life: architects and retired miners and library assistants and bikers and archaeology lecturers and policemen and billboard salesmen. Sometimes while naked and wet my dad would talk to his new friends at such length in the changing room that one of them would bring their towel over and begin to dry him. Just as my phone conversations with my dad would invariably end with him instructing me to 'WATCH OUT FOR FOOKWITS AND LOONIES' they would now tend to begin with 'THIS WEEK AT SWIMMING...' One week at swimming my dad was discussing a cashpoint in Nottingham which has the statistical reputation of being the scene of more muggings than any other cashpoint in the UK, and his policeman friend, also named Mick, told him that he had taken a statement from a student who'd been mugged down the road from the cashpoint. Not having any cash on him, the student had offered to pay the muggers by cheque. The muggers declined and escorted him back to his flat, stripping it of its most valuable contents. Another week at swimming my dad hid Malcolm's shoes. Another week at swimming, in late summer that year, when the wooden head's kamikaze dives from the porch wall were becoming even more frequent, my dad was getting unchanged and noticed that he had a black toenail. He showed the black toenail to Malcolm, who agreed that it was a black toenail.

I winced when my dad showed me the black toenail, remembering the pain I'd experienced when the nail of my thumb turned black in 2008 after I slammed a car door on it. But my dad said he had experienced little to no pain from the black toenail. He couldn't remember anything he had done to make it black and was told by his doctor not to worry about it and that the nail would fall off naturally when a new translucent one had finished growing beneath it. Presumably it was one of those minor injuries you sustain in the thick of strenuous exercise or physical labour and don't notice at the time they occur. I get a lot of these myself and currently even had a very slightly bad toe of my own, probably sustained on a steep rocky crevice during a long walk in a thinly populated part of Devon. I have inherited my dad's toes: long, thick and unintentionally violent. Because of this and the tiny unseen people who live in my house and steal socks in the dead of night, my sock drawer resembles a diverse but unsuccessful sock dating site: socks of every shape and colour, each of them alone, failing to find love. I stub my toes fairly regularly, and my dad stubs his a lot too, and toe length could quite feasibly be a factor in this regularity. Earlier in the year, many weeks before the black nail's appearance, my dad had stubbed his toe on a table leg in his office then immediately replied to an unsolicited mass email from Boris Johnson with 'FUCK OFF, BORIS.' Afterwards he told my mum about the email and – although certainly no fan of Boris Johnson herself – she told him it hadn't been a very nice thing to do. My dad immediately tramped back upstairs and sent a follow-up email: 'SORRY ABOUT THAT, BORIS. I OVERREACTED. IT WAS BECAUSE I'D JUST STUBBED MY TOE.'

There was quite a bit of speculation among my dad's mates at swimming about when the black toenail would fall off. Looking at how precariously it was hanging there on everyone's last swim before Christmas, Pat and Malcolm suggested that today could be the big day. 'What if it comes off in the water?' asked Pat. 'That wouldn't be good.'

'NO, IT WOULDN'T,' replied my dad. 'ESPECIALLY IF SOMEONE IS DOING BREASTSTROKE AND HAPPENS TO BE OPENING THEIR MOUTH JUST AS IT FLOATS INTO THEIR PATH.'

The nail, however, had been looking just as precarious for several weeks. I'd been getting little reports of it via text message from my mum. 'Your dad's black toenail is looking really bad now: I think it's about to come off,' she would tell me, but several days later there it would still be. My dad knew it would hold on for a bit longer still. He loves his early-morning swims and would, I am sure, have been reluctant to jeopardise his relationship with the authorities at the pool by defiling the water. Recently the pool had asked its regulars if they had any suggestions for things they'd like to change about the facilities. My dad came up with the following three:

1. A *trompe l'œil* panoramic landscape on the bottom of the pool to keep people amused when they were swimming with their heads down.
2. Mirrors on the ceiling, to enable swimmers doing backstroke to see where they were going and not crash into each other.

3. All-over-body airblade dryers for the
   changing rooms.

So far, there had been no response from the pool.

My parents and I spent that Christmas of 2015 at my house in Devon, where I was playing nurse to one of my cats, who was recovering from two large life-saving operations, having been attacked by a dog. My dad filled their car with several bags of firewood, which he'd very kindly collected for me. I felt bad taking this from him, as he stacked it in such beautiful formations, and I felt even worse when my mum explained the lengths he'd gone to in order to get some of it. 'He lost a big branch in the river again, like last year,' she told me. 'He walked back across the field and asked me to come over and hold his legs for him while he reached over and got it. I'm sixty-five.' Only just over a month had passed since the last time my dad had fallen into a large body of natural water: a lake in Lincolnshire into which he was dipping a jar in order to get goodies for his new garden wildlife pond.

'I should have known he would never be a proper grown-up when he asked me to go sledging on our first date,' said my mum.

After my dad and I had brought the logs in from the car, he went upstairs for a bath, taking the radio with him, and my mum and I attempted to catch up with each other over the booming sound of the Radio 4 *News Quiz* and my dad's laughter. Half an hour later, I went upstairs to the toilet and found a trail of bubbles leading across the landing to the spare bedroom. 'WATCH MY TOENAIL!' my dad shouted, charging past me and down the stairs, barefoot. A few moments later he could be heard making loud quacking noises at my cats while throwing huge rolls of greasy cooked turkey at them: a treat he'd bought them from Asda the previous day. Afterwards, as he arrived in the living room, I noticed he'd taken his shirt off again. He looked like a man who'd been unexpectedly invited to compete in a wrestling match in the last three minutes.

'CAN YOU PUT ROLLING NEWS ON THE TELLY FOR ME?' he asked, handing me the TV remote. I noticed the toenail was still not fully off. It really did look like it was about to detach now, but recent events had told me not to get too excited. It could be months yet.

On the second morning of my parents' stay I asked my dad if he wanted a cup of tea. My dad has not to my knowledge ever had a cup of tea, but I sometimes ask him if he wants one just to wind him up.

'NO, I WANT A COFFEE,' he said. 'STRONG, WITH A BIT OF COLD WATER SO I DON'T BURN MY OESOPHAGUS. YOU'VE KNOWN ME THIRTY-EIGHT YEARS. YOU SHOULD KNOW THAT BY NOW.'

'I'm forty,' I said.

'YEAH, BUT YOU DIDN'T REALLY KNOW ME FOR THE FIRST TWO YEARS.'

Increasingly, my dad's visits to my home are about recreating the rituals he enjoys in his own as assiduously as possible: the extravagantly bubbly baths, the loud radio, the bars of chocolate hidden under sofa cushions so – in his own words – 'THEY ARE FUN TO FIND LATER.' He also likes to go for an early-morning swim at the friendly local pool, which has an old-fashioned Speedo clock and doesn't appear to have been redecorated since the seventies. Today being Boxing Day, though, the pool was closed. We'd only got out for a very short walk the previous day, and I knew it would be important to exercise my dad, in much the same way it's important to exercise a German shepherd, so I suggested that he, my mum and I went for a walk along the seafront at Dawlish. I offered to drive, but he declined and said we'd go in his and my mum's car. I told my dad that I could easily navigate us to Dawlish from my house, just thirty-five minutes away, but he insisted on using his satnav.

After the female voice on the satnav had directed us down a farm track for the second time in ten minutes, my dad called her a bastard, told her to 'FOOK OFF' and permitted me to direct him the final quarter of the way. 'THIS CAR'S GOT AUTOMATIC BRAKING ON IT,' he said. 'IT GIVES ME MORE CHANCE TO WATCH OUT FOR FOOKWITS AND LOONIES.' As my dad drives, he tells stories from his life, slowing the car down dramatically as he gets to a climactic or highly descriptive point in the narrative, to the frustration of any drivers behind. On this occasion he told a story about an old man who recently went into a skid and flipped his Land Rover over on the main road not far from my parents' village. A farmer had been first on the scene and, upon helping the old man out of his Land Rover, noticed that the old man's dog was crushed beneath the vehicle, one floppy ear sticking out heartbreakingly from beneath the bodywork. After he pulled the old man to safety and discovered he was not seriously hurt, the farmer gave him the bad news. 'I don't have a dog,' replied the old man. The farmer and the old man walked back to the Land Rover. 'That's just my fur-trapper hat,' said the old man, pulling the floppy ear and releasing the remainder of the hat from beneath the wreck.

There were no exhibits or statues on the seafront at Dawlish so my dad did not stop to air-box or wrestle as we walked. It was also too cold for him to pause for a spontaneous nap in a starfish position. The stretch of railway line that runs in front of the beach here, where Deepest Devon ends and the cliffs turn red, is the Elizabeth Taylor of train tracks: beautiful but constantly troubled. When you're on the train, passing along it, you feel like you're in the sea itself. On a windy day, waves will often crash into and over the side of the train. This had been a rare winter when the sea hadn't broken the track into bits, causing lengthy closures and replacement bus services. Nonetheless, the wind was fierce, gnashing at our cheeks as we walked west, the waves thudding angrily against the track's new rocky defences. There were lots of other families walking the footpath but I noticed that, unlike mine, the dads in those families did not periodically shout 'KEEP AWAY FROM THE EDGE' as they strolled beside the steep drop to the beach.

'Have you been to get your bad tooth looked at yet?' my mum asked me.

'KEEP AWAY FROM THE EDGE!' said my dad.

'I was thinking that bamboo I gave you might be best planted on the far side of the garden – the same side as the oil tank,' said my mum.

'KEEP AWAY FROM THE EDGE!' said my dad.

'Mick, stop saying, "KEEP AWAY FROM THE EDGE!"' said my mum. 'We're miles away from it.'

'YOU'RE NOT. LOOK AT TOM. TOM, STOP DOING THAT. YOU COULD FALL IN AND DIE.'

During the drive back to my house my dad asked if I had used my new headtorch yet, a present he'd bought me for Christmas but had delivered to me several weeks early because he was so excited about it. I admitted that I hadn't and apologised. 'WHAT?' he said. 'I CAN'T BELIEVE IT. USE YOUR HEADTORCH. AND WHAT'S THIS YOUR MUM TOLD ME ABOUT YOU TURNING DOWN THE CHANCE TO GO ON BREAKFAST TELLY?' I told him I had no interest in ever being on telly, detailing another couple of opportunities I'd turned down in the last six months. 'I CAN'T BELIEVE YOU. YOU'RE UNFOOOKINGBELIEVABLE. YOU'LL BE BACK WORKING IN TESCO IF YOU'RE NOT CAREFUL.' The rest of the evening passed quietly, in contrast to the previous time my parents had stayed when, in his sleep at 3 a.m., my dad had shouted, 'THEY LET ME OUT SOMETIMES, YOU KNOW.' The next morning he got up early, threw some more cooked meat at the cats and packed the car, ready for the long journey back to Nottinghamshire. My mum checked my dad had not erroneously put any of my possessions in their suitcase, such as the four clean pillowcases he took last time. I felt much as I always do when I've seen my parents: tired, ready for a quiet sit-down, but sad to see them go and wishing I saw them more frequently. 'WOFFAL!' said my dad, which was the acronym version of 'WATCH OUT FOR FOOKWITS AND LOONIES!' that he'd become fond of using lately. 'WEAR THAT HEADTORCH!' he added as he and my mum walked to the car. I promised I would and tried to remember where I'd put it. I asked him if his black toenail had fallen off yet and he said it hadn't. When they arrived home five hours later, the wooden head was on the ground in front of the door.

My dad's black toenail finally fell off about four weeks later. Over the phone, my mum told me that it had dislodged in the swimming pool changing room, upon which my dad had proudly shown it to all the regulars. 'Was this before or after his swim?' I asked. 'Before, fortunately,' my mum said. I asked her where the toenail was now and she began to repeat the question to my dad, who was upstairs.

'IS THAT TOM? TELL HIM TO WOFFAL,' I heard my dad shout.

'I don't need to tell him. I'm sure he can hear you. He wants to know where the toenail is,' said my mum.

'IT'S ON A SHELF UP HERE IN MY OFFICE,' said my dad.

'Why?' said my mum.

'I WANT TO KEEP IT AND GET IT FRAMED. IT CAN BE A MEMENTOE. MEMENTOE! DO YOU GET IT?' said my dad.

'Yes,' said my mum.

21st-CENTURY YOKEL

My mum told me she had some other, bigger news: they had solved the mystery of why the wooden head kept falling on the ground. 'You will never guess,' she said, and she was right. I had turned all the facts over in my head numerous times, and even the most logical conclusions I had drawn – that the head contained the reincarnated spirit of an Egyptian demon from the year 11 BC, for example – seemed wildly improbable.

'Your dad caught Casper from next door throwing it at the door.'

'But...how?'

'He kind of scoops it up with his paw then flicks it at the handle. I think he just wants to be let in.'

My mum and dad's neighbours' cat, who is all white and named Casper after the famous friendly animated ghost, had been a regular visitor to their house for years. Between 2012 and 2014 he was never happier than with the tongue of my parents' previous cat, Floyd, deep inside his ear. After Floyd was killed by a car in the autumn of the latter year, Casper began a new love affair with George, a ginger and white stray I had rescued from the mean lanes of Devon then donated to my parents. Casper and George, who bears a startling resemblance to the Belgian international midfielder Kevin De Bruyne, sleep with their limbs entwined at least once every day and gambol about my mum and dad's garden, playwrestling and chasing one another up trees. Both of them have been neutered, but my mum has walked into upstairs rooms on several occasions to find George taking Casper roughly from behind. Casper is the heavier cat, but it is George

80

who plays the dominant role in their relationship. Casper knows how to be assertive too, though. Before he started asking to be let in by throwing the wooden head at the door he had already worked out how to bang the brass knocker on the door with his paw.

It wasn't until the beginning of summer that I next visited my mum and dad. The wooden head was on the flagstones near the porch's entrance when I arrived, its mean, furrowed face staring up at a heavy sky. I took my shoes off but chose not to leave them in the porch

beneath the head's perch. I entered the living room and found Casper sitting upright on the sofa, not unlike a small human. Missing only a remote control and a can of Tennent's Extra, his pose was one that brought to mind the term 'catspreading'. He gave me the most casual of glances then continued to watch rolling news. Not finding any sign of my parents in the house, I put my shoes back on and wandered down to their new wildlife pond, which had come on in leaps and bounds since last year. Broad-bodied chaser dragonflies flitted about above the water's shiny surface, and a little egret belted by overhead. 'I'M GOING TO GET A SWAN FOR IT,' my dad had announced when drawing up plans for the pond. 'Where from?' I'd asked. 'I BET YOU CAN GET THEM OFF THE INTERNET,' he'd replied. He had abandoned this plan, but moorhens, ducks, water beetles, frogs and newts had already arrived on or around the water, of their own volition. My parents had worked tirelessly to transform the space from the remains of an old pigsty into what it was now, my mum referring to their efforts as 'pondering'. I noticed too that the plants my dad had appropriated from my own pond were thriving.

My pond is a fraction of the size of my mum and dad's but was full of life in the summers of 2014 and 2015. At the start of this particular spring, the following year, it had become somewhat weed-choked and I'd begun to de-weed it but not got all that far by the time my mum and dad last visited me in March: the one time I'd seen them between now and our Christmas outing to Dawlish. My dad had dipped an arm in to take some specimens for his pond then got a little carried away for the next fifteen minutes. I'd left him to it, said bye and gone off for a walk on Dartmoor. Two hours later a photo popped through onto my phone from my mum, showing my dad in the middle of my pond, topless, up to his waist in water. I returned home to find the pond entirely clear of weed and algae. Tired and keen to relax and refresh myself with a hot bath after my long walk, I thought about what a kind gesture this had been from my dad. The feeling of gratitude lasted all the way to the bathroom, which, upon entering, I discovered now boasted much of the former contents of my pond, and subsequently took me over an hour to clean.

Despite visiting a couple of nearby large bodies of water with a jam jar in an attempt to restock it, my pond had been a bit bland and sleepy since then, so I was excited to see all the buzzing activity in my mum and dad's. Casper and George had now joined me to watch the hubbub. As they began to do cat kung fu on the water's edge, I tiptoed out onto a small rocky promontory in an attempt to see a water beetle.

'DON'T FALL IN!' said my dad, arriving behind me and almost causing me to fall in.

We walked back up to the house, past a bed full of thriving spinach, a riot of stoned-looking bees on a giant scabious, the stump of the fateful eucalyptus and the wooden head. In the kitchen my dad picked up a piece of rock from on top of the plate cupboard. 'KNOW WHAT THIS IS?' he asked.

My dad greeting me after several weeks apart by showing me an obscure object he'd found in the ground near the house was nothing new. Objects he'd found in the ground near the house before included some ancient dog teeth, a sheep skull, a sea of writhing, unusually colourful worms and an extremely bendy courgette. 'Is it some kind of old-fashioned brick?' I said, evaluating his latest find.

'GOOD GUESS. I'M GOING TO TELL YOU EXACTLY WHAT IT IS LATER ON, AND I WANT YOU TO LISTEN. I'VE JUST HAD A BATH AND SWALLOWED A BIG LOAD OF RADOX BUBBLE BATH BY MISTAKE.'

'Can you not just tell me now?'

'NO. DO AS YOU'RE TOLD, YOU BIG STREAK OF PISS. I NEED YOU TO SIT DOWN AND I NEED YOUR UNDIVIDED ATTENTION.'

My mum arrived in the kitchen and gave me a hello hug. She seemed a little flustered and explained that she'd lost her ticket to a literary event organised by her book group.

'IT'S BECAUSE OF YOUR CRAZY LIFESTYLE,' said my dad. 'YOU'RE WORSE THAN LINDSAY LOHAN.'

Later we sat down for dinner and I talked to my mum about the wooden head. I'd recently found a new home for the Devil-headed letter opener she bought for me – with my friend Jo, who had drained its dark power by keeping it in a pot on her desk alongside several brightly coloured plushies. Now some of the wooden head's occult strength had been compromised by Casper, I wondered if my mum might finally feel confident about giving it away. She said she'd rather not and that the head still troubled her. I agreed. At this point she turned to my dad, who was wearing a stained orange T-shirt. 'Mick,' she asked. 'Did you know that you're wearing one of my painting rags?'

We watched the extended Brexit edition of *Channel 4 News*, and my dad pointed out some politicians he thought were fucking bastards and some other politicians he'd previously thought were just bastards but now thought were fucking bastards too. Then we went into the other room and my dad picked up the piece of stone again. 'NOW THEN,' he said. 'SIT NEXT TO ME. AND LISTEN.'

'I need to nip to the loo first,' I said.

'IT'S ALWAYS THE SAME,' said my dad. 'PEOPLE ARE ALWAYS LEAVING ME.'

'I've already been holding it for half an hour just to be polite.'

'DON'T WEE IN THE TOILET. GO OUTSIDE AND DO IT IN THE BUCKET IN THE SHED. I NEED IT FOR MY COMPOST.'

My dad had found the piece of stone while he was doing what he calls fossicking. This is when, after very heavy rainfall, he walks down to the river to find good firewood that has been washed down it by the flood waters. After picking the stone out of the shallows, he had taken it to the swimming pool to show Pat, whose experience as a mining geologist, my dad thought, might enable him to identify it.

'You took it to the actual swimming pool?'

'NO, JUST TO THE CHANGING ROOMS. I FORGOT MY TRUNKS THAT DAY AND HAD TO BORROW SOMEONE'S SPARE ONES. BUT THAT'S NOT WHAT I TOLD THE HAIRDRESSER THE OTHER DAY. I TOLD HER I SWAM NAKED BUT JUST KEPT MY LEGS REALLY TIGHT TOGETHER THE WHOLE TIME.'

'And what did Pat say about the rock?'

'HE SAID, "It's just a bit of limestone, Mick." BUT I WASN'T SATISFIED WITH THAT. SO I SHOWED IT TO MY FRIEND PHILIP. HE USED TO BE AN ARCHAEOLOGY LECTURER. HE KNOWS ALL SORTS OF THINGS. HE'S SIX FOOT FOUR AND

USED TO LIVE IN A THIRTY-TWO-ROOM HOUSE. HE LOOKED AT IT AND TOLD ME IT'S A BIT OF MASONRY THAT WAS MEANT TO BE ON A MEDIEVAL HOUSE. THIS BIT HERE WAS A JAMB, AND THIS BIT WAS MEANT TO GO IN A WINDOW, BUT WHEN THE MASON GOT TO THIS BIT, WHICH IS CALLED AN OOLITH, HE REALISED IT WAS THE WRONG SHAPE AND CHUCKED IT. AND NOW IT'S MINE. EVERYTHING IN THIS WORLD HAS GOT A STORY TO IT. GENGHIS KHAN DIED OF A NOSEBLEED ON HIS WEDDING NIGHT. NOT MANY PEOPLE KNOW THAT. SOME PEOPLE ARE INTERESTED IN OTHER PEOPLE'S STORIES AND SOME PEOPLE AREN'T.'

'Yeah, that reminds me. I was going to the—'

'NOW LISTEN CAREFULLY, YOU, BECAUSE THIS LEADS ON TO SOMETHING ELSE. BUT I'VE FORGOTTEN IT NOW BECAUSE YOU'VE TALKED SO MUCH. I'LL HAVE A THINK AND COME BACK TO IT IN A MINUTE.'

My mum and I stepped back outside into the garden. The day had started wet, but now a fuzzy blanket of transparent warmth hung over my mum's plants. Everything seemed four times as fragrant as it had a few hours ago. The light had almost completely faded, but the stoned bees still clung to the giant scabious in cuddly gangs. Below it were three pots of lager: my mum and dad's attempt to control the garden's current slug population. My dad had offered me some of the same lager – which, bought in bulk, worked out at around 20p a can from Asda – and I'd declined. I asked my mum if my dad was still shouting in his sleep.

'Not as much. But he did wake me up by saying, "A FORTY-HOUR WEEK AT FOUR POUNDS AN HOUR? WHAT'S THAT?" the other night.'

George bounded up behind my mum and me, then cut in front and thwacked his strong tail possessively against our shins. I spotted a metal grass roller, passed down first to my granddad and then my dad, that my great-granddad had made – when? During the 1920s? Thirties? I'd never given it much thought before and now I felt like a short-sighted ingrate for never having done so since clearly this was one of the most amazing and precious things on my life's periphery. A few yards from it I spotted a familiar steel dish with a duckling pattern moulded into the outside. In it were a few chunks of leftover cat food.

'I remember that dish!' I told my mum. 'Didn't you used to feed the cat from it when I was a kid?'

'It was actually your baby dish,' she said. 'I use it to feed the hedgehogs cat food now.'

I'd gone through a brief phase a few years earlier when I wanted to get rid of all my possessions and live an entirely unencumbered life. That had changed and, even before it had, I'm not sure I was ever fully down with the idea of getting rid of my books and LPs. I still understand the whole 'You can't take it with you' philosophy but I'm not quite as emphatic about the way I subscribe to it. I know you can't take it with you but I still wouldn't mind having a small amount of it, for a bit. I can see how stuff can be a burden, but I like some stuff: stuff that doesn't boast of its intention to alter your life, but then proceeds to do so in small ways. I'd found a horseshoe on Dartmoor and attached it to my house late the previous year. It's just an old rusty horseshoe, but I'd be miffed if somebody nicked it. Originally, out of pure unthinking laziness, I hung the horseshoe upside down, and shortly after I fixed it to the large granite bricks on my house a few bad things had happened to me. I'd turned it the other way up a few months ago, and nothing quite as bad had happened to me since. I'm sure the events of my life are not directly connected to a horseshoe from near the village of Didworthy, but there is no way in a million years I'm turning it back the other way up. I related these thoughts to my mum as we strolled around the garden.

'Your nan used to say that if you hang horseshoes upside down your luck falls out the bottom, but I think it's nonsense,' my mum said as, once again, we walked past the wooden African head that my mum did not like but would not part with for fear it would unleash terror on anyone who owned it.

Although we'd only been outside for ten minutes, I felt refreshed. Every time I see my dad, he tells me dozens of great new stories – about Nottinghamshire, about history, about who he is, about who I am – but the narrative is of such a loud and experimental-jazz nature that I get easily tired. The theory has been put forward before by those close to him that my dad does not speak words; he haemorrhages them. I don't need a long breather from his lectures, but small breaks help, as they would anyone listening to someone holding six conversations at the same time, all on their own. Now, after clearing my head, I was ready again. I sat down in the perfect place to absorb the next part of his story, which would no doubt lead to another, and another. I was keen to find out what else he had to tell me about his new possession.

'OK, I'm all ears,' I told him. 'Go for it.'

But he did not reply, and when I looked more closely at him spread out lengthways on the sofa, I noticed he was fast asleep. He wasn't speaking or snoring or singing. For the first time that day, he looked totally serene. Beside him on the arm of the sofa was the novel he'd been reading, its spine bent back on itself, like every book he enjoys. Held tight in his arms, like a favourite teddy bear, was the chunk of medieval limestone.

3

TWO OTTERS, SEVEN BEAVERS, TWO RIVERS AND A LYNX

There was an escaped lynx on Dartmoor so I went up to Dartmoor, alone and unarmed, to try to find the escaped lynx. I took with me a map, an old book about ghosts, a bottle of water, a packet of crisps and some past-their-best walking boots. In packing for the trip, I had given arguably less thought than I should to the lynx's needs, but I was carrying a rucksack with a long piece of elastic attached to it that I could forcibly remove and coax the lynx to chase, in the event that the lynx turned out to be playful. The elastic – which formed part of an exterior compartment intended for the carrying of drinks or maps – hung off the rucksack in a perilous way and had been irritating me recently so it would be a relief to remove it anyway. The previous week I had been walking down the high street in town in the sun feeling fairly decent about myself when the elastic had caught on a pedestrian bollard, twanging me back up the high street four or five feet in the direction from which I had come, like a small allegory for the experience of being human.

Dartmoor Zoo, to which the lynx had been exported from Kent immediately prior to its escape, has a fairly infamous history, having been the scene of a few other animal escapes, including that of a jaguar in 2006 and a Canadian timber wolf called Parker in 2007, which was recaptured outside the pub in the local village and further emasculated by being described by the zoo's owner Benjamin Mee as 'a big girl's blouse'. A marginally limp film was made about Mee and his zoo by the mostly excellent director Cameron Crowe in 2011. The film was set in California, but Dartmoor Zoo is not in California; it is on the edge of Sparkwell, a few minutes' drive from the twenty-four-hour Tesco at Lee Mill.

In attempting to locate a Carpathian lynx on a 65,000-acre high-altitude moor, the most important thing to do is to try to think like a Carpathian lynx. Using my new lynx brain, my firm instinct was that the lynx, whose name was Flaviu, would head north from Sparkwell, away from Tesco and towards Burrator Reservoir, which was a good place for Flaviu to have a nice big drink. Flaviu, following his instinct, would then head to the very highest part of the moor, approaching Okehampton, where there would be snow later in the year, enabling him to put the large pads on his feet to use in a way that he probably couldn't in a zoo. En route he might well pass Raddick Hill, where a distraction could occur in the form of a sizeable population of sheep and a few wild ponies and cows. It was here that I planned to intercept Flaviu.

I parked in Princetown, a settlement architecturally anomalous to most of Dartmoor and Devon, where the greyness of the pebbledash houses and a sky colour that often matches them can make me forget I am not on a journey from Mansfield to Worksop in 1986 with my dad to buy some Swarfega and gravel. Here, like some part of industrial Yorkshire that went off on a downcast inward-looking wander and never came back, looms Dartmoor prison, scene of even more escapes than Dartmoor Zoo, including that of Harold 'Rubber Bones' Webb, who gained his freedom by contorting through the tight spaces between some of the building's heating ducts, and James Jennings, who, assisted by two fellow inmates, stole a tanker delivering oil to the prison and used it as a battering ram: more elaborate procedures than Flaviu's, which merely involved chewing through a cage.

I set off in the opposite direction to the prison, towards South Hessary Tor. It was a curious experience temporarily living inside the mind of a lynx, as it not only made me quite good at tracking but gave me a strong craving for chamois. You don't get chamois in west Devon and I am a vegetarian so I settled for the packet of crisps in my rucksack. The packet was one of those with GRAB BAG written on it, a thoughtful and liberating gesture from the manufacturers granting permission for assertive action to people like me who'd previously been hesitant around crisps and afraid to admit what we truly wanted. I climbed the tor and scanned the blasted and desolate

surroundings for the lynx. I could not see the lynx. I sat for a small number of minutes and admired the new iron cobra head on top of the tor, which stood next to the stump of the previous iron cobra head. The previous cobra head – one of four erected in 1867 to mark the boundary between Walkhampton Parish and the Forest of Dartmoor – had been snapped off by thieves a couple of years earlier. I puzzled over the mentality that had led to this surreal, nonsensical act of vandalism, conducted out of sight of any building save for the abandoned farmhouse down near Foxtor Mire. Did the thieves later transport the cobra head to Bude on the north coast and sell it at the sprawling Sunday car boot sale there, being haggled down from an ambitious show price to the one they'd actually hoped for? Or perhaps they listed it on eBay, with a 'Buy it now' teaser price, in the hope that somebody just happened to be using 'cobra', 'blacksmith', 'retro' and 'Duchy of Cornwall' as search terms that week?

I turned south-west in the direction of Raddick Hill, following the course of the Devonport Leat, which dates from the 1790s and was for a long time, before the excavation of Burrator reservoir and its accompanying dam, the principal source of water for Plymouth. There is rusty metalwork in the ground here from the Victorian age that can trip you up, and I hoped that if he followed this route Flaviu had been careful, since he was only two and, having lived in captivity his whole life, would not be used to negotiating rusty Victorian metalwork.

Via the local and international media, Devon police had been keen to get the message out that members of the public should not approach the lynx. Presumably this was for the normal lynx reasons but also perhaps because the lynx had a store of remarks that could be very cutting. I felt pleasantly alone in this region, where the moor gets big and yellow like a monster range of algaed sand dunes and begins to swallow a person. I thought of my phone, also alone, where it currently sat, on top of a cupboard in my living room. I often feel bullied by my phone and spend an increasingly large part of my life wanting to throw it forcefully into a builder's skip, so I frequently leave it at home when I walk, but it did occur to me that, were the lynx to corner me, I would not have any means of calling a friend or an appropriate authority and informing them I had been cornered by a lynx.

Dartmoor, like all three of the major moors of the South West Peninsula, already had its big cat legends: blurred sightings of big dark shapes slinking through the heather. Sheep carcasses too expertly mutilated to suggest the work of even the biggest domestic dog. In the late 1970s Mary Chipperfield, animal trainer and circus owner, set out to transport five pumas from the old Plymouth Zoo to Dartmoor Zoo, but only two of the cats ever arrived; the others, it is thought, were released, or escaped, onto the moor. A zoologist who lives on the moor – an acquaintance of my friend John – claims that she categorically identified a puma slinking across her driveway during the early nineties. The average lifespan of a puma in the wild is no more than thirteen years, but if Chipperfield's pumas bred, Flaviu might not be the only wild feline up here.

Near the aqueduct where the leat crosses the River Meavy I checked for lynx droppings, although I found this tough, having never previously seen any lynx droppings. I was so busy looking for lynx droppings that I dropped my OS map in the leat. The map flowed west with the current towards Tavistock for a few yards before I retrieved it. I shook the water off the map and skirted the bottom of Down Tor then headed over the high ridge to Crazywell Pool, another great potential drinking place for a thirsty lynx. For a long time there were claims that the pool was bottomless and that when all the bell ropes from Walkhampton church had been tied together and lowered into the water they still did not reach solid ground. But this was disproved early in the 1900s. Crazywell is in fact an old flooded tin mine no more than fifteen feet deep and, if you are someone like me who doesn't mind getting pondweed stuck to your legs, looks quite inviting for swimming and diving. Dusk was edging closer now, and as I sat by the pool I could not help remembering another legend: the one that said if you visited the pool at this time of day a ghostly voice would whistle along the wind and inform you of the next person in the neighbourhood to die. The breeze weaving through the grass behind me did seem to form words of a sort, but I didn't recognise them. They didn't sound like names, unless they were complicated, unusual names and doom was being foretold for the offspring of nonconformist middle-class West Country hippies. I was also more glad that none of the words sounded like 'Flaviu' than I was that none of them sounded like 'Tom'. At any one point you'll get loads of

Toms in west Devon. If the Ghostly Voice had whispered my name it could have been referring to virtually anyone.

From Crazywell I climbed past a restored medieval stone cross to the logan at the top of Black Tor, which forms a ledge of sorts. I thought this was a possibility as lynxes like to make their dens under ledges, but I found nothing save for the marbled shapes of crab's lichen and a small circular hole in the ground, probably made by an adder. A few hundred yards on I encountered a sheep with a pronounced limp. Was this the first sign of the lynx? The keepers at Dartmoor Zoo had said that the lynx was unlikely to kill any livestock but this was not to say that the cat could not inflict a leg injury on a sheep. Upon review, I decided the evidence was inconclusive. I was almost back at my car and I had not found my lynx, but to be honest that was OK, as I hadn't had any decisive plan of action for a scenario in which I did. I certainly wasn't going to dob Flaviu in to the authorities and probably would have decided against taking him home. I already had four cats, which was more than enough. I tend to find that, with cats, neediness increases in a ratio directly in accordance with size. My smallest one was fairly aloof and got on with her own thing, but the biggest was constantly following me around, dribbling on my clothes, sitting on my chest and watching me sleep in a slightly unnerving way or asking my opinion on stuff that he really should have been confident enough not to need affirmation about.

Back at my house a browse through social media suggested that opinion on Flaviu was split into three main camps. A few people were concerned that Flaviu might head towards Plymouth and eat one of the city's many schoolchildren. The *Plymouth Herald* ran a story about a pair of lovers who were due to have their wedding at the zoo in the near future and were worried that Flaviu might choose that moment to return, gatecrashing the festivities. Some people were keeping their fingers crossed Flaviu was soon rescued and returned to the zoo. Others – and I tended to side with this camp – were rooting for Flaviu to make it on his own and hoping his escape was an early step towards the rightful re-wilding of Dartmoor, which would hopefully soon also include the appearance of wolves and bears. The parts of the Norfolk and Suffolk countryside that I stomped around before I lived in Devon were similar to the South West in that they had lots of famous ghost animals roaming about, many of which were of a wild nature. But in Norfolk and Suffolk people rarely talked about reintroducing actual living wild animals to the countryside. There had been a re-flooded fen a mile up the road from my house but at no point did anyone discuss the logistics of introducing a moose or hippo into it. Here, however, people talk about that sort of stuff all the time.

'I'm going to Ireland,' a neighbour of mine in Devon announced earlier in the summer.

'Ooh lovely,' I said. 'Why are you going there?'

'I'm going to a wedding,' she said. 'I might bring back some pine martens too, and release them into the woods. If we had them here it could lead to a strong resurgence of red squirrels. I'm taking my van, so I'll have plenty of room.'

She showed me a space in the back of her van beneath one of the seats which she'd cleared out, where the pine martens might be able to sleep in what for pine martens would be relative comfort on the long journey across the water, down through the convoluted roads of Wales and round the hook of the Bristol Channel back to the South West Peninsula.

One reason I was not more dejected about not locating the lynx on Dartmoor was that I'd already had a bumper week for spotting unlikely wildlife in my home county. Just a few days previously I had, for the first time in my life, had a close-up sighting of beavers swimming around in the wild. This occurred on the River Otter, about forty miles east of where I live.

Nobody knows exactly how the beavers first appeared on the Otter. The most likely theory is that they were

captive beavers from a beaver farm, released by the owner of the captive beavers or someone loosely or not at all affiliated to the custodian of the captive beavers. Sightings of them by members of the public began in 2010. Not long afterwards, the beavers began to breed. The Conservative government then decided to have the beavers removed from the river, owing to the fact that it does not like the UK to be in any way a fun or diverse place. Fortunately, the Devon Wildlife Trust, with overwhelming support from conservationists, opposed this removal and – having tested the beavers for diseases and found them to be in rude health – managed to get a licence for the beavers to live on the river for five years and their effect on the environment to be monitored. There were now thought to be around twenty on the River Otter.

I did not travel to the river expecting to see wild beavers. Just to have known I was within a hundred yards of some wild beavers and seen their teeth marks on some trees would have been exciting enough for me. But as dusk fell and my friend Sarah and I and Stephen Hussey from the Devon Wildlife Trust made our way quietly along the riverbank, we heard a loud splash and, about twenty seconds later, two otters dipped past us at speed. The otters had a rattled look about them, like thugs who'd picked the wrong target for their thuggery and were now beating a regretful, chastened retreat. The size of the initial splash we'd heard, Stephen said, suggested that the commotion was about more than just these otters and some other otters. A larger animal had been involved: perhaps a dog, perhaps a beaver.

My friend Hayley once described to me a very spiritual evening encounter she'd had with an otter in the River Dart, less than a mile upriver from Totnes. Hayley had been staring into the water, seeing only her blurred reflection and stones and vague fish and the blackening ripples of the water, but then her reflection grew slick fur and whiskers and a button nose and became brunette not fair and was no longer in the water but out of it, only four inches in front of her face. She and her reflection – which she now realised was not a reflection but a real-life breathing medium-size otter – held one another's gaze for what felt like a minute but was probably an unusually long eleven seconds.

I have seen an otter in a similar spot on the Dart, but it was a far more ordinary sighting: a shiny head of dampened fluff several yards away that I only fully realised did not belong to a bird as it made a dive for the riverbed. There are lots and lots of otters six miles upstream though, including one called Mr Squeaks, who is too old to swim properly any more and, when requesting fish, makes a noise suggestive of a forty-a-day Benson and Hedges habit, and another called Sammy, who sits on the head of a man named Tim upon request. These otters are not wild, and neither is Tim; they, and Tim, belong to the otter sanctuary at Buckfast, but the water in which they swim is pumped directly from the Dart, which runs alongside their enclosures. The river gets volatile here, as it arrives on flatter ground from the moor, and when it overflows its banks, otters – wild ones, not from the sanctuary – have been found out of their element, washed away into the surrounding farmland. In the 1800s otters were hunted a few miles north of here on the west branch of the river by men with poles who compounded the asininity of their actions by shouting, 'Hoo-gaze!': the otter hunting version of 'Tally-ho!' The otters did their best to escape by running at speeds up to eighteen miles an hour, hiding in their parlours – deeper, safer places than holts, beneath hanging rocks – or running up trees, a little-known otter skill I learned about from Tim when I visited the sanctuary.

After the fast stretch below Buckfastleigh the river widens and dozes for a few miles, even while it prevaricates most dramatically about its intentions, then hits Totnes and goes tidal with a dramatic seabird flurry. In the sludge beneath the main bridge over the water in the town there is typically at least one upturned shopping trolley. The muddled clangs of the business park drown out the sound of cormorants and greenshank. Close by are the railings, hooped barbed wire and graffiti of the long-abandoned former Dairy Crest site. But the river still has an old-fashioned way of feeding the mythology of the place. Even at its most urban it retains a wildness that has not quite been buried. Stories from its banks find their way up the hill into the pubs at night. Over a pint my friend Ru told me he'd watched the town seal sitting on the bank a couple of weeks ago, munching casually on a huge salmon. There is almost certainly more than one seal, but everyone seems to have made an unspoken agreement to amalgamate them into a single town seal, possibly because the idea of him gadding about on various adventures between the weir at the northern end of town and Baltic Wharf at the southern end creates a more pleasing image. Sometimes I feel like I am the only person to live within a five-mile radius of the place who has never seen the seal, and this can be very socially isolating.

Teenagers hurl themselves into the water en masse down near the weir on the first semi-hot day of the year, and on every other subsequent one. You can walk past them in the garb of a counterculture fool from the middle of the previous century and they don't bat an eyelid. After nearly three years I am almost accustomed to it and have to remind myself it is nothing like the places where I spent my own youth. I seriously toned my look down the last time I went back to the town where I attended school, and kids still hurled abuse at me from across a street. I won't go into the details of the conversation, but suffice to say it was significantly less polite than when a stranger in Devon shouted, 'Get back to Woodstock!' at me and I assured her that I'd been trying my hardest to do just that for several years with only sporadic success. The town where I grew up did not have a river; it had a park, which sometimes had puddles. You went to the park, drank Special Brew and either had a fight or a snog. My training from that habitat kicked in last summer when I was walking parallel to the Dart and a tall, slightly lairy-looking teenage boy dripping river water from his shirt started striding purposefully towards me. I put my guard up, expecting trouble. 'Would you like a hug?' he asked very sweetly, with arms outstretched. I told him I'd better leave it, having not long got out of the shower and only just applied deodorant. The only criticism I can really level at these kids is their taste in music, which runs largely to dubstep and drum 'n' bass.

The music on the banks of the Otter was gentler, but that fitted in with its character: it's a redder and sleepier and narrower river than the Dart, more crowded in by its banks. The early 1980s heroin party anthem 'Golden Brown' by the Stranglers tinkled through the trees from a portable stereo near a tent on a rocky inlet just downstream from the spot we chose for our beaver stake-out. Stephen, Sarah and I stood quietly in a dark spot under an ash tree and waited for it to finish and, almost exactly on cue with its final bars, a beaver of not dissimilar colour to the one celebrated in the song swam out from the opposite bank. It was far more serene than I imagined, much more serene than the otters we'd just seen, but when it clambered out onto a small sandbank just upstream and began scratching itself that serenity abruptly vanished. 'It looks like a giant tea cosy,' observed Sarah, accurately. 'Is it scratching its nipples?' A few nights earlier Sarah had gone down to the kitchen in her house to get a glass of water and seen a larger-than-average badger munching through a dish of her housemate's cat's food then watched, alongside the cat in question, as it waddled out through the cat flap. 'I really didn't think my week could get any better after that,' she said. 'But I was wrong.' As for me, any bitterness I'd been quietly nursing about Hayley's encounter with the otter on the Dart or Ru and the town seal abruptly vanished.

Beavers are vegetarians, and – contrary to what you might have read in the fiction of C. S. Lewis – not the kind who sneakily eat fish as well. What is a little mind-boggling is that not more than twenty human generations back seeing one would have been a fairly normal thing. 'I saw a beaver today!' would still have been a more noteworthy statement than 'I saw a duck today!' but not by much – maybe, say, comparable to a person from our present British century seeing a particularly excellent swan. Beavers were last spotted in Britain in the sixteenth century. The thickness of their pelts and the fact that their castor sacs contain castoreum, which was used as a tincture in perfume, meant they were hunted to extinction. You don't hear many people banging on about wanting a perfume that smells of castor sacs these days so you'd hope that, were beavers to return to the UK in large numbers, they'd have a much easier time. Their ability to fell trees – earlier, upstream, Stephen had shown us teeth marks in fallen willows – and dam rivers also has a positive effect on the environment, preventing floods and creating wildlife-friendly pools and bogs. After a grooming session, this one – a female – swam another fifteen yards upstream and began to munch loudly through a bank of Himalayan balsam. I thought instantly of my mum, who'd had big problems with balsam in her garden in the past, and I drifted off into a daydream set on her birthday next year: me and the beaver, driving up to Nottinghamshire, Crosby, Stills and Nash on the stereo. 'Don't worry,' I tell the beaver. 'We'll be there soon. I know it's a long way but we're almost done. Try not to scratch your nipples too much.' I pull up outside my parents' house, leaving the car in the lane, not the driveway, out of sight of the house.

I ring the doorbell then instruct the beaver to hide behind the hedge or one of my mum's larger plant pots, just to make the occasion that bit more special for everyone.

Whereas otters live in holts, beavers live in lodges. This is one of many things I love about beavers. It tells you what you need to know about them straight away: they're a bit fancy but not too fancy. This particular beaver lodge had been built into the bank of the river directly opposite us, amid the roots of overhanging trees. Spotters from Devon Wildlife had thought there were three kits living in the lodge with this beaver and her far more publicity-shy male friend, but six days after my visit, a couple of days after my fruitless search for Flaviu on the moor, a photo was taken by a resident of the local village which clearly showed five kits sitting in the shallows at the edge of the river. The evening I saw this, I instantly dropped everything and drove back to the Otter and, after sitting on the bank for very little time at all, saw what I had been not quite optimistic enough to bank on: two kits swimming out, serenely, following the exact same route that their mum had the previous week, climbing the bank and chomping on the balsam, albeit with considerably less volume. After a quarter of an hour a dog walker called David arrived. David had been there the previous week, standing close to Sarah and Stephen and me on the bank, and in total had been watching the beavers for over three years, since before their presence on the Otter was even revealed in the news. 'The male never comes out,' he told me. 'The female's very casual now, though. I held a branch of willow in the water for her not long ago and she started to chew it.'

David is a mechanic who walks his obedient and lovely dogs along the Otter every night. He probably knows the beavers' movements as well as anybody. The largest number of otters he's seen in one night on the river named in their honour is seven. There was a slight worry about the otters trying to eat the beavers' kits, but now the kits were larger that danger seemed to have passed. The otters were clearly intimidated by the sheer bulk of the adult beavers. Stephen had said that the adult beavers were around the size of a cocker spaniel, but looking at David's cocker spaniel, Willow, I decided this was an underestimation. The adult female beaver looked like she'd be a fair match for his Labrador, Bracken, on the scales.

The kits returned to their lodge, and David and I walked back along the river in the direction of my car. The hills roll more modestly here in the eastern part of the county, and as we walked the sun went down over those on our right, like a party balloon losing the friction that had attached it to a wall and gently falling to rest behind a squishy sofa. About forty miles beyond that, or maybe closer, Flaviu still roamed free despite the zoo's attempts to lure him back with some ocelot urine donated by a concerned keeper. He would roam for over a fortnight more before being captured, in that time toughening up a little and committing the rite-of-passage murder of four lambs. The night felt lively, the particular buzz and hum and rustle that only summer evenings in the countryside in July contain. David, who clearly had more finely tuned hearing than me, stopped abruptly every minute or two to investigate a distant splash or a rustle in the reeds. I had to remind myself not to get complacent about what had just happened: in less than a week I had seen three examples of an animal that just a few years ago I'd assumed I'd never see in Britain during my lifetime. On top of that, I'd seen two very clear examples of another animal I'd only seen in the wild twice – and much more fleetingly – before. But now it seemed oddly normal. Maybe a lot of this was about the power of scarcity? But it *was* about more than that too. When I was shopping for second-hand records and found rare, forgotten albums, they excited me because they were rare and forgotten, but that wasn't the whole story: I wouldn't buy them if they didn't look and sound great too. Beavers were rare, and the role they'd once played in Britain's ecosystem had been a little forgotten, but they looked and sounded great too.

At David's commanding point and whistle, Willow shot off into the field to our right at speed and completed two ecstatic circuits of it. Upon returning she arrived at my feet and gazed at me keenly. I gazed back at her eager floppy-eared face, the face of a perfect spaniel in rude health. If you'd never seen a face like that, or one remotely similar to it, and you just stumbled across it living contentedly wild on some desolate moor, you'd go a little nuts. Or perhaps you knew about it, this mythical spaniel creature, but only via drawings or the passed-down, subtly altered tales of centuries of folklore. Even so, you'd be excited. 'Oh my God! Look at this!' you'd shout. 'Come quick!' But after that you'd remember you were on your own, and there was nobody to tell. You would reach for your phone and recall that it was at home on top of a cupboard. You'd shout a little more. Maybe someone was over the next ridge? But your shouts would echo coldly into the big surrounding nothing, unanswered. There would be a vague disappointment about that initially, but you'd get over it. In not much time at all what you'd seen would become your little secret: something that you'd put away somewhere warm and safe for ever that was all the more special for never being touched by anyone else.

4

THE HILLOCKS HAVE EYES

'Is that my underwear catalogue?' asked Annabel.

We had just arrived outside the studio where Annabel, an artist and university lecturer, worked, near Woodbridge, seven miles from the Suffolk coast. As we emerged from my car we had watched a man in off-white overalls with a sandpaper beard and darting eyes emerge from the front door of the studio. In his hand he clutched a glossy magazine produced by Bravissimo, the lingerie company that caters for women with bra sizes of D cup and above, showcasing their spring range.

'Yeah, sorry, I wanted it for the men's stuff,' said the man, returning the catalogue to Annabel.

'That's Brian,' said Annabel, opening the door to her studio when Brian had gone. 'He works in one of the other buildings. He's harmless, but he doesn't like dipping his hands into things. There's a water butt around the back filled with rainwater. I offered him a tenner to put his hand in it and he wouldn't do it.'

Annabel and I were about to head off to find two scarecrows she had seen a few miles north, on the edge of the village of Blaxhall, but first she had to check on her zebra finch, which was currently living in the rafters of the spare room next to her studio. The zebra finch did not reside at Annabel's smallish house in Ipswich, as there was no room, what with the amount of Annabel's art stored there plus the giant collection of 1980s pornography dominating the first floor. This collection did not belong to Annabel but to her recently deceased landlord, or more precisely to his daughter, who had inherited it and had, for sentimental reasons, declined all requests for it to be removed. Annabel's studio was in a former school built in the mid-1800s, featuring tall rooms with high windows purpose-built to begin their ascent to the ceiling at the average head height of a ten-year-old Victorian child, to prevent pupils looking out of them and becoming distracted. The dark places behind the beams in the zebra finch's annexe – a bigger room than Annabel's studio – were ominously quiet for two or three minutes when we entered, but the finch eventually fluttered out from his hiding place to investigate the latest fatball and seeds that Annabel had provided for him. He had been part of a pair but had recently, in Annabel's words, 'shagged the girl to death'. Prior to this, in happier times the two of them had made a nest in Annabel's first-aid kit out of needles from last year's Christmas tree, cotton wool buds and the clippings from Annabel's fringe left on the cold studio floor when she had self-tamed it with her art scissors, but, not being in need of first aid during this period, Annabel would not find this nest – adorned with two perfect cold eggs at its exact centre – until several months after I visited her. At my birthday party the following month she would bring me a gift of half a dozen owl pellets, attractively presented in cellophane-topped tissue paper, which, already under the influence of alcohol, I would incautiously place on top of the sideboard in my dining room amid beer bottles and cake. 'Do you think Tom will mind if we have a couple of these truffles?' I overheard my friend Seventies Pat ask my friend Louise later in the evening, when I was still fortunately just about steady and swift enough on my feet to move across the room and intervene before Pat had fully removed one of the pellets from its packaging.

Annabel could not promise that the scarecrows she had seen would be out today, as they sometimes hibernated, but she had high hopes that we might see them, if we were very quiet. If you are going to spot a pair of scarecrows in Norfolk or Suffolk, the part of the year we were now in – early spring – is as good a time to do so as any. Both of the Blaxhall scarecrows, a male and a female, used department store mannequins as their base and like all proper self-respecting mannequins were known to regularly change outfits, their preferences usually being clothes of a 1940s or 1950s vintage. Despite their local notoriety they were not the best-known instances of esoteric agricultural spookiness within the boundaries of Blaxhall. This distinction went to the Growing Stone at

Stone Farm. Allegedly the stone was first excavated by a
Blaxhall ploughman in the nineteenth century, at which
point it was no bigger than two fists, but it has been
expanding steadily ever since, to the extent that it has
far surpassed liftability. Old Blaxhallians swear by this
legend, although there is no photographic evidence of the
stone's diminutive childhood, nor of its adolescence, when,
according to an old man from the village who spoke to
the oral historian George Ewart Evans in the mid-1950s,
'a cat could not walk under' its now formidable lip.
Arguably more than its alleged growth, what makes the
stone eerie is that it stands alone in a part of the country
that is anathema to big rocks. You could comb the whole
of England and not find a less craggy place than here.
Stones – flints specifically, the picking of which provided
an important income for poverty-stricken villagers in
the area before the metalling of roads began in the early
twentieth century – are an important part of the terrain in
Suffolk and the eastern half of Norfolk, but they are as a
rule small, just like almost everything here except the sky.
It is a countryside of sleepy waterways, geometric fields,
gently rounded churches, satisfying meetings between
stubble corridors and spirit-level horizons. If you return
here after a long time away in a more vertiginous place,
doing so can make you a peculiar kind of dizzy. I can't
quite compare the feeling to anything else in my own
experience, but I imagine you'd get a similar sensation if,
after living in a normal-size place, you were shrunk and
given the chance to explore a model village for a weekend:
maybe not shrunk really small so you were to scale with

the houses and parks and shops, but reduced to perhaps the size of a hare or a young fox. Everything seems so soft and mild here, but to put it down solely to the flatness would be an error. Where East Anglia is at its flattest, from west Norfolk into north Cambridgeshire and south-east Lincolnshire, a distinctly harsh and unmild ambience is created. By contrast the delicately sloping fields of the rest of Norfolk and Suffolk can feel like a Trivial Pursuit Young Players' Edition of the south-west of the UK, with hillocks taking the place of hills, and heaths functioning as bonsai moors. It is possible to be lulled into the erroneous belief that it is a place where nothing bad could ever happen.

There is a treachery to this place but it is a subtle treachery: the treachery of a dastardly hypnotist with a kind face. Scarecrows to me are a big part of this treachery: disorienting comedy humanoid figures redolent of death, shaking in deceptively flinty breezes on distant hazy cotton ridges. You see so many of them in these lowlands, and I don't think it's just because they have fewer places to hide. I hadn't come to East Anglia looking for scarecrows, but they soon found me, as they would anyone who truly seeks to get to know the place on foot, which to my shame I did not until 2008, by which point I had been a resident of the region for almost seven years. That was three springs before I went to Blaxhall with Annabel, and in that time I had photographed over a hundred scarecrows, or mawkins, to use their old Norfolk name. Admittedly some of these were at village scarecrow festivals – such as the one in Barton Mills, at whose 2008 celebrity-themed festival the class system of the village was inadvertently revealed in fake humans on sticks, from the Stephen Fry scarecrow in the north (big detached houses) to the Katie Price scarecrow in the south (1940s council houses) – but these never interested me as much. They were overdone – the commercial 'all the gear and no idea' side of scarecrow culture. I far preferred the more rudimentary, minimalist kind I chanced upon on walks, made by farmers and vegetable gardeners with few raw materials and a barnload of imagination. Upturned paint buckets on dusty boiler suits under cloth skies. Gnashing faces from the crypt scrawled in black Sharpie marker on polythene stuffed with old newspaper. Angry one-armed junkyard freaks with car-door-panel torsos. Millennial CD heads on eerie ripped safety-tabard bodies, drenching a fussy allotment in the macabre. Collecting pictures of them became a compulsion in the way that collecting anything lovingly made and not easily located in the mainstream can become a compulsion. I acted decisively on tip-offs, abandoning engagements ostensibly more beneficial to my time. A text arrived from a friend who was almost certain he'd seen a couple in a cornfield just south of Attleborough while travelling back to Norwich from London on the train. I was there within the hour, pogoing a ditch, ripping my best jacket on barbed wire, to get the money shot: ominous greatcoat, traffic-cone wizard head. When Annabel told me about the couple in Blaxhall I did not waste time. As it transpired, they were nowhere to be seen. All we found was an austere allotment. An upturned rusty wheelbarrow. An inkling of young carrots. She comforted me and I tried not to act as disappointed as I was.

We continued towards Snape, making the most of a bright almost warm day with a breeze made of small needles, the dusty-coloured countryside fervidly evolving to mustard and green all around us. Near the church we stopped to say hi to some sheep. Blaxhall has a good strong sheep history, and these ewes seemed aware of it, upholding their heritage by wandering over to gently headbutt our fists. The name of the inn in the village, the Ship, comes not from a vessel on the sea or the nearby Alde estuary but from the old Suffolk word for sheep. In the nineteenth

century the man responsible for dipping the sheep in the village proudly displayed the sign CHARLES SMITH: SHEEP DRESSER outside his house. The shearers here drank lots of ale, sang songs and slept outdoors. In the off season they found what other work they could. Poaching, smuggling. One, legendarily, cut the villagers' hair, using his shears to 'take off the rough' then trimming the rest up with scissors. I told Annabel about this and took a second to admire her fringe. She'd cut it herself again and it was looking particularly smart and sharp. In my bag was my phone, which still displayed an unreturned text from my hairdresser in Norwich, a hairdresser about whom I'd initially felt quite positive before having the cold realisation that she was just like all the other hairdressers I had met in the past and only pretended to listen to me when I told her about the stuff that was important to me. I resolved to return the text later in the evening, explaining assertively that I had moved on and since our parting had found out a lot about who I was and what I truly wanted in life.

After a false alarm – two old wellies on sticks on the ditchy margin of a mini-valley of oilseed rape – we turned south-west and hit pay dirt: a good solid mawkin a quarter-mile down the road towards Tunstall Forest. Paint-pot head, wax coat, 1982 power ballad stance. Nothing special, but getting the job done without an undue quantity of fuss. The scarecrow wore cords, like my own garden scarecrow, Warren, but his, unlike Warren's, were more the workwear kind. Unflared. Practical. He looked healthier than Warren too, who – with arms still outstretched – had recently almost keeled over into some

ivy in a pose that brought to mind the phrase 'death by disco'. Even when he'd been healthier, before his false beard began to rot and his parka became stained with mud and rain, Warren's life had been checkered by failure and insult. 'Why have you got a corpse in the corner of your garden?' my neighbour David had asked, completely within his earshot, only days after my friend Jo and I had filled Warren with straw and erected him. Even before he'd begun to ail, he'd done little to protect from birds the grass seed I'd put down. I suppose he'd just never seemed like an assertive figure. Right from the start he'd failed to command the necessary terror or awe of his kind. I am thinking particularly here of the day I collected his frame – part of an old tree my dad had found down in the field behind his garden – then headed off to meet Hannah for a walk on the moors west of Sheffield. It was my debut date with Hannah, and my forward planning, as it so often does, left something to be desired. *I am a man with a scarecrow in the back of his car, driving to meet a woman who hardly knows me for a walk on remote moorland*, was the realisation that hit me as I reached the outskirts of Sheffield, on the way to collect her from the train station. 'What is that?' Hannah asked, pointing to Warren's frame half an hour later, as we headed in the direction of Froggatt Edge and Grindleford. 'It's the structural base of my new scarecrow,' I replied. 'Oh, cool,' said Hannah casually and continued to talk about a Dusty Springfield record she had recently purchased.

Upon my return home to south Norfolk from Blaxhall it began to rain lightly: long streaks on windows and grey brick, like crap finger-paint. I checked on Warren. Had he lost weight? His flares had slipped down to reveal a glimpse of straw tradesman's bottom, and he had fallen even further down into the ivy than yesterday, the weather gradually pressing him into the earth. It would soon be time, I decided, to put him out of his misery. I opened the door of my study and wondered vaguely about continuing work on my Norfolk-based folk-horror novel. I knew I wouldn't. I had left it too long, lost momentum, again. I'd had a notion of the book way back when I'd first moved to Norfolk in 2001 as a twenty-six-year-old of puppylike idiocy: a misty flicker of inspiration first felt on holiday in flat fields abutting the North Sea and on an atmospheric early-morning walk across Blackheath near my old flat, amid fat crows, with plague-ridden corpses beneath me, listening to pastoral witchcraft-infused music recorded in low fidelity three decades earlier. A fictional epic of occult happenings and misguided hippy idealism on lonely lanes beneath dun clouds that I had neither the skill nor commitment to bring to fruition. Did it feature musicians? Maybe. I had no idea what it was really going to be about, whether it was going to be serious, or funny, or both, but it agonised me that I could not write it. I reached a point not far short of 30,000 words, twice, and abandoned the manuscript, twice. I told myself I'd done so because I had a mortgage to pay, a partner to support, and I needed to prioritise work that paid rather than fanciful self-indulgent nonsense. All this was broadly correct, but there was another reason, harder to look square in the face, for my inability to persevere: the simple fact that I could not fully believe in a single sentence of what I had written. I had been writing about Norfolk and Suffolk as a lover of the countryside and as a casual student of its folklore, but I hadn't truly been out *into* Norfolk and Suffolk. A large portion of the first part of my life there had been spent in estate agents, tile warehouses and B&Q, which might have been fine if I wanted to write about estate agents, tile warehouses and B&Q, but I didn't. I wanted to write about life – and possibly death – in the fields, but how could I if I almost never ventured out into them? All my life I had been a walker, even when I didn't categorise myself as a walker. I walked endlessly as a child with my parents, endlessly as an adolescent golfer, endlessly, even, as a carless resident of London with no particular enthusiasm for public transport and a keen nose for exploration. For my initial stint in Norfolk, however, I was not a walker, and if you are not a walker and you want to write believably and truthfully about rural life, you are off balance, on the back foot, before you even begin. This seems obvious but didn't actually occur to me until I had lived in the county for almost seven years.

When I did begin to walk, in late 2008, my attempts to write about make-believe characters in familiar but make-believe places improved, but something still stopped me pressing on as doggedly with my fiction as I desired to: a realisation that I was not ready, that I had some flavour but barely any filling. Despite this realisation's presence I did not fully confess it to myself because the thought, as I turned thirty-three, then thirty-four, then thirty-five, then thirty-six, that I *still* wasn't going to write this bastard book I believed I had been born to write, or the film script I sometimes considered writing instead, was too painful for me to address. Instead, without ever quite intending to, I did the next-best thing: I lived physically in a different story, also of a spooky nature, which did not require the typing of so much as a word. My walks became a folk-horror book or film of their own where nothing terrible ever quite happens but always might. This wordless physical novel had none of the dramatic plot twists that I'd always envisaged my real book as having, but it was long on atmosphere. That was OK, though. I was losing faith in dramatic plot twists. A film such as 1968's *Witchfinder General*, about the seventeenth-century reign of the country's self-appointed mysogynist-in-chief

Matthew Hopkins and his mission to rid East Anglia of dark magic, much of which was shot in my prime Norfolk and Suffolk walking territory, and whose church I made a pilgrimage to on one of my earliest local rambles, does not stick with you because of its dramatic plot twists, many of which were downright hammy. It sticks with you because of its atmosphere, which, in its low-budget way, is so powerful that it makes you forgive the hamminess of the plot twists.

Like *Witchfinder General* and so many other British films and TV shows in the horror genre from the late sixties and early seventies, my walks were powerful in a low-budget way, and, like those films and TV shows, it was their very lack of resources that was partly responsible for imbuing them with the power. My boots, the one bit of walking equipment I'd shelled out for – alongside my maps – had cost not much more than twenty pounds. So much exercise in my past had been costly or off-puttingly pedagogical. When you first walk out into the deeper countryside, especially when you do so alone, it feels amazingly rebellious: to be able to do something so soul-quenching for nothing, with no authority figures to drain the fun from it, seems like it should have some kind of catch. Even as someone with a lengthy history of not following the paths in life I've been told to, I remember feeling a little nervous, turning back shyly on early walks when I lost my way. Soon I learned to embrace the disorientated moments, thrived on the extra challenges of a flooded towpath or vanished hedge indentation, developing the understanding that the countryside's job has never been to pander neatly to the needs of foot traffic and never will be. Then I went fully rogue, no longer even accepting the AA or Pathfinder as my teacher, mapping my own routes. My OS Explorer maps were in themselves as fecund with language as many a great literary novel. I became familiar with the minor complexities of multifarious gate types and began to open and shut them less in the manner of a person apologising for being alive. I eschewed GPS, as I did in the car. Looking at a map might distract you from the scenery – particularly if, like me, you sometimes found said map smothering you as you tried to refold it – but maps were more at one with the scenery than a screen could ever be. A screen sucks you in, away from the moment. You can miss all manner of stuff while staring at a screen, and who knows what it might cost you? My graduation from walking books to self-mapped routes was my rambler's equivalent of the phase where a cook breaks free from the shackles of the recipe book or a musician starts to experiment outside their customary genre. There was something massively liberating about looking on OS Explorer 230 and seeing, say, something called Alecock's Grave a mile to my east, then thinking, *I'd quite like to know what Alecock's Grave is*, then thinking, *HOLD ON! I actually can go and see Alecock's Grave and nobody is going to stop me!* GPS fostered the opposite of that, a zombified extension of something the musician and rural warrior Julian Cope bemoaned fourteen years ago: 'People don't go anywhere nowadays unless there's a sign.'

My trust in maps, in the Ordnance Survey itself – that artful, loving institution, simultaneously historical and progressive, which as far back as the 1950s made a point of paying male and female employees equal wages – became immense: a renewed love affair that had begun on walks in my childhood and on long car journeys with my parents when I was often the one in charge of the atlas. Perhaps the trust was *too* immense at times. When maps were old and beginning to lose their marbles, they still seemed wise to me, which gave me an unwavering faith in what they told me, even when it made no sense. On an eight-mile walk near Sheringham on the north Norfolk coast I learned one of the big rules of East Anglian coastal rambling: avoid using maps more than a decade old, as this can result in erosion-themed death. I noticed that I was drawn to the darker places maps told me about, as well as the ones they didn't. On a more successful walk in next-to-zero light I guided my friends Jack and Hannah to one of the two Bronze Age barrows in south Norfolk alleged to be the burial place of the first-century Iceni warrior queen Boudica, then on to an isolated orchard two miles north where the annual Kenninghall village wassail was taking place. 'What is wassailing?' asked a friend from London. 'Is it a bit like abseiling?' I texted him back to say that it was quite a lot different, and that you had to be a fair bit braver to do it, attaching a photo of the master of ceremonies at Kenninghall, a robed figure with a face made of leaves known as the Lord of Misrule. In truth, the wassail – which means 'be healthy' in Old English – was definitely the warmer, more comic side of the physical novel that I was now living inside on my walks, a manifestly unscary gathering around a big bonfire, involving the singing of Kenninghall's own wassailing song, 'Dance Around the Firelight', and the splashing of apple trees with cider to banish the frost giants and encourage a healthy crop for the coming season, all led in jolly fashion by the Lord of Misrule, who explained to me that when he was not wassailing he was a homeopath named Steve. You could call it silly, but most of the best things for the human spirit are, and it would be a mistake to see such rituals as being conducted in a purely postmodern way. In the contrast between the upbeat chatter in the heat of that fire and the stark place we had walked to an hour earlier was an illustration of the immense necessity of such events in centuries past: the communal respite they provided from the cold, stripped vertebrae of the land in winter. Back at the foot of that burial mound, as the oaks and whitethorn on it above us bent back in the January wind, there had been no levity. It was a pocket of old black something enfolded in weather and history. It retained its own energy – magic, threatening, unviolated by architecture.

That mild-faced demon in Norfolk and Suffolk that I'd perceived even as an unprobing tourist in my own region stayed mild-faced when I became a walker, but grew fangs, subtle ones, deep-rooted, their edges poking up just above the flat earth. I met the demon head on, often very close to home, alone with only an OS map to hand for protection. In a field straddling the Norfolk–Suffolk border within plain sight of the brown tourist sign that welcomes visitors to the historic market town of Diss, with its fourteenth-century church and cut-price Friday market Duracell multipacks, I met one of my first scarecrows.

Even a few hundred scarecrows later, it would remain the most literal and chilling in my scarecrow backlist: half a bag of sand and a subhuman arrangement of six old dark grey planks, the top two of them more eye-catching than the others, owing to the three dead crows nailed to each. In all the sub-*Wicker Man* imaginings of my failed novel there was nothing this starkly horrifying. In Rumburgh, near Bungay, I happened upon a field of ten immaculate white bedsheet ghosts, not dissimilar to the one seen in the 1968 BBC adaptation of the M. R. James ghost story *Oh, Whistle, and I'll Come to you, My Lad*. The ghosts were overseen by a fake bird of prey on a wire. This was crop protection escalated to performance art. But on closer inspection there was even more to the tableau than I'd first assumed. In the far corner of the field I found a faceless scarecrow 'boss' in a turquoise boiler suit, hanging from a tree by a noose. A foreman of death. At the north Norfolk village of Wolferton, during the same summer, I queued to park with crowds stretching into the hundreds to witness organised and elaborate scarecrow exhibits, but found nothing nearly this inventive or disturbing. The scarecrow censors would have banned it. It found its place, out of necessity, Off Grid, outside the rules, where it had space to be itself – as increasingly did I.

Similarly agriculturally enthused spiritual brethren sometimes told me about scarecrows via the Internet and gave me the grid coordinates of their locations, but if I followed their leads I always felt like a fraud. A lot of the thrill of the hunt came from the fact that it was not meant to come replete with a user-friendly digital guide.

I didn't want to be a customer at Scarecrow Argos. I had no wish to browse laminated or virtual pages for the scarecrow I wanted, type the scarecrow's number into a keypad and wait for it to emerge, flat-packed in wastefully proportioned cardboard. Scarecrows weren't supposed to be accessed via a gleaming online portal. If anything they were supposed to be behind a real, three-dimensional door set in an old wall, made of heavy oak, weathered with arcane scratch marks and opened with a long iron key that you usually had to rattle in the lock for three minutes before it worked. I found most of the best scarecrows – and most of the other finest examples of the macabre lurking in the soft creases of rural Norfolk and Suffolk – by the ancient art of Going Outside And Looking Really Hard, or by the almost as ancient art of Going To A Small

Settlement Of Houses Based Around A Place Of Worship And Talking To Some People Who Might Know. On a regular walk which circled the villages of Old Buckenham and New Buckenham I became intrigued by the remains of Buckenham Castle: a keep of an unnervingly perfect circularity, thought to be the oldest of its kind in Britain, guarded by a moat and a padlocked gate. A patron of the Gamekeeper pub in Old Buckenham who sat and chatted to me in front of an inglenook fireplace he was visibly proud to have built told me that you could visit the castle but only if you gave John at the Robin Reliant garage in New Buckenham two pound coins. On the brink of Guy Fawkes night 2012 I visited the garage – one of those charmingly shabby ones at which Norfolk still excelled, harking back to the days when you still needed to say petrol pumps were 'self-serve' to acknowledge they were different to the norm – half-expecting John – sixtyish, blue overalls, blue dungarees – to sigh at another practical joke his friend had played on an innocent, but sure enough, after I had handed him a couple of quid, he bestowed upon me the hallowed key to the padlock, but not before he had extracted a promise that I would return before closing time and spun me a yarn about the castle being the place where the gunpowder plot was born, members of the castle's owning dynasty, the Knyvets, providing sanctuary for the plotters. 'Is this confirmed?' I asked John. 'Yes,' he said. 'By me.' I got the distinct impression that he had a different story like this for every big date on the national calendar, this innocuous pile of stacked earth and old flint a few minutes' walk from the local butcher's, vitally, inexorably, shaping our island's history.

I had driven past John's workplace countless times, but it was not until I walked away now, turning back to admire its proud fleet of Robin Reliants, that I took in its name: Castle Hill Garage. Not totally a statement of sarcasm. It was a hill, of sorts. You got a few of them in this soft sandy twenty-mile run up to Norwich from the south, where the heaths of Breckland and the last fragmented chunks of Thetford Forest fall away. Norwich itself was built around one, with another castle on its summit. I stood halfway up it that same autumn with another shadowy Norfolkian storyteller who favoured a monochromatic colour scheme: the Man in Black, the host of Norwich Ghost Walks. Pointing to the steep grass bank above us, the Man in Black told me and the rest of the evening's crowd about urban Norwich's own sort-of-scarecrow, the rotting spectre of the sixteenth-century rebel leader Robert Kett, who was often still seen up there, wobbling in the breeze in his phantom gibbet. The Norwich Ghost Walks didn't begin until 1997. Their original host, Ghostly Dave, retired four years ago to open a pub in King's Lynn, allowing the Man in Black to step in: a narrator with a skull-headed staff and an impressively hawkish, Victorian face. His mystique was in sharp contrast to, say, the ghost walks in Dudley, which Seventies Pat, who lived there, reliably informed me were hosted by a man simply called Craig. That said, the Man in Black's blood-red business card did lose something of its spine-tingling aura by having an ad for his other business, Richard's Driving School, printed on its flip side, which promised a 'friendly and patient service'. As well as the ghouls and witches paid to jump out at punters on the walk – including the Faggot Witch, who will curse you with her sticks, a skull-faced man to whom one member of the party offered a tenner to stop growling at her, and the Grey Lady and the Lonely Monk, who lurk amid the plague pits in the city's Tombland district – we got a few uninvited additional guests. In Cathedral Close a stout figure limped aggressively out of the fog towards us, and we braced ourselves for another ghoul, but it was only the bag lady who had been living on one of the benches there for a couple of years and had once thrown an apple at my friend Jenny for no apparent reason. Later a wino tagged along for a while to see what all the fuss was about, and the Man in Black stole away into a dark corner in

St Andrew's churchyard to make a deal with the owner of a new Chinese restaurant, the outcome of which being that the restaurateur was permitted to hand flyers out to us advertising cut-price chow mein. Part-way through the walk the Man in Black stopped outside the window of the London Street branch of Bravissimo. 'There aren't any ghosts here,' he told us. 'I just like it.'

That switch between light and dark which I'd never got quite right in my written novel was seamless in this physical lived one: it was often funny, but it could be scary too, and neither quality ever jarred with the other, because that's what living in this part of the country, really living in it, was like. Upon leaving Buckenham Castle and returning the key to John, I stalked off on one of my regular routes, my coat dusted with the persistent mansize cobwebs of early-medieval flint. It was a great walk, an unassuming favourite, past old marl pits and wild ponds and through intensely adhesive ploughed mud which made your boots twice as heavy as they were when you started walking (a common phenomenon that has

given rise to its own East Anglian word, honkydonks).
Scarecrow country did not come much more prime than
this. I'd found many of my best ones here or nearby: a
sexless helmeted figure who somehow managed to be more
futuristic space horse than person. A mechanic not totally
unlike John, but with green, not blue, overalls and a head
formerly containing turps. Another who, due to barbed
wire and young crop conundrums, I'd never been able to
get close enough to photograph clearly; even though I'd
tried my best and dropped my phone in a stream as a by-
product; and who was preserved as nothing more than
a grey banshee cotton blur soothsaying about a coming
ecological unkindness with empty billowing non-arms.
My route took me via Old Buckenham church, whose
early-1600s font is described in the 1958 *Shell Guide to
Norfolk* as featuring 'hairy animals'. In the graveyard I
said a silent hello to a tombstone inscribed with the name
Richard 'Dick' Cocking. I knew nothing about Richard
but always took it as read that he had lived abundantly.
I passed a stile that made me think of the habits of

Richard's Driving School.
Sponsors of Norwich Ghost Walks.
Friendly and patient service.
Phone 07765 854784
http://thebestdrivingschoolintheworld.co.uk

rats, not because I'd seen rats near it, indulging in their habits, but because I'd once talked to my parents about the habits of rats as we climbed the stile. Stiles and gates had that effect, I had discovered: you recalled something that happened when you climbed a stile or opened a gate, but on thinking harder it was something that had happened at another time that somebody had merely told you about when you climbed the stile or opened the gate. In early 2013, when my friend Russ and I opened a gate at the edge of Tyrrel's Wood while walking near Pulham Market, Russ had not brought his football mate who lived with a pet wolf and permitted it to accompany him to Norwich City's home games; Russ just told me about his football mate who lived with a pet wolf and permitted it to accompany him to Norwich City's home games. I only met his wolf-owning football mate in a Norwich pub later. Regrettably, I never met the wolf.

Two miles south-west of Old Buckenham, November started to call time on its meagre excuse for daylight. Unseen pigs I passed in stone sheds grumbled good-naturedly about the state of affairs. Unseen pigs in stone sheds in Norfolk and Suffolk always sounded restless, like pigs in a disaster film just before apocalypse hits. Later, when I'd moved far away, to the other side of the country, unseen pigs preparing for apocalypse would become one of the sounds that distinguished East Anglia from elsewhere in my mind. Another was its silence, which has a different timbre to the silence in the rural west, or the rural north, or the rural south. My walk finally took me back behind Buckenham Castle, to a lonely space occupied by New Buckenham's graveyard, a more orderly cemetery than Old Buckenham's (although neither village is anything close to 'new', almost everything in New Buckenham is orderly and compact, where Old Buckenham is scruffy and sprawling) but a less welcoming one. Being lonely and being alone are frequently two extremely different sensations and, despite the cemetery's loneliness, I did not feel entirely alone as I walked through it. On my solitary Norfolk and Suffolk walks, particularly in the chillier months, I would often feel this 'followed' sensation, have the impulse to spin round to see who was behind me. I had walked in plenty of topographically threatening environments in other parts of the UK countryside but never had the same impulse. It sprang at least in part from that peculiar silence, combined with the vastness of the horizon. There are so many hiding places for the malevolent in an undulating landscape it is almost as if the brain refuses to accept them. In East Anglia the malevolent hides in subtler places, nearly in plain sight, which is ultimately more troubling. It's the camouflage-enthused kid in a hide-and-seek game who eschews the big wardrobe on the far side of the house and instead blends seamlessly into a long vintage rug two feet in front of you. This aspect of Norfolk and Suffolk tells you a lot of what you need to know about why the nuanced ghost stories of M. R. James are the scariest and most enduring ghost stories of all, and why he usually chose these two counties as the setting for them. James, who was provost of King's College Cambridge between 1905 and 1918, liked to use the crumbly seascapes, old manor houses and mildly sloping heaths and lings of eastern East Anglia as settings to supernaturally taunt the lonely academic sceptics often at the centre of his stories, and had a recurring interest in the malevolent capacity of inanimate objects. Perhaps he had noticed that inanimate objects radiated that capacity more here than elsewhere. James wrote of Parkins, the protagonist in *Oh, Whistle, and I'll Come to you, My Lad*, which, both in its written and original TV form, successfully reproduced that 'followed' feeling I felt on many of my walks, 'the spectacle of a scarecrow in a field late on a winter afternoon has cost him more than one sleepless night'. The main demonic object in this case was not a scarecrow, however, but an old dog whistle, found by Parkins while digging around on a monastic site on a Suffolk cliff top. I did not do any DIY excavation as an East Anglian walker – I would defy anyone to be brave enough to, after watching my favourite M. R. James adaptation, Lawrence Gordon Clark's 1972 BBC version of *A Warning to the Curious*, with its unforgettable barked instruction from beyond the grave, 'No digging here!' – but there always seemed to be at least one cabbalistic metal object gnashing its teeth at me from the edge of a bridleway or thicket during my hikes through the silent parts of Norfolk and Suffolk: forgotten robots of the fields, their purposes becoming ever more recondite as they sank into their surroundings, contravened by iron oxide and weeds.

What those with an overactive imagination, such as M. R. James or myself, might have seen as malevolent was of course nothing more than practical to many. All those old drag harrows and tractor wheels and Allen Scythes and hay tedders served an everyday purpose before they were left to rot and get groped by nature. Scarecrows, too, were not just there to enhance the folk-horror film-cum-art-gallery in my head. They warded off birds, even though there are crop scarers to do the same job now (which, for all their monotony, can add an aptly spooky and unexpected *Pop!* to that engulfing lowland silence). But I was convinced there was more of this ominous, backward-looking aspect of agriculture here. Even if it hadn't been agreed upon in a barn somewhere with a handshake, it was a trend that had spread visibly – perhaps in a classically Norfolkian, taciturn way, prompted by clandestine farmerly nods, not words. In the other twenty or so counties outside the east of England where I'd walked, I'd seen scarecrows and toothy rusting metal monsters but never nearly as many as here, and it surely wasn't *just* because they had bigger humps and bumps to hide behind in other parts of the country. When it came to necromantic mannequins and unwholesome, rudimentary heads in particular, Darkest East Anglia seemed to have a unique affinity that went beyond just scarecrows. Norfolk's sole waxwork museum, the Louis Tussauds House of Wax in Great Yarmouth, had for several decades been full of shoddy monuments to the power of the inadvertently macabre, showcasing, among others, a Neil Kinnock which looked like someone had simply burned the hair off a Margaret Thatcher waxwork and made do, and a Michael Jackson which gave an impression of what the King of Pop would have looked

like if he'd aged naturally from 1982 onwards, died in 1997, been buried then dug up a fortnight later and stung by a passive-aggressive remark. In this alternative universe, far more entertainingly odd than any scarecrow festival I'd attended, Daley Thompson in his prime was no longer the figure my mum once cited as the Most Attractive Famous Man of the 1980s but a slightly melted version of Burt Reynolds with zombie ears.

In 2012, at the end of a straight sixty-mile line west of Yarmouth where the last vestiges of the Brecks tumble into the Fens, three friends and I walked to the village of Stow Bardolph, opened a mahogany cupboard in the church and were confronted by the funerary wax effigy of Sarah Hare, an eighteenth-century member of the wealthy Hare family, who owned the Stow Bardolph estate from the 1500s onwards. Following an Oliver Cromwellesque line of thinking, Hare had requested to have her appearance rendered exactly as it was in life, without prettification, so wax Sarah remained in her precise mid-1700s state, with the exception of the original whalebone in her corset, which had been devoured by insects. As we perused her warts and zombie hair, we were kind of nonchalant. Our insouciance could be blamed on context. Less than an hour earlier we'd chanced, unwarned, upon a more chilling humanoid, or perhaps scarecroid or even zomboid: the macabre, huge-mouthed, broken-lipped Marilyn Monroe dummy at the deathly quiet Hollywood Legends Diner off the westbound carriageway of the A47 near Narborough. Normally if you look at a dead woman in a cupboard you're going to be able to say unequivocally that that was the most disturbing part of your day, but this was a different kind of day, a Norfolk kind of day. Did the diner realise how intimidating their Marilyn was, with her dark-eyed, chipped face hiding behind early-1990s grunge festival hair? I gingerly stepped up and gave her a kiss, not quite touching her cheek. It wasn't a hollow gesture, like the air kisses I used to reluctantly receive as a young man in the newspaper business from members of the media I'd never previously met. I was just frightened. Wrapped around Marilyn's neck like a noose was an electric cord which, when plugged in, looked like it would release air from the grate below her in a facsimile of the famous billowy dress scene in the 1955 Billy Wilder film *The Seven Year Itch*. Something made me deeply thankful the device wasn't switched on.

In the Cambridge Folk Museum I saw arguably the most disturbing inanimate quasi-humans of all: two Aunt Sallies. Angry wooden heads on sticks, black-painted, thick-lipped, buck-toothed, penis-nosed. A male and a female, the difference in gender signified only by a bonnet. At village fairs in the 1800s people would jeer and throw rotten fruit at them. From the perspective of the early twenty-first century, they are deeply unsettling, drenched in provincial racist fear and angry carnality. But who knows? There was probably a point when they seemed far more innocently comical. Time has a way of coating the mildly disturbing in an extra layer of darkness. I heard it in a lot of the songs I listened to when I drove to the starting points of my East Anglian walks: acid-folk tracks intentionally tinged with the occult when they were recorded in the late 1960s and early 1970s, enhanced by an extra patina of mystery in the decades since, as if the sounds themselves had been left in an an unused room to gather dust. The 1970 song 'Graveyard' by the short-lived Lincolnshire band Forest, for example. At the time Forest were ghost-obsessed kids barely out of their teens, messing about on recorders and violins in a budget studio, but by 2012 they had become somehow the perfect evocation of M. R. James eeriness and solo walks in empty pockets of land shadowed by a nameless, invisible beast. Stone Angel's self-titled 1975 debut album was recorded by the Norfolk husband–wife songwriting team Joan and Ken Saul on the equipment at Joan's teacher training college,

just south of Norwich, due to financial constraints. Only three hundred copies were pressed, and in the early 1990s Joan and Ken still had ninety of them languishing under their bed. Approached by a record dealer, they sold them all to him for £2.50 each, save for a couple they kept for themselves for sentimental reasons. One of these originals will now sell on eBay for well over £600. The fragility of the recording eerily evokes the Norfolk and Suffolk legends Stone Angel sing about: the underwater bells of the sea-sunk churches of Dunwich village which allegedly still ring beneath the waves, wind-whipped marsh reeds, smudgy light, the footsteps of a demon beast. A dog endemic to eastern East Anglia, but not a normal dog you feed and stroke and patronise with a thrown stick. Black Shuck, he has been called, or Old Shef, or – presumably by the very short-sighted – Old Scarf. He is red-eyed, made of history, the rub of the earth. Above all this, Joan's voice is a gossamer cry on an icy east wind, coming from somewhere behind old stone. She works in a library now. Ken is the secretary of the Norfolk Moth Society. 'Don't get him started on moths,' Joan told me when I met the two of them in a pub in the village of Spooner Row. 'You'll be here until next week.'

In 2012, when I did a short stint of volunteering at the Cambridge Folk Museum, I got more of a sense of how time could darken a work of art, particularly those characterised by minimalism or naivety. With thoughts of relocation, I was beginning to clear out my loft at the time and had noticed how much more interesting a lot of the stuff in my loft had become in the years since I'd shoved it up there. That is the big rule of lofts: everything becomes more interesting once it is in one. If you were a dull person and you spent a few years in a loft it could probably do a lot for your character. Attics aren't quite the same, as they are posher and generally have more refined and expensive stuff in them. The museum was like a giant living loft, everything in it getting more darkly interesting all the time. It was different to Kettle's Yard, the museum next door, which was smarter, more attic-like. If a well-groomed person in neat clothes came into the Cambridge Folk Museum, nine times out of ten it was because they'd got the wrong door. Two staircases led to the first floor. The narrower of the two functioned as a downward-only staircase. A visitor would sometimes attempt to ascend the downward-only staircase, and one of my fellow volunteers – a retiree in her late sixties – would shout, 'STOP!' nearly causing the visitor to fall back down the stairs in fright. Time palpably slowed once through the doors of the museum because any concept of 'catching up' with the world beyond the threshold was rendered moot here, since there would always be more social history to record. My job was to work behind the scenes, archiving the constant flow of new potential exhibits, sometimes guessing at what they were with wild inaccuracy. Another of the more elderly female volunteers had recently mistaken a black cylindrical candle mould of Victorian vintage for an early dildo. I was warned to watch out for vodka beetles, who had a bad habit of chewing through ancient cloth and carpet – especially, I presumed, when on one of their signature benders. I opened a box to find an exquisite dress accompanied by a letter explaining that the owner had first worn it in 1952 at a ball with her late husband on a ship bound for the Gold Coast. I formed a shield around it with my arms, fearful of what vodka beetles might do to it if they got their way.

I began to picture an alternative life for myself amid all this gentle, cranky beauty, caring for early-Victorian horses' sun bonnets and corn dolly windmills and eventually inaugurating my own Scarecrow Wing in the furthest corner of the building, rescuing Zombie Marilyn from an East Norfolk household waste recycling centre when the Hollywood Legends Diner met its palpably imminent end, giving her a home for eternity where she could graduate from nightmarish to downright wake-up-screaming-for-your-mother-in-the-night terrifying. But in total honesty I had reservations about my pedigree as a curator of folk artefacts. I had been genuinely thrilled to find a five-foot wicker man at Myhills Pet and Garden in Swaffham in 2003, but in time I had taken him for granted. Over two winters, uncherished, forgotten, he had rotted into my hedge until he was nothing but a couple of brittle brown ribs, barely distinguishable from the twigs around him. A true social history archivist would not have allowed such a demise to take place. *There will always be generously sized garden centre wicker men*, I'd thought, much like people before me probably thought, *There will always be rudimentary Edwardian traffic lights*, or, *There will always be rusty Georgian mantraps*. I'd looked high and low at garden centres across East Anglia for his replacement, but no dice. Wicker geese? Yes. Wicker owls?

Certainly. Wicker men? No. I replaced him with Warren the scarecrow, lovingly stuffing and clothing him, vowing to be a better mannequin parent, but he did not last. In the same spring that I proudly worked as an archiver of rural folk objects, I set Warren alight on my garden bonfire. I saw this as ritualistic, a ceremony marking my decision to move away from Norfolk, the end of this physical folk-horror book I'd lived inside, this era of straw men. But there was a more basic desire at work too: I just really liked burning stuff.

I do not class Cambridge as part of true folk-horror East Anglia, nor its surrounding villages, which are more Camberwick Green than anything you see in even the most genteel stretches of Norfolk or Suffolk. Cambridge is a different drink, served in fragile bone china with milk and two sugars. But it is still an early gateway to the Badlands of the East, a point where a rustic wheel very slowly starts to turn after miles of patchy post-London almost-countryside and repressive commuter sprawl. It was a very convenient base for M. R. James to make the excursions north-east that inspired his stories. On the coldest day of 2013 I went to the Leper Chapel of St Mary Magdalene, on the city's harsher, less leafy north side, to watch a man called Robert Lloyd Parry – another Cambridge academic – spend an hour and a half pretending to be James. Parry's one-man theatre company, Nunkie, doesn't settle for simply reading aloud the stories that James wrote in the first three decades of the last century but attempts to recreate the experience of the author himself reading them to rapt students and fellow scholars at

King's or Eton College in the final part of his life. Parry's shows invariably sold out well ahead of opening night. He was only forty-two but looked uncannily like James did in late middle age, albeit much taller, his huge shoulders crammed into a waistcoat and jacket, with thin-rimmed round spectacles and a slicked-down flick of receding mousy hair. He's toured the eight stories in his repertoire all over England, but tends to favour old buildings in East Anglia. 'Remember to wrap up warm,' he told me before I set off for the Leper Chapel to see him perform the stories *Count Magnus* and *Number 13*. I took this for nothing but a pleasantry, something anyone would say to another going anywhere on a snowy January evening, but it turned out he really meant it. Nine centuries old, with no heating and a ceiling of such a towering nature that its finer details remain a mystery, the building smelled like every damp cellar that I'd ever been in had got together and formed a damp cellar supergroup, but also like the damp itself was suffering from hypothermia and needed help. The temperature inside hovered an elk's hair above freezing. At the interval everyone in the crowd of fifty or so got up, not because we had anywhere to go – in a toiletless one-room building like the Leper Chapel there *isn't* anywhere to go – but because we needed to stamp our feet to bring some semblance of circulation back to our legs. Candlelight waltzed up walls, illuminating the drooping tongues of gargoyles. Not your everyday gargoyles, but serious, primal gargoyles who remembered a time before clocks. I began to realise that the performance had been mismarketed. It was not a solitary show after all. There were two performers here, both equally vital: Parry and the building.

In the century and a bit since James's first stories emerged, human brains have been voluntarily reprogrammed: they flit between forms of entertainment at an infinitely higher speed, distracted by the tyranny of choice. In an era of compressed attention spans how do you get an audience to focus on James's slow-moving world of solitary academics weekending in off-the-beaten-track hotels and admiring the cupolas on Suffolk churches? Parry's method is to make as few concessions to the present as possible, pulling you with a primitive *thud* back to the dark of an early-twentieth-century room then, in his storytelling itself, pulling you even further back to an earlier era – typically the 1880s or 1890s. 'Turn off your mobile phones,' we had been told by the man on the door. 'Don't just put them on silent. Turn them off properly.' Parry read without preamble or thanks to his audience, illuminated only by a couple of candles. 'Some people complain it's too dark,' he told me afterwards. 'But I'm afraid I ignore them. The pale light, uncertain shadows and flickers of candlelight reflect James's storytelling method: the sense that there is something just out of sight, on the periphery of your vision, something you have to peer at to see, and even then you don't see it clearly.' He adds to the atmosphere with props, including old books, photographs, a vintage armchair, a leather bag containing notebooks and, often but not tonight, a bust of Zeus and an old coat stand. In the Leper Chapel he paused at turns in the narrative to take a swig of brandy and milk. His style was somehow exasperated, troubled, wry and utterly commanding all at the same time, an exaggerated amalgam of two or three very old tutors he had had at university, 'terrifically erudite men with very dry wits and faintly satirical twinkles in their eyes'. When he deliberately, violently dropped the leather bag on the floor at a crucial juncture in *Count Magnus* – another James tale featuring a disbelieving, lonely academic being haunted by a terrible presence – I jumped in a manner that I hadn't since the first time I watched Jamie Lee Curtis walk home from school through the ominous suburbia of John Carpenter's 1978 film *Halloween*: a testament to how thoroughly Parry's performance had transported me. Three years later, when I saw Parry perform *Oh, Whistle, and I'll Come to you, My Lad* in a smart, conventionally decorated theatre in a converted early-twentieth-century factory he was equally commanding and convincing, but something was palpably missing: the vital extra element called Place.

The general thinking is that the fictional setting for *Oh, Whistle, and I'll Come to you, My Lad* is based on the area around Felixstowe, but it's Dunwich, thirty miles further north along Suffolk's coast, that I always think of when I read the story or – particularly – see the original BBC adaptation: the drowned port, Britain's Atlantis, the place where Scarecrow Country begins to be nibbled by the sea. When I see Michael Horden, who plays Parkins in the 1968 TV version, finding the dreaded dog whistle in the weeds and sand above the sea, it's the crumbling cliff beyond Dunwich's ruined thirteenth-century Franciscan priory I think of. When I have been alone, walking along Dunwich's ever-shifting shingle, soundtracked only by the cries of terns and the rough indistinct conversation of my footsteps with a wind made garrulous by a long lonely journey over water, I can't help thinking of Horden being chased along the beach by the white sheet ghost in his dream. 'Who is this who is coming?' reads the inscription on the whistle, translated from Latin. In Dunwich on a cold lonely day the something-behind-me feeling of emptiest Norfolk and Suffolk reaches its apotheosis: the sense that, while you have no place to hide here, whatever might follow you has plenty of very subtle ones. For my last decade in Norfolk it was the nearest stretch of coastline to my home, a place I visited regularly to read, to swim, to think, which got a few feet closer to me every year. When I revisited Suffolk for the first time after two years in Devon, in 2016, it was, for reasons of a magnetic nature, the first place I headed for.

I passed through Blaxhall on the way, stopping to watch corvids and buzzards weave above geometric fields. Twenty-four months had given hills enough time to alter me. I felt the full force of that dizzy, shrunk disorientation for the first time. The Blaxhall scarecrows were still not there, but outside a farm shop near Middleton I stopped to photograph a couple of others, also apparently joined in matrimony. They were good ones, especially the husband, who sat on an old camping chair dressed in a brown suit jacket and cravat, with a cheap toy scarecrow cat – *Great Yarmouth gift shop* was the thought that sprang to mind – on his lap and an expression on his white cotton bag face that found the middle ground between

dreamy and psychotic. I'd have liked to have seen him a bit more weatherblasted but that was nitpicking. I was forty now, the age when people should be writing novels, and the written version of my scarecrow novel had still not emerged. I was much more relaxed about that fact than I used to be. It either would happen, one day, or it wouldn't. I'd written a couple of other books in the meantime, very different books, which I felt proud of and had enjoyed writing, tuning in to a frequency that suited me. My novel, if it had happened in one of its initial forms, probably would have been inferior. I saw now that in the writing of it I'd been striving for something unreachably big while neglecting all the little stuff that was a vital part of making something reachably big or even something reachably medium. Some of us, especially if we have perfectionist tendencies, want to create our best work when we're unblemished. But that's not typically the natural pattern of events. Sometimes the best work doesn't arrive until we're a collection of wood in a mud-caked boiler suit, alone in a field, being buffeted this way and that by a cold wind. Of course we have to learn this for ourselves because one of the central characteristics of being temporarily unblemished is not having any awareness that you're temporarily unblemished.

I'd chosen one of my old walking mixes of spooky folk songs for the drive to Dunwich, including Lal and Mike Waterson's 'The Scarecrow', a song so broken it barely exists, but so ripe with death metaphor and circle-of-life awareness it cannot help but exist for ever in the mind of anyone who's ever heard it. Aptly, as I drove past Dunwich Heath, Stone Angel's 'The Bells of Dunwich' kicked in, although 'kicked' wasn't really the word. It floated in on a ghostly tide. Underwater sounds. Sounds as smudgy as the light let in by an M. R. James story. Even if the bells had been ringing right now under the sea and I had listened very closely, I doubt I'd have been able to hear them above Poseidon's violent whistling breath. Extreme weather warnings had gone out across the UK the previous evening. In other parts of the country people were mocking them as a false alarm. Not here. A tree was down, blocking the main route to the beach, although because of the angle at which the trunk had fallen and the ivy overwhelming its limbs my initial impression was that a lane I've travelled dozens of times had vanished into thin air. This was not the part of Dunwich most associated with the supernatural, but it was a junction I'd often thought of as singularly enigmatic and eerie, perhaps the nearest to an archetypal blues musician's Devil's crossroads as you'll get on the Suffolk Heritage Coast. Arriving at it on foot one early-winter evening in 2011 I'd come face to face with a huge stag, the two of us staring each other out for what felt like an eternity. During those thirty seconds or so I felt like I'd crossed some sort of metaphysical divide. In another incident flavoured with arguably no less paranormal excitement two years prior to that, I had happened upon an unmanned table of home-made jam in some woodland on the other side of the road.

Now, in 2016, I took the longer route around to the deserted beach car park. Miscellaneous fragments of tree and bin and fence were flying through the air, and everyone who was outdoors – essentially me, a bold crow, a man hurrying towards the village pub and a woman wrestling with her weekly rubbish – looked like they'd just had their eyeballs pressure-washed. I hadn't planned to come here in the middle of the most destructive storm of the year, but for appropriate historical ambience I could not have chosen a better day. Is there another part of the English coastline that has been more altered by strong weather over the last thousand years than the four-mile stretch from Walberswick, a couple of miles north of here, to Sizewell, a couple of miles south? It's doubtful. In the early 1300s Dunwich was one of the major ports of East Anglia, but over the next six centuries the sea staged a series of devastating attacks on it, bringing the coastline over a mile further inland and destroying all of the town's original eight churches. The last one crumbled down the weakened cake-like cliffs in the 1920s, its final standing buttress being removed and placed safely in the graveyard of the current, relatively modern (1832) church on the furthest side of town from the waves. Despite the place only having around one hundred residents, a trace of the fish trade remains. 'Do you have any Dover sole?' a man in the queue ahead of me once asked at the beachside fish hut. 'I'll just check,' said the man at the counter, disappearing around the back in the direction of the beach. 'You're in luck,' he said, upon returning thirty seconds later. 'The boat has just come in.' In the 1800s it was still not unheard of for herring to be used as currency in nearby inns.

I could easily have stayed overnight with friends in Norwich or south Norfolk, but I checked into a B & B up the road, in the neighbouring village of Westleton, alone. It seemed the M. R. James thing to do. I used my debit card to pay for my room, not having any herring to hand at the time. I noted with pleasure that the B & B had the Jamesian name of the Crown, instantly evocative of an item another James protagonist, in *Warning to the Curious*, finds buried near the eastern seashore. 'Brian is finding it difficult under the table with his legs,' said a talkative woman at breakfast with a strong West Midlands accent. Everyone in the room except me had a strong West Midlands accent, which of course made perfect sense, us all being only 179 miles from Walsall if we stuck to major road networks. It was a ridiculous thing I had done, coming double that distance from my own home in Devon to stay in this place amid holidaying strangers, but the ridiculousness was freeing. I crossed the road to a second-hand bookshop in a converted chapel, where a lovely man in apparent nightwear sold me five books and loaned me three more, and his impossibly polite adolescent assistant offered me a cup of tea. When I came back the following day to return the loaned books the shop was deserted, but there was a stick and a dented sunflower-oil can next to a sign reading BASH CAN WITH STICK TO GET ATTENTION, an instruction that came across as much as a recommended life philosophy as a retail-themed instruction. I bashed it, and the lovely

man appeared, again in apparent nightwear. It turned out he'd been to school ninety yards from where I now lived. I didn't find out if he also wore apparent nightwear back then.

In 2003 I had viewed a house for sale directly across the heath from the bookshop that I couldn't afford, motivated by the regular optimistic thought of my late twenties and thirties that I would imminently become a person who wasn't constantly scrabbling around for next month's mortgage. The man who showed me the house, which seemed to have last been updated in the less auspicious part of 1974, had not lived in it; it had belonged to his late father. He confessed that, while it was

peaceful for much of the year, the 'kiss-me-quick crowd'
going past on the nearby road in the direction of the
beach could be a problem in summer. It had struck me
as a strange observation then, and did so even more now.
There could be few less intrinsically kiss-me-quick places
in England than Dunwich. Drag-a-cold-icy-finger-down-
my-spine-slow maybe. Kiss-me-quick? No. And that way
it had stayed, with its excellent museum and seasonal
1950s fish and chip hut the only concessions to tourism, a
lack of development potential being, along with a strong
supernatural ambience, one of rampant coastal erosion's
undervalued plus points. Dunwich is that bit more
desolate and ragged than its near neighbours Southwold,
Thorpeness, Aldeburgh and Walberswick, especially on a
gale-wrecked March day. A wooden gate swung furiously
in the wind as I arrived on the beach, revealing a rusted
generator like some deeply anticlimactic birthday surprise.
As I climbed the sea wall, I was lifted slightly off my heels
and almost knocked onto my back on the shingle. These
are itinerant stones, moving constantly southwards, and a
few centuries ago many of them might have cited Norfolk
as their home county. Half an hour's walk further up the
coast a dead porpoise provided another reminder of the
sea's ever-encroaching bully-boy wishes. It was pushed up
against the last shelf of shingle, beyond which was only
sandy heathland and heathery marsh. It was the second
porpoise I'd found on this stretch of lonely coast, to add
to the pristine one I had discovered in almost the exact
same spot five years earlier. I'd called the coastguard
about its predecessor and would like to think the body

was put to good use: an example of perfect porpoiseness to be shown off for generations in a museum. This one was smaller, and birds – herring gulls, oystercatchers and the terns from the light green, sandy, sectioned-off nesting area behind me – had already begun to feast on its face.

The murky waters of Dunwich conceal so much: not just more porpoises but old merchant houses and graves and churches and even, perhaps most astonishingly of all, an ancient aqueduct. It is still an aqueduct of sorts now, wherever it is. One of Dunwich's most calamitous storms, in 1740, not only destroyed more of the cliff but, to the villagers' horror, uncovered bones and buildings lost to the sea centuries before. When you're on the beach in summer and burying a person to her neck in pebbles, as I did with a group of Norwich friends here one summer, a macabre note is added to the activity by the realisation that a matter of yards away actual human remains are submerged beneath dark water and turbid stone. In March with a storm raging and the beach full of fresh driftwood and flotsam, it's even more possible to look at the horizon and picture Dunwich's old frontier, more than a mile out there, in the waves: a place that, had Poseidon been feeling more benevolent towards it over the last millennium, might have gone on to outshine Norwich as East Anglia's finest city. Staring at the sea is always a cathartic reminder of human insignificance, but there's an extra cathartic element on this stretch of coast that perhaps gives it its unique power: a reminder not just of our insignificance but of the way the things around us with a strong illusion of permanence can crumble, a

reminder of change and the lack of choice we have in life to do anything but embrace it.

Looking back in the direction of the rest of Suffolk and Norfolk from the back ledge of the beach here I sometimes get the sense that the angry saltwater has already got the better of the land, imprinted itself onto it: that, lacking the big rocky walls which defend so much of Britain's west coast, East Anglia's big horizons and quiet spaces, its horror-film emptiness, are creations of the sea's force – or at least its strong salty air. I feel another aspect of this nine miles north of Dunwich at Covehithe, a very different stretch of beach, possibly even more desolate. Since 1830 its cliffs have been forced back more than five hundred metres, and there is no sign of a slowing of the erosion. Almost exactly a year after my Dunwich trip, on another dizzy day when my suppressed love for soft scary East Anglia tripped me over, I walked from Covehithe's double church – a vast ruin, courtesy of Cromwell's armies in the Civil War, and a smaller, newer church inside it – north up the beach and was rendered open-mouthed by the latest dramatic leap the shoreline had taken backwards. It was if someone had popped a balloon or crisp packet next to the shoreline when it had not been expecting it. What I thought impossible had happened: Covehithe looked even more post-apocalyptic than it had half a decade before. The remains of a cliff-top copse I had walked through on my way to Benacre Broad in 2012 were now scattered on the beach, the salt-blasted roots of its trees being shaped by the tide more each day into something an elaborately branded corporate think tank might give a sculptor in Southwold or Aldeburgh a handsome cheque to produce. The stretch of beach beside the broad itself – already becoming a salty lagoon on my last visit – was now unnegotiable unless the tide was right out, freshwater and saltwater having finally become an irreversible cocktail. 'Can we get across that?' I asked Isabelle, a long term walking companion I'd been reunited with for the morning, assessing the churning sandbanked natural well where sea met broad. 'Yeah!' we chorused. But we couldn't. We didn't even give it a proper try. We'd have been up to our waists in no time. Bad things could happen here despite the soft lull of the land. This was the place where Charles Halfacree, an Essex factory worker, made a failed attempt to float the body of his sister's transsexual ex-husband out to sea on a lilo, in one of the less run-of-the-mill East Anglian murder cases of the last two decades. The church had its own infamous personal interior breeze, which still whistled inexplicably around the pews on the calmest of days.

Sea bishops – fish creatures with episcopal headwear – were said to rise from the deep here in the sixteenth century and raise earth-shaking storms. In 1912 the Norfolk-based writer Lilias Rider Haggard wrote to her famous adventure novelist father Henry to say she'd seen a sixty-foot-long sea serpent next door to Covehithe, at Kessingland Beach. Down south at Orford in the twelfth century a bearded man was found in the sea and brought back and treated as a pet by the villagers: a fish-like figure with no hair on the top of his head as close to a sea scarecrow who has ever existed in folklore.

As Isabelle and I gazed back across the tilted farmland from the crumbling toffee-coloured cliff top to the village, I saw what I'd been hoping to see: a scarecrow, juddering in the breeze. There was no breeze, which made the juddering curious. Perhaps it was that phantom church breeze, escaped into the great wide open.

'Tom, that's just a guy with a metal detector,' said Isabelle, who has better eyesight than me.

I missed living close to this bit of sea. I missed this long straight line of islandless shore with its old shingle monsters and its residual effect on the land beyond. I missed the unimpeded sky – not that I didn't adore the impeded sky where I now lived. I missed more about this region: my friends, the way my existence here had seemed more effortless in many ways, less necessarily toughened up, although in others less challenging and less brightly, scarily alive. There was nothing to be done about it, though. History has proved that people can't have two lovers – not successfully, not on a long-term basis where all three parties feel equally rewarded. I had to keep choosing just one. Besides, there was an almost-four-hundred-mile gap in the middle. It didn't make the process of two-timing easy. On what might be seen as the plus side – although not if you are currently living in one of the buildings a hundred yards inland from Covehithe's shore – my two romantic interests were getting closer every year. Visibly so, in the case of the eastern one today. The large amounts of polite nineteenth-century-holidaymaker graffiti scratched, with excellent calligraphy, into the church windows suggested a time when Covehithe might have almost been a small resort, rather than a dystopian non-village at the rim of the planet; there was even the mark of a visitor from Buenos Aires, dated 1889. Nowadays the church didn't even bury bodies in its grounds, anticipating the deeper more forsaken place where coastal erosion would soon take them. As well as the desolate tree corpses, a boxy red-brick structure languished, smashed and part-submerged, on the beach. I took it for an old lookout shelter I once sat in, but the Suffolk artist Kate Batchelor later told me it was a septic tank, which I had definitely not sat in. On my last visit, in 2012, the tank had still been buried unseen in the hillside.

Back then the road through Covehithe ended in a jagged precipice over the shoreline, like a dismantled piece

of unusually crude Scalextric track. That bit of tarmac, serrated by nature, had long since been washed out to sea. It was a beach with an unusually fluid exchange of eclectic paraphernalia. Plenty went out, but plenty came in too. As Isabelle and I walked south towards Southwold we found rounded glass pebbles, a sea-blasted lunchbox, various lengths and colours of old rope, a wristwatch. I remembered the second time I had come here, in 2009, when large planks were scattered all over the shore: strong-looking joists, good quality, probably fallen off a cargo ship. A group of men – opportunists in the timber trade perhaps or just people who, like me, really enjoy wood – were carrying the planks up the beach, one at a time, two men to a plank. The image had stayed with me, and I remember thinking at the time how much they looked like pall-bearers.

5

WORLD TURNED UPSIDE DOWN

'Bees?' asked a lady with a badge on her lapel as I entered
Exeter's Royal Albert Memorial Museum.

It was a busy Saturday morning at the museum and
I'd estimate that only about 5 per cent of the foot traffic
through the front doors during this small window of
time was for the bee identification course I was due to
attend in one of the building's upstairs meeting rooms.
Perhaps I just had a bee look about me. 'Yes,' I told the
woman, confirming that I was some bees, and not having
a problem with that. In his book *The Twits* Roald Dahl
wrote that if people have good thoughts 'they will shine
out of your face like sunbeams and you will always look
lovely'. Possibly, in a not dissimilar fashion, a long period
of musing about bees will bring something of the bee to
your personal ambience: a look that somehow combines
peacefulness, industry and dopiness in equal measure. I

had been thinking about bees a lot recently, ever since the day a few months ago when a stranger had approached me in the countryside not far from my house and said, 'Excuse me. Did you know two bees are having sex on your flares?' and I'd looked down and seen that two bees were having sex on my flares.

What is the correct course of action when two bumblebees are humping on your clothing? Mine was to take a flyer for a local charity jumble sale from my rucksack, gently slide it beneath the two bees then place them on a low branch of a nearby mulberry tree. They were extremely involved in what they were doing and did not seem to notice the change of scenery. Who knows? I might even have spiced things up a little for them. I had considered the option of just walking on and leaving them to it, and despite the worry that they might fall off at the wrong moment, I could see the possible advantages in this, especially had I been single at the time. It would have been such a great story to tell. 'How did we meet? Oh, I didn't have to do much at all. Elizabeth was very forward. She marched directly up to me and informed me that two common carders were making love a few inches below my groin.' You could imagine it perhaps being a hindrance later on though: the realisation that you had grown apart, yet not wanting to admit it, years of your life frittered away as you stayed together just for the bees and the anecdote they had gifted you.

It is not uncommon for insects to have it off on me. A few weeks after the bees shagged on my flares, two flying ants landed on my hand and went quite hard at it doggy style as I sat in my garden and attempted to concentrate on an intricate novel about a century of family life in the American Midwest. But I felt particularly honoured to function as a bee knocking shop. I'd always loved bees, a love that has burned more brightly since I moved to Devon, where there appear to be as many bees as there were in the Nottinghamshire and Derbyshire countryside of my childhood. Sometimes one of them will fly into my front room, headbutt numerous items of furniture and leave. I would not put up with that kind of behaviour from a human friend, but from a bee it feels like a compliment. I would probably even go so far as to say that I'd fight anyone who thinks bees aren't great, were it not for the fact that loving, not fighting, is the bee way.

There was a time when my friends would have been surprised if I had told them I was doing a day course identifying bees. Actually, that's not true. There wasn't. The course I attended at the Royal Albert Museum was taught by Stephen Carroll. Stephen is the county recorder

for hymenoptera, which essentially means he is in charge of all the insects in Devon. When insects are obscure and aren't sure what they are, they can go to Stephen to find out. As well as showing us how to identify more regular bumblebees, such as the common carder and the buff-tailed bumblebee, he told us about bumblebees particular to Devon, such as *Bombus muscorum* and *humilis*. I decided that of all of these the buff-tailed bumblebee was my favourite, having a certain satisfying chunkiness about it. I pictured myself befriending one and teaching it to sit on my shoulder like a fat stripy parrot.

Later on during the course we learned about some other rare bees who hang out in other parts of the country but don't make it this far south-west. At this point I found myself bristling and getting a little Devon-proud. *Why does Northamptonshire have red-shanked bees, but we don't? What is so good about Northamptonshire? I* wondered. *Surely it wouldn't hurt to nip up there and bring a few back in a medium-size van?* We traipsed out into Northernhay Gardens with perspex bee pots, gently trapped some bees inside them, identified the bees with Stephen's help then set them free. It was amazing how many bees you saw, even here, in the heart of a small city, once you truly opened your eyes. A couple of homeless men who had been sleeping under some blankets in the gardens also joined in at one point and seemed equally fascinated.

Most of the bees I see in my garden are bumblebees, but every so often a honeybee will turn up, probably on a reconnaisance mission from my friend Hayley's bee sanctuary, less than a mile away. The sanctuary is behind the graveyard of an extremely old church, an apt home for creatures indelibly associated with death and birth and so crucial to our continuing prosperity as a species. In the ancient custom of Telling the Bees, which dates back to pagan times and is still practised to this day, bees are viewed as highly intelligent, sensitive beings who should be informed of all big life events, as you would a close human friend. If any flying insects are good listeners, you sense it is bees. I like the idea of keeping them abreast about the significant stuff happening in my life.

'Hello. Is that the bees?'

'It is.'

'I am having a big party for my fortieth in May.'

'Great. Thanks for letting us know. Remember, it's better to overestimate on food than underestimate.'

Hayley seemed unsurprised when I told her about the two bees having sex on my flares. 'It happens a lot,' she said. I assumed she meant generally, rather than specifically on flares, but wasn't totally sure. 'I watched two of them going at it for ages recently. They will often last an hour. They tend not to suffer from premature ejaculation. The guy wiped himself off very carefully afterwards.' Hayley has just one hive, built with great love by her carpenter boyfriend Tom, which sits amid ox-eye daisies, lady's mantle and dwarf comfrey. Hayley cuts the grass in the sanctuary with her scythe. I know this because when she gave me a lift back from the pub once in her van she said, 'Mind you don't sit on my scythe!' when I got in and almost sat on her scythe. Whenever I've sat in Hayley's sanctuary with her, honeybees have buzzed gently around us and a special soft quietness has been in the air. Hayley does not wear a mask when she's around her bees, and I did not feel the need to either, even when a bee landed on my earlobe. A few days later as I drove past the sanctuary with my car windows open one of her bees flew in and joined me. I wondered about turning round and driving it back home, but it flew back out again after less than a mile. I have to assume it made it back OK but I can't be sure.

There are all sorts of dangers for Hayley's swarm every year. Bees from elsewhere can come in and hijack the hive. Many years ago Hayley opened one of her hives and found a mouse corpse inside, which, in self-defence, her bees had entirely encased in wax. The previous year she'd lost her swarm when wasps drove them out. I think I know the exact wasps she means too: I'm pretty sure they were the same ones who'd been waging war on my garden furniture, weakening it to the extent that one of the chairs finally gave way beneath me, sending me crashing to the ground. I doubt my weight was much of a factor in the breakage since I am, in the words of a man I once paid to adjust a shirt, 'built like a whippet'. The wasps had been nibbling industriously at the wood for two and a half years, and although they are very small and their work is gradual, my hunch is that their adherence to a diligent long-term plan weakened the structure. The chair was the second part of the patio set to break in the space of the year – the other being half of the sofa section, which came in useful as fuel in an unusually cold late spring, when I ran out of logs.

If the weather is dry, in the warmer months the wasps and I often sit on my broken garden furniture in the morning and have breakfast together. I normally have muesli. The wasps are quite content with wood, which they take straight, without milk. I look carefully at what I'm eating and drinking before I put it in my mouth, as I don't want my tongue to get stung and swell up and suffocate me, but I don't think the wasps want any trouble. They get on cheerfully with their thing, and I get on with mine. They're in good spirits in spring and summer, far different to what they're like later in the year, when their tempers flare due to being, in the memorable words of my gardener friend Andy, 'drunk and out of work'.

On paper I have more reason to be nervous around wasps than most, and as any wasp worth his salt will tell you, paper is important. When I was eight, a few days after I'd fallen through a garage window, ripping open the underside of my arm and getting rushed to hospital for several stitches, an Italian wasp planted its sting deep inside the fresh wound. I should point out that I was in Italy at the time of the sting, and the wasp had not travelled overseas specifically to hurt me, although I sense that its malevolence was such that it probably would have thought little of doing so. If I close my eyes now I can still feel the spiteful acid furnace of pain I experienced. It was one of many examples I'd seen of just how formidable insects were in Italy, a country where on the same family holiday I'd witnessed thirteen ants successfully carrying a whole baguette along a medieval wall. Wasps then left me to get on with my life in peace for many years after childhood until one day in Norfolk in 2013 when four of them simultaneously stung my bottom while I was in my garden. I had just mowed over their nest though, so who could blame them? I hadn't realised the nest was there, but you know what it's like with wasps: they are not interested in going back over the nuances of a fracas.

I have since come around to wasps. They're formidable architects, they kill lots of garden pests, they pollinate much more than people tend to believe and they helped humans invent paper – a fact that contradicts the long-held view of them as the anti-book thug counterparts to bees' gentle selfless intellectuals. In mid-summer any defects they might have are also put into sharp perspective by the horseflies across the road from my house. To date I have never encountered a nice horsefly. Even the one horsefly I met who seemed sort of OK and didn't bite me probably later turned out to be a Scientologist. I must have been bitten by fifty of them when I went alpaca trekking in Norfolk in 2011. 'I will never forget what your legs looked like on that day,' my friend Will told me. 'Oh, Will. That's such a beautiful thing to say,' I replied before realising he was referring to the runnels of blood that turned my shins into a painted horror show as we walked along the North Norfolk Coast Path. I don't know how the Jersey cows who live near me cope. If I had as many horseflies around me as they do in July, I'd be sarcastic and hard to get on with, but they're always up for a cuddle when I walk the footpath through their field.

Insect Day arrived behind schedule last summer. This is the twenty-four-hour period when all the insects in the south-west of the UK get together and agree to all crawl and fly into my front room at exactly the same time. I remember the exact day, as it was the one when I saw my cat Roscoe pummelling a small creature against the French windows of the room with her paw. I hurried outside and removed Roscoe from the creature, which turned out to be the biggest cockchafer beetle I had ever seen. The cockchafer flew into the air, its wingspan covering such an area it could have been mistaken for a dragonfly. It was a warm night and I was drinking beer with my friend Charlotte, who had never seen a cockchafer before. 'Do you get many moths here?' she asked. 'I have a bit of a phobia of moths.' Remembering the two hundred or so that make my house their home between June and October, I felt it was best to phrase my answer carefully but without factual inaccuracies I might be called on to account for later. 'Some...but I haven't seen any so far this year,' I said, opening a window and watching seven of them fly in at once, in the direction of Charlotte's hair.

I save a few of these moths from an early death at the hands of various foes – cats, running bath taps, spider's webs. 'Good moth!' I told one not long ago. I praise moths so they distinguish good behaviour, such as leaving the house through open windows, from bad, such as flying at lamps. But in many cases my efforts will be futile: over the course of the summer many moths will be eaten by bats. Moths are a favourite snack for bats, along with cockchafers, dung beetles and gnats. A pipistrelle bat – the most common breed in Britain – will eat around 3,000 gnats in one night. I know stuff like this because

last summer I went on three guided bat walks in the space of three months in the fifty square miles surrounding my house. Most of these revolved around lesser and greater horseshoe bats, species once common in the south-west of Britain, whose numbers dropped dramatically through the twentieth century but have risen again in recent years. Seventy per cent of Britain's current population of around 10,000 horseshoe bats can be found in Devon. They like the mild climate here, and the hedgerows, which as Anna, a member of Devon Wildlife Trust's Greater Horseshoe Bat Project, told me, 'make for excellent bat commuter tunnels'.

If you visit the footpath leading down to Buckfastleigh town centre from the ruined church at the top of the hill at dusk on a rainless summer night, you'll see precisely what Anna means. It's like a bat motorway: dozens of horseshoes speeding up the leafy corridor towards Dartmoor, weaving expertly between branches and your face, like X-wing Starfighters negotiating the artificial canyons of the fragmenting Death Star. I luckily managed to photograph a couple of these bats on my second visit to the spot. In the background of one shot is a ghostly figure that I would like to boast is one of Devon's infamous Green Lane sprites but was actually another bat spotter, further down the hill. Bat spotting is a common hobby here. Earlier in the year, Chris, who co-runs the community radio station where I volunteer as a DJ, had been walking in the area at nightfall and saw a gang of tough-looking adolescents approaching who appeared to be up to no good. Their threatening aura dissipated when he noticed that all of them clutched bat detectors in their hands.

A top-of-the-range bat detector will set you back well over a hundred quid but, on a tip-off from Bea, another Devon Wildlife Trust volunteer, who hosted a bat walk in the village of Dartington earlier this month, I discovered

that Argos do a surprisingly good children's version for around a tenner. Sadly, when I went into Argos in Exeter and typed 'bat detector' into one of their terminals, the item turned out to be out of stock. The woman behind me in the queue saw and offered a look of sympathy, perhaps less in recognition of my disappointment and more because I was the kind of person who goes into Argos and types 'bat detector' into one of their terminals.

In June, at Berry Head Nature Reserve, I sat with twenty other bat enthusiasts with more advanced bat detectors and waited for the local horseshoe population to emerge from their roost in the old quarry overlooking the sea. The age of my fellow enthusiasts ranged from early twenties to late sixties, and no archetypal bat enthusiast attire was in evidence, although I could not help noticing one younger couple who looked about as much like bats as any two *Homo sapiens* I had ever seen. Their style was something that stepped boldly and spikily beyond goth: an all-black mix of tough fabric, elaborate piercings and violently angular hard-glued hair that suggested a life lived in darkness, on the wing and on the edge. Sadly the batlike couple appeared to have a muttering disagreement part-way through the evening, and made a low-key but semi-dramatic exit towards the car park so did not get a chance to witness any actual bats. All we'd really done as a group by that point was root through some cowpats for dung beetles, which I found fascinating but am aware might not be everyone's idea of a quality Friday night.

The pipistrelles came out first at Berry Head, common bats you'll see in most rural areas of the UK in summer, only around a quarter of the size of a greater horseshoe. We were instructed to change the range on our detectors ten minutes later, when the greater horseshoes emerged, since they echo-located at a higher frequency to the pipistrelles: around 80 kHz. Several bat experts had told me that the noise horseshoes made was like nothing else on earth. Bea described it as 'like a long wet fart'. To me it sounded like the highfalutin work of a rural acid house DJ who lived by his own rules. It mixed with the music drifting across on the wind from a nightspot in the nearby town of Brixham to create a mash-up that many would have agreed managed to be simultaneously rinsing and banging. Three teenage fishermen walked up the hill past where we were sitting and turned goldfish-mouthed. 'I'm going to say something damning about this scenario,' their faces said to each other, 'but I will need to take a number of hours to process it first.'

Bats are divided into microbats and megabats, but it gets confusing as you get large microbats which are bigger than some of the smaller megabats. Greater horseshoes, which can live until they are thirty and are one of suprisingly few species of bats that actually hang upside down, are an unusually large microbat. People often expect and want categories to be clearly defined in nature, as if when weasels were invented they were all brought out on a large tray marked 'Weasels', which was very separate from another tray, which contained all the planet's original stoats. But that's not always the case. As the ecologist John Walters explained to me in an orchard just outside the village of Stoke Gabriel, the line between butterflies and moths, for example, is not a line at all, as it does not exist. Some moths are surprisingly cool with flitting about in the daytime; some butterflies are a bit reclusive and nocturnal. Some moths have a Laura Ashley beauty to their markings that they don't get nearly enough credit for. Some butterflies – such as the numerous marble whites in the orchard with us – are a bit mothlike in their wing decor. You get the feeling Donald Trump could learn a lot about the complexities of genetic identity by spending a day in a never-fertilised, insect-heavy field such as this, but of course, as a massive closedbrain fuckshined pissface, he wouldn't. He'd be too busy nuking it and turning it into a golf course.

I could have got flat on my stomach in the orchard, as I did in my parents' garden in Nottinghamshire so often on summer days when I was six or seven, and watched the activity in that tiny never-fertilised jungle for hours, the communities-within-communities playing out their lives between the reeds of grass. I could then have gone home and identified everything I'd seen, but I'd still not have known a fraction of what there is to know. There are apps on phones for that kind of thing nowadays but they're not always a guarantee of help. My friend Jenny, who had joined me in the orchard, had been walking along a path near Totnes a few weeks previously and stopped to let a furry orange caterpillar cross. A crowd of walkers soon gathered around the caterpillar, fascinated as to what kind it could be, since it looked quite exotic. Nobody knew the answer. An authoritative man in the crowd told everyone not to worry as he had just the thing, then

photographed the caterpillar and fed the information into the appropriate part of his high-grade smartphone. There was a dramatic pause as the crowd waited anxiously for the voice on the phone to reveal the identity of the insect. 'Orange caterpillar,' said the phone, finally.

One of the most visually impressive finds when Jenny and I were with John in the orchard was a large emperor moth caterpillar, a beautiful plump specimen with a punk-rock back of soft yellow studs. After pupation John will sometimes release a female emperor moth on Dartmoor, up on one of the high points above Postbridge. 'Within seconds I'll see about a hundred randy male emperor moths flying over the ridge, having caught its scent on the wind,' he told me. Since the previous autumn I had been following John on a few of his talks and expeditions, trying to soak up some of his vast entomological knowledge and sometimes carrying his butterfly net for him. At home John has a glass bee house, where his bees sometimes sleep on their backs. In March, at a talk in Dartington Village Hall attended by Hayley and me, he showed his audience photos to prove this, as well as his stunning watercolour illustrations of insects, snakes and birds, all of which he composes live, outside, in front of his subjects. 'I can't do it any other way; I'd have no way of capturing the movement,' he told me. John also took the first ever photo of the extremely rare horrid ground-weaver spider and will tell you a great story about a fellow naturalist who once escaped unharmed after having an adder up his trouser leg on Dartmoor and reacted to the experience with Buddhist equanimity.

I remember that outside the village hall that night, as Hayley and I set off in the direction of home, there was a full moon, and Jupiter was clearly visible next to it. The planet burned so bright I began to worry if perhaps they had trouble up there with a fire. There was a pregnant feel to the air, as if spring was behind an invisible wall, scratching to be let out, and not far behind it was summer, yawning and rubbing its big eyes. But that summer, as a lot of people in this area knew, could signal an ominous change for the local ecosystem. A couple of hundred yards behind Dartington Village Hall is one of the most fertile small valleys for rare wildlife in the area, a refuge for dormice and another horseshoe colony. Beside it is the social housing of the Brimhay development, occupied by over-sixties and built by the same 1930s architecture firm which constructed many of the utopian buildings of the nearby Dartington Hall estate. These are slightly draughty structures, tired and in need of an update, but they were designed with community vision and kindness, and placed in a sociable green space, abutting the wild and precious valley. For many of their residents – such as Liz, a nature lover I met who'd not long recovered from a broken spine – the proximity of the valley has a huge bearing on quality of life. The council, however, had decided to bulldoze Brimhay and a large portion of its wildlife to make way for gardenless blocks of flats in which its residents were to be rehoused.

In a court case a few months later, a proposal put together by the Don't Bury Dartington campaign for a more moderate, more wildlife-friendly and significantly cheaper alternative for Brimhay was put forward. Heroically, Dartington won the case, the result of eighteen months of hard work by Liz and Trudy, the founder of the campaign. 'If they'd gone ahead with their plan for the flats, nobody who lives here would see each other any more,' Liz told me. 'As a community, we socialise because of the layout of our houses and gardens. At the moment, when I'm in my garden I see owls, jays, two different types of woodpecker. I've got flowers and butterflies everywhere. All that would have been gone.' Liz and Trudy raised the £17,000 needed to fight the court case through neighbourhood curry evenings and a groundswell of community support, Liz making the long journey to London despite health problems. The case turned, apparently, on a chewed nut, which was submitted as evidence of the presence of dormice in the area. The outcome represents a simultaneous victory for people, dormice and rare bats, and perhaps the question is, why should the needs of people, dormice and rare bats ever *not* be mutually compatible?

Weird is a word with two very polarised meanings. Good Weird can be the best thing ever. If someone whose opinion I revere tells me a film or book or record is weird, and I can tell from the tone of their voice that they mean Good Weird, it means I need to consume it as soon as humanly possible. Bad Weird is very different: it's a warning. It could mean a lot of stuff, none of it particularly salubrious. I can kid myself that loving bats and insects is generally thought of as Good Weird, but that's because I spend a lot of time hanging out in a cocoon of people who love bats and insects. I know that a lot of people would view it as Bad Weird. I know that not giving a nocturnal flying fuck about horseshoe bats and wanting to park your four-by-four and executive home on top of their rapidly diminished habitats is the norm. I know that not wanting a moth in your house because you've just vacuumed and Colin and Sue are coming over later is the norm, as is getting Brian to come in and swat it. This view – seeing a love of nature as Bad Weird – seems to be at the root of so many of the ecologically damaging decisions made, big and small, by humans. 'Oh, look at the oddballs fighting not to kill all these innocent creatures and to keep the entire world from turning into an unfeeling concrete monolith. What's all that about? Ignore them. They're just oddballs. They probably don't even own any new coats.' Too often, nature is perceived as an outsider's hobby. In reality, though, it's not some quirky extra to the main business. It *is* the main business.

It's easy to look at history and find out when a king or despot was born or died but hard to pinpoint precisely when a prevailing attitude shifted. Most history is written by old people who, despite being wise, often have very poor memories, which means it is rife with factual inaccuracies. Nonetheless, it can be said with some certainty that at some hard-to-specify point in the past man lived closely connected with nature, not viewing himself as especially, if at all, superior to it. Then one day he started to view himself as more important and nature as being something to subjugate and treat without respect. Of course this was nonsense and soon created more problems for him as well as for nature. Despite regularly using face scrub, I am nowhere near as pretty as a small magpie moth. I am not better than a bat because I am able to watch Netflix and a bat is not. If anything, this probably makes me worse than a bat. In fact, out of solidarity with bats I recently cancelled my Netflix subscription. I am also almost 100 per cent sure I ate at least a couple of midges when I had a drink in the dark with the bedroom window open the other night. Now I just have to learn to echo-locate and fly through the overhanging branches of an overgrown drover's road and I will be very nearly there, in full eternal unison with bats.

Naturally, we all have our favourites and our black spots when it comes to nature. I, for instance, try not to spend time around hamsters, as they push me towards a melancholy state of mind. But as soon as you start getting too specific and prescriptive about what it's OK to like or not like in nature, you become the equivalent of somebody who holds the view that all people who wear hats are dickheads just because they wear hats.

I try my best to endorse it all, and I want to be better at accepting that nature is better than me, but I know I have work still to do on this score. Bees are easy to love. It's taken me years to fully forgive wasps their trespasses and accept that they are much cooler than me in terms of both physique and artisanal craftsmanship. But I am sure I will swear violently at another wasp before my life is over. After one particularly heavy day of insect bites, not long after my final bat walk of the year, I was bitten harder still by another horsefly on my cheek. I raised my hand to squash the horsefly, but I managed to resist. I considered the horsefly for a moment. It had not bitten me because it had taken offence at an out-of-context screenshot from a piece of my writing, or because I liked a piece of music it didn't, or because I voted Remain in the EU Referendum, or because I sometimes splash out and buy carrots from a supermarket unbefitting my low-born nature. It was just a horsefly who had seen a juicy, half-decent, freshly suntanned cheek, and was being a horsefly. And its equivalents in future generations of insects would probably continue being horseflies long after my kind and I had wiped ourselves out, and somehow there was a curious comfort to be taken from that.

6

THE BEST WAVES

The tiny Victorian terraced house where my nan lived for most of my life was on a steep, narrow street where cars drove a little too fast, children shouted a little too obnoxiously and dogs defecated a little too freely, in the same Nottinghamshire town where, as infrequently as possible, I attended secondary school. At lunchtime on the majority of school days for five years I walked to my nan's house, which took an average of eleven minutes. I turned right out of the school gates then left into a council estate of pebbledashed post-war houses, where in the summer of 1990 a boy called Ian threatened to hit me with a hammer, then towards the newsagent where my friend Bushy had once legendarily pointed to a jar of halfpenny chews and asked, 'How much are halfpenny chews?' From here I cut half-right down a jitty and downhill across a small patch of parkland to the railway embankment, which was frequently peppered with white dog turds and seemed to wear a permanent invisible cloak of its own past, both dark and light, but mostly dark. Afterwards I turned sharp left along a short public footpath, then sharp right, past the town brewery. This was a beautiful, proud, sprawling, red-brick Victorian building which, because I lacked an enquiring mind, only interested me due to two things: a tunnelled footbridge, which I thought was kind of cool, and the fact that Josephine Shaw, the mum of my classmate James Shaw, worked in the reception there, because when you are a fourteen-year-old boy the fact that your classmates have mums can be a surprisingly enduring form of amusement.

My nan's house was one of the first row you reached after the brewery. The town is called Kimberley, which its residents generally pronounce as 'Kimbleh', leaving their mouths open for a fractional but noticeable moment on the final syllable. The street is called Hardy Street and is named after the beer-making brothers who erected the brewery in 1861.

I normally walked to my nan's alone or with Graham Basten. At school my social life awkwardly spreadeagled the cool, tough, sporty kids and the more nerdy kids, whose maths and science work I could sometimes copy and towards whom, as I became more mentally and physically absent at school, I gravitated increasingly. Graham was one of the latter. He lived on a new estate five minutes further up the road from my nan's, and his dad was a butcher, not a supplier of sustainable timber and building materials, although my memory sometimes alters this due to the fact that his dad was a dead ringer for the man who fronted the TV adverts for a famous supplier of sustainable timber and building materials. Graham and I saw ourselves as mild and well behaved, but I now realise that was less to do with us being mild and well behaved and more to do with having plenty of contemporaries to compare ourselves with who were the diametric opposite of mild and well behaved. If we were feeling a bit lairy, we would shout, 'Josephine Shaaaaaw!' at James Shaw's mum as we passed the brewery entrance then run away up the hill. Further up the hill from my nan lived a tall hairy man with big teeth who always wore para boots and an anorak and was, so my nan alleged, a poet. Sometimes when we walked past him, or anyone else who strayed from the tight parameters of late 1980s Kimberley fashion, Graham and I would say, 'And there it is!' just loud enough for our targets to hear us.

The hill and the greater area around my nan's house always smelled pleasantly of hops due to the brewery. This was in contrast to the area around my auntie Jayne and uncle Paul's house, on the other side of town, which smelled strongly of white bread due to the nearby Sunblest factory, a smell too redolent of migraine and chemicals to merit a term as benign as 'yeasty'. There was a small area in the centre of town which smelled neither of hops nor white bread. This usually smelled of chips.

The front door of my nan's house, which was always unlocked during daytime when she was in the house, led directly into her living room. When I arrived I walked in without knocking, just as the rest of the family always did. My nan lived alone for the final thirty-six years of her

186

life but was often surrounded by people: children, spouses of children, grandchildren then great-grandchildren. Until I was around nine she also had a questionably disciplined chihuahua called Beau, who once ate fifty quid. She said there was a ghost who lived with her: a man a few years older than she was who she sometimes heard walking down her stairs, but she said he was a shy ghost who didn't like to be a bother to anyone. He was an apt ghost, since not liking to be a bother to anyone was also a central trait of my nan's personality. When my nan moved into her terrace, in 1985, from her even tinier house half a mile away, 'Easy Lover' by Phil Collins and Philip Bailey was relentlessly on the radio, and the whole family mucked in, scraping tired, dirty old wallpaper from some walls and slapping paint onto others. 'Easy Lover' was the best song I discovered in my nan's house, the second best being 'Stop' by Erasure. My nan's house was not on the whole a place synonymous with the discovery of exciting new music. She only owned about a dozen albums, all on cassette. One of these was the 1971 album *Imagine* by John Lennon, who like her was from Liverpool. The others were all by the country singer Don Williams. My nan rarely played music, preferring TV and radio news. Besides the news, she stuck exclusively to three other types of programme: snooker, tennis and *Coronation Street*. Nobody in our family was more passionately up to date on current affairs or the heartbreaking near-misses of Jimmy White at the Crucible Theatre than my nan.

In my mental picture of my nan's house two ever-present smaller objects stand out: a 1950s wooden backscratcher and a large, shiny seashell that looked like a toothless mouth – not in fact entirely unlike my nan's own mouth, on the occasions when I stayed overnight at her house and saw her after she'd put her teeth in a glass to soak. It could be argued that the wooden backscratcher was a poignant symbol of the fact that, for many years, my nan had not had anyone to scratch her back, but in reality it was probably just a really nicely crafted backscratcher. The significance of the seashell – which in the mists of time had been attached to a living conch – is in less doubt. Living in this most landlocked of places, my nan missed the sea terribly. 'Put this to your ear and listen, son,' she would tell me when I was little, in a Scouse voice as gentle as a couple of intertwining lines of silk thread, and hand the shell to me. 'Can you hear it? That's the actual sound of the waves.' Even now, long after doubting the logistical possibility of this, I still fail to completely shut myself off to the idea of it being true.

'Which waves?' I once asked my nan, being the annoying kind of child who was always looking for specifics.

'The best ones,' she replied.

When I was a little younger than school age and my nan used to look after me while my mum and dad were at work, my nan and I would walk into the centre of Kimberley to the Co-op, where she would do her grocery shopping. We would then go to the newsagent, where she would settle her newspaper bill and purchase a packet of twenty Embassy Number One cigarettes from a man called Richard who stroked the palm of your hand very lightly as he gave you your change and had astonishing bouffant hair that some people claimed was visible from space. If I was very lucky, she would then buy me a Matchbox car from the toyshop directly opposite the Co-op, under the big black shadow of Kimberley's soon-to-be-demolished Wolseley factory. One day my nan, a non-driver, bought me a Lamborghini Countach, and the two of us hatched a plan: on another day, in the distant future, when I was old enough, I would buy a real Lamborghini – my nan was by no means wedded to the idea of it being a Countach – and drive her over the hills of Derbyshire in it. In retrospect, I wonder if this plan, which was as much my nan's brainchild as mine, contained an ulterior motive. If you drove to the high part of Derbyshire from Kimberley, then pressed on in the same direction, the second-to-next big place you'd get to after Manchester was Liverpool. The Peak District is always a bit of a bugger to get across, but in a Lamborghini with the traffic gods on your side the journey could surely be completed in less than two hours. That seemed like a long time to me as a four-year-old, but to my nan, who was forty-nine, it must have seemed like no time at all: less than the duration of an average Wimbledon or World Snooker final, less than a week's worth of *Coronation Street*, even if you chopped out the ad breaks, which my nan would, since she hated them.

There's a tendency to assume that a family settles in an area for solid and organised or at least logical reasons – a business, a collective plan, the binding roots of history – but just as often a family can end up in an area like they have been dropped there out of the cargo hold of an uncertainly piloted plane then picked themselves up, dusted the dirt from their knees and hair and made the best of it. My mum's side of my family – my nan's side, the big side, the female-dominated side – all lived in Liverpool until my mum was in her mid-teens. My nan, my granddad, my mum and her two sisters moved to Lenton on the outskirts of Nottingham when my granddad got a job there with the Co-op. After my auntie Mal gave birth to my cousin Fay she and my uncle Tony bought a house in Kimberley because it was the cheapest subrural area half an hour from the city in which to buy a decent-sized semi, and my parents and my uncle Paul and auntie Jayne followed nearby for the same reasons. It was only practical that my nan should live in the same area, especially after the unexpected early death of my granddad. Within time, my cousin Fay, then I, then my cousins Jack and Jeff attended the comprehensive school in Kimberley, and in a half-accidental way, despite a strong awareness that there were better places in the world to live, the family became tethered to the area. I know though, from my later conversations with my nan, that she never envisaged living out her final years there. There was talk of a nice bungalow in a different Nottinghamshire town, a little to the north-east, on a quieter street without swearing schoolkids, without neighbours who took air rifle potshots at birds and cats. But I think in her truest heart she would have liked to have ended her life on the edge of the country. As someone who did not believe herself to be remotely important though, and liked to be anything but the centre of attention, she would never have expressed this desire to us in any assertive way. Instead, as she drifted off to sleep at night, she liked to imagine that the hum of cars behind her house, heading along the A610 towards Ripley – harmonising with those on the M1, if the wind happened to be in the right direction – was the sound of the sea. On the same side of the house, in the stone shed at the back of her tiny backyard, she also made a quiet monument to her longing: a grotto containing hundreds and hundreds of seashells, which she glued to the shed walls using tile cement.

There's a photo of my nan and me walking hand in hand, from a family holiday in 1987, taken on Blackpool Sands beach on the south Devon coast not all that far from where I live now. With hindsight it strikes me rather sadly that, although it was over twenty years before her death, this would have been one of my nan's last handful of visits to the sea. It is also almost certainly the trip during which she collected the first batch of shells for her grotto. It was around this point, while she was cooking Supernoodles or Findus Crispy Pancakes for my school lunches every weekday, that she would have been clandestinely beginning her grand project. Soon word of it got around the extended family, and if anyone was going to the seaside, they knew what to do: collect some nice shells for Terry's shed. Terry – that was what she was known as to those not related to her by blood, short for Theresa. To everyone else she was mum or nan, never – *never* – grandma. The distinction was very clear from as far back as I can remember: a grandma, while technically the same relation to you, was a much sterner and less relatable character than a nan. A grandma might knit you a jumper just like a nan would, but it would be less comfortable. You could talk to a nan about a girl you liked at school, but never to a grandma. My nan carried off her nanness well, possibly partly owing to the fact she'd had it thrust upon her so early. She was still a year shy of forty when she first became a nan, which strikes me now as a dizzying bit of worldly-wise-before-its-time artistry, like finding out that Cat Stevens was just twenty-one when he wrote his *Mona Bone Jakon* and *Tea for the Tillerman* albums. By the time her second grandchild – me – came along, six years later, she was in possession of all the classic accoutrements of 1970s nanhood: the fluffy-toed slippers, the pension, the false teeth, the hair curlers, a plentiful and magical supply of cake and wool beyond her means. Look at photos of her from the mid- to late sixties though, with her beehive hairdo, and you get a sense of just how swift a transformation this really was: 1968, possible lost member of the Shangri-Las; 1975, full nan. Dependable. Timeless. Classic. It wasn't that she seemed old as such, more that she suited the paraphernalia of oldness.

Some of my nan's nanness was a reflection of the era – a period when young people transformed into old people at a very early age and made less effort to kick against it – but there was also no doubt that it had been hastened by having her soulmate snatched away from her in the prime of life. Her husband was called Tom, and it is in memory of him that I am named. When my mum was very small, Tom worked at the English Electric factory in Liverpool. My nan looked after my mum and my auntie Jayne and auntie Mal at home and worked part time in a sweet shop.

When my mum was five, the family moved from a three-bedroom Victorian villa in the Anfield region of the city – where all five of them had been living in one room, sharing the house with my nan's parents, three of her sisters and their families – to the vast new Kirkby council estate, which had been created as a place to rehouse families living in the Liverpool slums created by the Blitz.

In my nan's dreams of returning to the north-west coast of England, I doubt it was this house in particular she was thinking about. I drove to Kirkby to see it not long ago, and it looks not dissimilar to the pebbledashed council houses I used to walk past on my way from school to see her. Since 1972 the M57 motorway has roared along only a hundred yards or so from its front door, meaning that had my nan returned the sounds she would have heard at night would have been louder, more obnoxious versions of those in Kimberley that she creatively recast as waves in her sleepy mind. These days Kirkby is an eerily silent zombie apocalypse sprawl of three-quarters-empty sports pubs, illegally dumped waste and lonely bus stops, whose crime rate is rarely out of the local news, but in the 1950s Terry and Tom's house on the edge of the estate looked out onto a country lane and fields which, in August and September, were full of stooks of corn: a scene an old master could could contentedly render in oil as long as he was careful not to turn his vision more than ten degrees to either side.

My nan made all my mum's, Mal's and Jayne's clothes from fabric she'd bought in the sales at T. J. Hughes in Liverpool, and – in interests of fairness – dressed them identically, which my mum, being the eldest, complained bitterly about. My mum remembers my nan being permanently at her sewing machine and her hands looking constantly sore. While Terry did outwork making window-cleaning cloths out of scraps of chamois leather – a thankless, repetitive job that my mum remembers as akin to slave labour – Tom worked to get the qualifications he had not got at school, attending night school and studying late into the evening at home, learning about economics and politics. As a mark of his commitment to a better life, he purchased a bureau on which to write, a piece of post-war oak Utility Furniture, cheap as chips at the time but now a very fetching example of mid-century modern for which you might see someone charging obnoxious prices in a shop in Brighton or Greenwich. Through his trade union work he had become friends of a distant sort with his fellow Scouser Harold Wilson, the soon-to-be Labour prime minister. One of the wooden slots in his bureau was reserved especially for all his correspondence from Wilson. I am looking at the slot at this very moment, as I write this, sitting at the same bureau.

Tom was very active within the community in Kirkby and eventually became a justice of the peace. Word got around about this, and coupled with the fact that his daughters' clothes looked so clean and neat all the time, the family was marked out as 'well off' and the house was burgled several times. Through the trade union at English Electric, Tom received a scholarship to Oxford University in his thirties, where he read economics and history. He clubbed together with a couple of fellow students to buy a beaten-up old Ford Anglia – 'a tatty black box on wheels', as my mum remembers it – which they used for a week at a time each, enabling him to drive back to Kirkby from the south to see Terry and his daughters once every three weekends during term time. His degree eventually led to his job with the Co-op in Nottingham, in Personnel. The way my nan told it, by the early seventies everything was going well for her and Tom: their money worries had finally begun to dissipate, they'd bought their first house and their own car, and, after a brief, regretted move from Liverpool to Pinner, on the edge of London, they were in a new city where they felt comfortable. But Tom worked too hard and smoked too much. One weekend in 1973, upon returning home from buying a new lawnmower, he vanished behind the sofa in the living room, never to get back up. He had suffered a brain haemorrhage. He was forty-six. My nan was forty-three.

In the first photograph my mum possesses of my nan and me, from two and a half years after this, I am bawling my eyes out, and my nan is laughing hysterically. Perhaps at just a couple of months old I am already feeling the pressure of being the next Tom: the knowledge that I am never going to be able to live up even close to his strong sense of social justice or his calm and methodical ability to repair electrical appliances. My nan's face displays the pure joy she almost always felt around young children. She had been one of sixteen brothers and sisters in Liverpool, living in extreme Catholic poverty. When her dad ate bacon at the table, my nan and her siblings watched him hungrily from the floor, occasionally being treated to a little of the rind. Until she was fourteen, neither of her parents worked.

Shoes were shared between her and the ten of her siblings who also lived beyond infanthood, as there was not nearly enough money for everyone to have their own pair. The only chocolate to enter the house was consumed by her dad – a Cadbury's halfpenny bar, which he slowly and methodically ate in front of his children once a week. My nan developed less than positive feelings about large Catholic families and decided she would not make the same mistakes. She would not have sixteen children; she would have three. In her family, even if there wasn't money, there would be room for plentiful love for children and grandchildren. Every bit of her pension that she could save for birthdays and Christmas, she did, and her presents were always carefully considered. The only time she came even close to not getting it quite right for me was when she bought me a six-pack of Stella a year after I'd told her I'd stopped drinking it. This miniscule error of judgement was vast by her standards, so carefully did she mentally note down all her family's enthusiasms and loves. Nobody was a better listener or adviser. My cousins and I competed jealously over which of our houses she would come to on Christmas Day. My nan seemed incapable of making the decision herself, as it meant letting someone down, so stood aside and let our parents hash out the details. I cannot recall a single instance when I visited her house and there was no chocolate waiting for me in a cupboard or drawer.

My nan brought with her from Liverpool a plentiful supply of catchphrases, which became assimilated into our everyday speech. If something was on the floor it was on the 'dog shelf', if something left a bad taste in your mouth or irritated you it 'gave you the pip', if you felt the cold too easily you were 'nesh', if a partner was behaving badly you should tell them to 'sling their hook', if someone was looking nice they were 'all dolled up', if you were fed up you were 'browned off', if you were pleased but a little too much so you were 'like a dog with two tails'. One of my nan's catchphrases when speaking to me alone was 'I told you you'd be famous one day.' This gave me a unique feeling of combined warmth and unease that increased exponentially over the years, all the way to her death. Warmth, as I became more and more grateful to have the love and support of a nan like my nan. Unease, because, having inherited a combination of my nan's desire not to be the centre of attention and Tom's dogged autodidactic desire to forge a career a little bit different to the one expected of him, I was becoming more and more aware that being famous was something I would definitely never want to be. My nan might once have told me, 'You'll be famous one day' – perhaps during the outlining of our plans vis-à-vis the Lamborghini and Derbyshire – but all I can remember are numerous instances when she said, 'I told you you'd be famous one day.' This uncharacteristically self-congratulatory reference to her own soothsaying ability usually came after reports from me of personal achievements that could be optimistically perceived to hint at some miniscule notion of future fame, but not exclusively.

ME: I beat a boy three years older than me in a competition at the snooker hall down town on Saturday!

NAN: I told you you'd be famous one day.

ME: I got sent some free records from a record company this week!

NAN: I told you you'd be famous one day.

ME: I've been offered a music writing job at the *Guardian*. I think I'm going to take it!

NAN: I told you you'd be famous one day.

ME: I'm going to New York in a few weeks!

NAN: I told you you'd be famous one day.

ME: I just bought some cheese. It's marginally more expensive than the cheese I bought last week and has a fancy foreign name!

NAN: I told you you'd be famous one day.

OK; so I made the last one up, but you get the idea.

Another of my nan's catchphrases when talking to me was 'You're getting ever so tall,' which she said to me regularly from around the time of my fourteenth birthday until she died. In fact, if you overlook her enquiry about how I was and our actual goodbye, my nan's last words to me were 'You're getting ever so tall.' I was thirty-four at the time. In my nan's defence, during her last few years of erroneously informing me that I was getting ever so tall she was getting noticeably smaller. Almost impossibly so by the end, to the extent that, if you happened to be wearing a decent-size parka at the time, you might have looked at her and genuinely wondered if she would fit inside one of its pockets.

I remember being aware that my nan struggled with her health from the moment I was old enough to understand such a concept. I knew that you couldn't jump on her and ask for a piggyback, like you could with most adults. She couldn't come on country walks with the rest of the family and you certainly wouldn't even think of trying to involve her in a game of football. I knew that the problem was somehow connected with the cigarettes she smoked but also that it wasn't so simple that all you needed to do was take them away for her to be better. In fact, she'd had a small heart attack not long before I was born, and the doctor had said that her clogged arteries were down to years of chain-smoking. From that moment on, my mum, Jayne and Mal lived in constant awareness of her fragility. They'd lost their dad suddenly and unexpectedly, and it seemed eminently possible that they could lose her too.

Like a lot of working-class family get-togethers in the mid- to late seventies, those of my relatives – even those where children were present – were conducted in a thick miasma of cigarette smoke. But by the early eighties almost everyone save for my nan had given up. She had smoked constantly since she was thirteen, when her mum had handed her her first cigarette and taught her how to inhale and the best way to hold it. One time when I was doing some drawing at her house when I was eight or nine I asked her why she needed to smoke fags. Were they like food? 'Not exactly, son,' she said. I handed her my felt-tip pen and asked if she could pretend that was a fag instead. She said it wasn't that simple and, besides, it was far too late now. Who could deny her that one pleasure, when she'd lost two of her primary others, her soulmate and the sea? But the nagging of her offspring and their offspring finally paid off: directly after her sixtieth birthday, for which the family bought her a precise total of sixty presents, she found the willpower to give up. For the final couple of decades of her life she did not touch a cigarette and lived almost exclusively on the healthy diet of a pescatarian chaffinch. All that oily fish appeared to have a positive effect on her brain. She still nearly always went through the roll-call of almost all her children and grandchildren when addressing one of us – 'Can you pass me my specs, please, Fay, Jack, Jo, Jeff, Tom...? Oh dear!' – but she'd been doing that more or less for ever. She began to read more, devouring the novels my dad passed on to her until reading got too much for her failing eyesight. Her awareness of news and politics was more razor sharp and up to the minute than ever. As I became a hungry reader of novels myself and started to spend time with people far more educated and wordly than me, nothing I talked about was intellectually beyond her, even though she made a good job of pretending some of it was. Because she underrated herself so comprehensively, she ended up playing a character during these discussions: a small person cooped up in a small house who was bewildered by far-off places, erudite, ambitious people, new gadgets, constantly shaking her head at the size of the world. She believed in the character, but it wasn't her. She was actually a big person, wise enough to relate to and empathise with lives far outside hers, skilled at detecting the real from the fake, fundamentally more worldly and, in the most important sense, tougher than most of the erudite, ambitious people whose worldly toughness she shook her head in amazement about.

By this point – the late nineties – her shell grotto was really starting to take off, spreading out, covering all four of the interior walls of the stone shed, which a hundred years earlier had been the outside toilet of a brewery worker. In this small, glittering, unlikely fairy wonderland, in a town smelling of beer, pappy white bread and chips, were shells of almost every size and colour, every one of them once containing a life. Limpets, cockles, whelks, shark eyes and ponderous arks, none of which, if they'd had the brainpower to imagine their own future, would surely have pictured themselves so posthumously exalted. Ever since I had reached that height my nan defined as 'ever so tall' I had been able to get across her backyard in any direction in not much more than three strides, but in that tiny yard space were packed as many plants as it was physically possible to fit. Soon the shell grotto at the rear of it would be the same: a vast, multi-faceted universe squeezed into a modest space without fanfare. You'd think she'd done all that she could with it then it would expand some more, shapes within shapes appearing within it. I missed this peak period of the grotto's development and, not travelling to the sea for a long time, due to the location and somewhat nocturnal nature of my new job, failed to contribute any raw material to it.

In 1999 I had accepted a job as a full-time, contracted music writer and relocated to London. My nan was suspicious of the south of England as a whole, but truly hated the capital, spitting the name of the place out only when she had to. I only saw her more venomous when she was talking about Thatcher. She never went back to the capital for so much as a day trip after her brief move to its outskirts with Tom, my mum, Mal and Jayne, as part of a council-house swap with a family in Pinner, when Tom found himself working for a chronic bully at the Confederation of Shipbuilding and Engineering Unions. I did not hate London and had a high time there for a while, but like my nan I often found it icy and insincere, and after a little over two years realised it was not for me. To her credit, my nan never for a second tried to dissuade me from going and knew I had to find this out for myself.

For me, living over a hundred miles away, first in London, then in Norfolk, it would have been unthinkable to return to Nottingham to see my parents and fail to visit my nan as well. As always, I'd walk without knocking through her front door and invariably find her in her favourite chair with a cup of strong tea next to her, watching the news, the backscratcher and big seashell on her mantelpiece as ever, and she'd not seem remotely surprised at my arrival from several counties away, even on those occasions when I'd not warned her with a phone call. If you knew my nan and her general relationship with unheralded occurrences you might find this curious. She disliked shocks intensely – understandably so, since her life had been defined by a huge, terrible one. It didn't require a burst balloon or crisp packet or smoke alarm to set her off. She'd jump out of her skin at the smallest abrupt noise. At the sound of her phone, she would levitate to a height of between two and seven inches from her seat, dark orange tea splashing the upholstery. I like to believe that this was simply another way that she was slightly hip and ahead of her time: loads of people get excited by phones nowadays but my nan was already all about that way back in the early 1980s, before anyone even had text or the Internet.

When I was younger I laughed at my nan for being scared of the phone and for calling me by my cousin's or uncle's or mum's name by mistake. I also laughed – and still do – at her habit of clutching her house keys for up to an hour before returning to her house on any day when she'd been away. *Wasn't it silly, that key-holding thing my nan used to do?* I was remembering last year, about twenty minutes from home, on the walk back to my house from my local supermarket, silently chuckling to myself. *So premature and ridiculous of her!* I thought, looking down at my own right hand and noticing my front-door key clasped tight within it.

It was probably inevitable that I would become parts of my nan as I got older, but what was strange was how abruptly I became some of them immediately after her death: the premature key-clutching, the tendency to jump at the buzz of my phone and other smallish technological noises, a sharp increase in the strength and volume of my tea intake and, finally and perhaps most noticeably, a visceral, all-consuming need to have the sea in my life. I could have started doing any of these things as a tribute to my nan, in the same way that I began to wear the small green terylene scarf I inherited from her, but that wasn't it. It felt almost as if, as part of her death, there had been some kind of transference, without me having any say in the matter. But maybe that's an integral part of becoming a nan, or even becoming part of a nan: it's willed upon you by an independent force.

The year of my nan's death, 2009, was the toughest year of my life. In the same month that I discovered she was terminally ill, a friend died very suddenly and my marriage broke up. During this period the sea became my solace and therapy, its hugeness dwarfing any feeling I had of lostness or fear for the future. The sea's aim is always to make you feel better but never in an unrealistically flattering, emboldened, inspirational, Internet-quote way. When life turns against us in the modern world we often retreat into technology for some reassurance: a small virtual shoulder-rub from a stranger, often executed with the best of intentions but from a safe distance, confirming for thirty glorious seconds that the way we feel is all right. The sea doesn't give us any of that; its approach is far more Tough Love. 'My mind is heavy and troubled today,' you'll say to the sea. 'Properly stare at me for a moment and get a grip on yourself,' the sea will reply. 'Do I honestly look like I care? I'm the fucking sea.' It is inconceivably vaster than any of us, will still be here when we are gone – eventually drowning all that we once knew without a moment's deliberation – and doesn't care about our problems. Strangely this is often the biggest reassurance of all, especially in those moments of worry that derive directly from the delusion that as humans we are in some way important, which is ultimately all moments of worry, when you really think about it.

The nearest bit of coast – that belonging to north Suffolk – was just three quarters of an hour away from

my house on the Norfolk–Suffolk border, but until then I'd made pitifully little use of it, not frequently enough thrown myself into its howling, flecked winds on the kind of January day that makes your gums throb, rarely done backstroke above its shifting shingle and let its rejuvenating salt seep into my scalp. Now I rapidly made up for that. If I felt anxious or creatively blocked or stymied by indecision or even euphoric, I often went to the sea. Over the next couple of years I traversed around 70 per cent of Suffolk's coastline on foot, in all weathers. The summer of 2010 was one of the best of my life, and on the first warmish day of it I ran into the cold waves at full pelt, carelessly discarding clothes on my way, like a man in a bad film. It was only when I looked back to the shore that I realised the four friends I was with had not joined me and, moreover, clearly viewed what I had done as a minor act of insanity. But I felt comfortable with my actions. I knew this bit of sea now as a friend. Also, not to do what I had would have struck me as, well…a bit nesh.

How could I have not thought to bring my nan to these places in the years when she was well enough to come? I'd not grown up into the kind of person who would drive her to Chatsworth in a Lamborghini, or even, in fact, who had any awareness of what Lamborghinis themselves had grown up into, but surely I could have spared the time to at least drive her to Lowestoft in a second-hand Toyota Yaris? This is sad, but it's merely my own version of a standard heartache of family life, experienced by people the world over in their various ways: you can spend your life very close to a relative but, due to the cruelty of time, in some areas of mutual interest still manage to miss them slightly, like two people who've entered the same forest on footpaths that come agonisingly close but never quite converge. All I could do in my situation was posthumously take my nan with me on my excursions to the sea, although to be frank this wasn't hard since by this point I had become my nan in so many ways. My own nanness has only increased since then, and I feel that the part of the coast where I walk most frequently now, in Devon, is one that she would have liked even more than Suffolk's. Would it be too bold to claim that it has those 'best' waves she told me I could hear through her shell when I was little? Perhaps, but it has certainly seen some very impressive, and historically very destructive, ones.

It's always a little unfair to compare one unadorned example of nature to other unadorned example of nature, and to say that the craggy, towering, dog-bite coast of the South West Peninsula is better than the linear, eerie, ghost coast of East Anglia seems particularly harsh. It's as harsh as comparing one large piece of really lovely cheese to a whole shop full of really lovely cheeses made by people with far more cows than the people who made the one large piece of really lovely cheese. There's an awe to be experienced at the fact that two such dramatically different seascapes can exist on an island as small as this one, but there's another kind of awe inspired by the diversity of terrain from the mouth of the Dart to the mouth of the Erme. Bigbury and Bantham, with their art deco island and sliced-tuna-steak cliffs. Bolt Head, which in sea mist is the closest the coastal West Country gets to Middle Earth. The stone steps precariously rounding

Sharp Tor, which would befit the climactic battle scene of any great fantasy film and tower above the deep, folklore-charged Black Bull Hole: a passage named due to the legend that a black bull passed through it and emerged all white, so traumatised was he by his subterranean experience. Prawle Point, with its microclimate within a microclimate, where on a July day you walk through clouds of butterflies above turquoise water and want to wrap the whole place up and lock it in an old ottoman where nobody else can steal it. Start Point, a long, arthritic wizard's finger of land pointing out into the watery dark, where before the construction of the lighthouse at the end of the headland the relationship between ships and weather catastrophes was roughly akin to the relationship between toddlers and falling over: two whole ships, the *Marana* and the *Dryad*, sank here in one night in 1891, with every hand on the latter drowning. The long flat Slapton Sands, where the road bisects sea and freshwater lake but which, viewed from above near the village of Strete, looks like an unnervingly straight highway running through the ocean itself. Blackpool Sands, where my nan picked those first shells for her grotto and, with its leaf-framed natural windows to France and pine rows and brontosaurus coastal road, which brings to mind a chilly miniature version of Italy's Amalfi Coast. The cascading gorse terraces, wild-pony ledges and hidden coves surrounding Dartmouth and Kingswear. All this and more in less than forty miles.

I am not a tremendous observer of anniversaries. For one thing, they come around a bit too quickly nowadays and take me by surprise. But not long after a recent anniversary of my nan's death I walked from the high zigzag village of Stoke Fleming down to Blackpool Sands to find some shells. A day previously my friend Hayley had seen me walking along the roadside near my house, stopped her van to say hello and handed me the shell of a small beautiful limpet, and since it was the only one I owned, I thought it would be nice to add to it. As I walked through the trees to Blackpool Sands a girl called sweetly to a dog named Holly as girls with dogs called Holly often do on beaches, but when I arrived on the beach there was no girl and no dog, creating the impression that what I'd been hearing was an ambient beach soundtrack superimposed over the scene rather than noises from the real life of a dog and its owner. It was November, but at the scrubby back corner of the beach chamomile was still thriving. Blackpool Sands is the most benign cove for miles around and regularly packed with semi-naked bodies on a summer's day, but now I shared it with no more than three or four other chilly walkers. As I walked along the hard-packed stretch nearest the waves, the bank of shingle behind me got steeper until I realised that, in a matter of less than an hour, with the tide rushing in, I would become totally blocked off, in the far corner of the beach. I am not sure exactly where shingle becomes small enough to be classified as sand, but the shingle here was not that far from it. There were not many shells, or maybe I wasn't looking hard enough.

After my nan died, my mum, Jayne and Mal sold her terrace with the forlorn, unalterable realisation that her shell grotto would probably fall into alien, uncaring hands. Would it be torn down? Replastered? Filled with pesticides and air guns? We decided it was best not to know and best not to think about it. The street outside began to look more down at heel. The brewery had been bought by a large corporation and was closed down shortly before her death, many of its windows soon being broken by vandals. Schoolkids drank Special Brew in the empty building, just as I had in the park up the road. Despite the brewery's demise, a phantom smell of hops lingered in the air as far as where my auntie Jayne and uncle Paul lived, which was now a few streets away and no longer within sniffing distance of the bread factory. In 2012 my mum received an unexpected postcard from my nan's house's next-but-one owner, Jackie, informing her that she was continuing my nan's project with the help of her granddaughter. Together they had filled the remaining spaces on the walls with yet more shells and begun to plaster the ceiling with shells too. Supporting photographs ensued. Jackie wrote that she had got the contact details for my mum from Liz and Andy, the house's previous owners. Due to her slightly scrawled handwriting I read what she'd written as 'I got your address from Lizard Andy,' which made me wonder who Lizard Andy was, what he looked like, and caused me to speculate on the various ways he might have acquired his nickname.

'Loves the heat, does Andy. But it's done bloody awful stuff to his skin.'

'Remind me to tell you the story about Andy regenerating his tail. It's a long one though, so reserve plenty of time for it.'

'Andy? Everyone knows Andy. He's like the Kimberley answer to Jim Morrison.'

I found only a few good shells on Blackpool Sands beach, none of them a match for the best in the grotto, but that was nothing new: my contribution to my nan's

20 07 2012

Dear Mr. Cox,
my name is Jackie Gurnhill, I moved into
last week.
I fell in love with the house including your mums'
beautiful 'shell house' - Just thought you might like to
know that my granddaughter (5years old Milly) and I
cannot wait to continue the Job of sticking sea shell
or anything that means something to us on the walls,
ceiling etc..
we already have a selection of shells that Milly
presented me with last monday (moving in day)
I also found a box of shells here in the cupboard where
the gas/elec meters are!
Got your address off Lizind Andy hope you don't mind
me giving you an update. Regards, Jackie.

project had always been derisory. As I walked west around Start Bay, towards the cliffside wraith copses above Hallsands, the light slowly dripped away. In the brown gloom, with the long wizard's finger of Start Point ahead, it was more possible to imagine the terror that must have been experienced here during one of those shipwrecks: the utter helplessness in the face of the dark hugeness of roaring drunken waves and the unforgiving black humour of impassable cackling cliffs. When you go away from the sea, your mind has a way of making it smaller and more manageable. Its size in three dimensions, especially here, never fails to shake me. This is a big lonely landscape where there is room to think. Not in an obsessive, counterproductive way, where thoughts are folded repeatedly in on themselves, but in a bigger, more philosophical way. I had chosen solitude recently, opted to spend time alone in places like these, to live alone, to end a relationship, to resist entering a new one for a while. My nan chose solitude too, in a different way. There had never been any question of another man after my granddad. She had lost the love of her life. Nobody could ever replace him and that was that. The weight and earliness of that decision had never struck me more forcefully than it did now, as a single person, only a couple of years shy of the age she'd been when he died.

Hallsands was once a busy fishing village but is now totally abandoned, having been ravaged by a series of storms during the early part of the 1900s. It was finally evacuated in 1917 after numerous houses and the village pub had fallen into the sea, all the result of a protective bank of sand and gravel being greedily and negligently removed for construction use at a dockyard on the edge of Plymouth by a local MP. Hallsands women were a notoriously tough breed, rescuing crew from sinking ships and habitually wading out to the fishing boats with their husbands on their backs to save their menfolk's feet from getting wet prior to a day's work. One of them, Elizabeth Prettejohn, remained stubbornly and heroically in her house right up until her death in 1964, at the age of eighty, surviving on fish and crabs she caught herself and eggs from a tough gang of hens which roamed through the glorified rubble that constituted the remainder of the village. When tourists came to see the infamous place that the sea had swallowed, Prettejohn, as its one remaining resident, was only too happy to show them around, but you can't help wondering what else she did for amusement. 'I know! I'll found the Hallsands WI!' you can imagine her saying in a lightbulb moment. Then, with a sigh, 'Oh.' Prettejohn could have moved but didn't. She chose solitude instead, a tie to landscape instead of people. On a night like this it was possible to get a mental picture of what that solitude must have felt like here, at the edge of the world, and on fiercer nights when, in her own description, 'the sea was like mountains'.

It was lung cancer that finally killed my nan, although she'd only narrowly survived another heart attack a couple of years prior to that. For somebody who'd talked up her own frailty and imminent demise for a long time, she was very keen to hold on at the end. Her repeated refrain was that before she went she wanted to know everyone was OK.

Going through the break-up of a marriage at the time, I found it a little more difficult to convince her on this front than everyone else, but I think she believed me. She died at home, surrounded by almost all of her closest family except for me. It was hard to know when the end would come and, living over three hours away by car or train, to ensure that I would be there for it. She died listening not to the fake swells and rip tides of motorway traffic but to a CD of birdsong, which continued to play at a lowish volume after the moment of her death. My cousin Jeff arrived at this point and stayed with her in her bedroom while my mum, Jayne and Mal went downstairs to make the appropriate phone calls. This was during a lull in the birdsong CD so Jeff had not been aware that it was playing. As he sat with my nan's body the recorded sound of a vituperative crow pierced the room as if out of nowhere, causing Jeff, in a fitting final tribute, to levitate even further than my nan used to when her phone rang.

I can put an exact date to the last time I was clean-shaven because it was the day of my nan's funeral. She disliked beards, and I thought it was the least I could do for her to get rid of mine. I might shave again, but in seven and a half years I have not felt compelled to. I can look back at my nan's funeral and see that it represents a threshold for me: the moment when I put on a couple of permanent extra layers – one made of hair, one made of something else less tangible. In the weeks before her death I returned the gold wedding band she'd passed down to me as the first of her grandchildren to get married, the same ring Tom had bought her. At her funeral in Nottingham each of us took turns to touch her coffin to say goodbye. I did not cry. I felt solid and accepting and slightly insulated from what had happened, as if I had an additional coat on made of nothing. Afterwards, I went for a drink with my cousins and hoped we'd all stay in touch, having lost the main glue that held us together. That night, in the space between wakefulness and sleep, I heard a light, gossamer Scouse voice say, 'It's all going to be OK, son.' Whether I had willed it or it had come from some other place was not important; the important thing was that it was nice.

My nan was the final grandparent I lost, but I believe I have had a relatively easy ride as far as the death of those close to me is concerned. Age brings the perspective to see this, but something that sometimes gives me an additional insight is that I have two friends who are funeral directors. The funeral directors' names are Ru and Claire. When I moved to this part of Devon I was told by one of our mutual friends that I should get in touch with them because we'd undoubtedly get on. Was the reason I did not act on her suggestion straight away that classic one that makes people shy away from those who work with death: that I did not want to be reminded of my mortality? Or was it my appalling short-term memory? Perhaps a bit of both. So it wasn't until many months later that we got to know each other, after Ru, who'd recognised me from a photo online, tapped me on the shoulder when I was browsing the beer shelves in our local 7-Eleven and announced his presence with the unforgettable words, 'Hi. I'm the funeral director.' Everyone who knows Ru and Claire loves them. 'Oh, they're fucking brilliant,' a friend told me not long after I'd met them. 'They set fire to my nan a few years ago.' A couple of summers ago I was walking past Ru and Claire's office, which is in a barn, and the doors were open, so they called me in and asked me to settle a disagreement they were having about whether a paisley coffin they had in the back room was pretty or not. Claire thought it was; Ru wasn't so sure. I took Claire's side although this was perhaps due to the comparatively low number of coffins I had seen boasting intricate floral designs.

Only a small percentage of the time I've spent with Ru and Claire has been spent talking about death, but in that small percentage an extra awareness has been created for me of what people have snatched away from them and what people are finding the strength to deal with, everywhere, all the time. Ru lost both of his parents when he was young and started the Green Funeral Company in the years directly following his mum's death, having seen the impersonal way the traditional ceremony was conducted and wanting to provide something different for others in the same situation. He remembers the feeling of being excluded by undertakers he describes as 'a cross between removal men and bouncers'. He and Claire – who quit her job in the London music industry to join him as a business partner, and subsequently a romantic one – do not wear suits when conducting their ceremonies. They transport coffins not in a hearse but in an old Volvo estate which doubles as the family car. Their conviction is that grieving people fall back, very understandably, on tired rituals and ceremonies that don't reflect their beliefs because they don't have the energy to look for an alternative. What they try to provide is something based not on quasi-Victoriana and fake solemnity but on honesty and participation and appropriateness and a respect for the earth. The opening ceremony of a new music festival in the area was performed by them recently: an incantation conducted above a rotating skull, evoking the swirling nature of time and genetics, which was probably something of a surprise to outsiders who'd come purely for the indie rock and limited-edition vinyl. But what Ru and Claire do should not be lumped in with some of south-west Devon's more preposterous hippy excesses. There is no room for air quotes during their rituals; the importance of the subject matter will wash them away like violent weather.

Ru and Claire's natural burial ground is on a very high point above the Dart, over a chicane in the river shortly after it becomes tidal, and its curvy, oaky sweep to the sea – and that favourite bit of coastline of mine – begins. I saw my first wild Devonian barn owl not far from the burial ground, a daytime ghost vanishing as if embarrassed into a blue sky over the reed beds. Steep, shale-banked sunken lanes overrun with rubbly rocks and hart's tongue fern race down from here towards Totnes and fill up with fast water in the winter so the line between footpath and stream blurs. Dartmouth sits on its rocky perch at the end of the estuary as imperiously as an old naval captain assured that his family has owned the spot since time immemorial, but despite being seven miles inland, Totnes was once the bigger port of the two. The river stays wide enough to support a small ferry up all the way to the town weir, which seals and gulls tend to mark as the northern point of their territory. You can't see the sea here but you can smell a hint of it on the wind. This proximity is a continuing marvel to a person like me, a product of Britain's interior, and at my first sight of blue on the horizon beneath the skyline I always do a little cheer, either internally or – to the bemusement of any complacent South West Peninsula natives who happen to be with me – out loud. I have used this proximity as one of several landscape-based arguments in favour of my continuing residence here, in the face of counter-pressure, both intentional and unintentional, from friends and family to move back in the direction from which I came. In this way I am like Elizabeth Prettejohn, standing firm at my beloved wild outpost on the edge of the world, resisting a more convenient life, more densely packed with other humans. Except I'm nowhere near as tough as Elizabeth Prettejohn. I have BBC iPlayer, don't live in a ruined village and don't have chickens, just cats, who cannot give me eggs and probably wouldn't even if they could. But in these tussles with myself about what I want, landscape is the deciding factor. Good people I've met here – Ru and Claire included – win, but landscape wins too.

Some days I feel the tussle more than others, though. In early November 2015 I'd just returned from a cross-country car trip, over the course of which I'd seen my family, several of my best and oldest friends, returned to the county of my previous home and felt deep regret that I wasn't able to do it all more often. In the days I'd been away, late autumn's dimmer switch had been turned. The lawn had had its last mow of the year and paths and roads were overspattered with marauding leaf mess. The granite on houses and churches was getting that inky rain-lashed look again that is synonymous with shorter days and pinched light. I was back alone in a house that I'd initially found for two people, still raw from my recent decision to end that partnership. Before I'd embarked on my trip I'd noticed a troubling smell in the small room where I keep most of my book collection but had not had time to properly investigate its source, and now I noticed that the smell was getting the opposite of better. I called a cat over for a cuddle, told it how much I'd missed it. It ignored me and headed for the garden, slamming the cat flap on its way out.

If you live in the countryside and have cats what you're essentially saying is, 'I permit narcissists to hide dead things in my house.' Cats are ardent creatures of habit but they also do not like to get in a rut. Cats only sleep regularly in one place for a month. After that, by law they must move or they stop being cats. They select and switch their abbatoirs with similar fastidiousness. For a spell the dining room had served as the killing floor for my two most bloodthirsty cats, Ralph and Shipley, then the bathroom, but recently they had preferred the book room. The chief problem had been rabbits. I'd managed to save a few, thanks to my advanced tackling skills. One had escaped and hidden behind the freezer, and I'd managed to lure it out, in cartoon fashion with an old carrot, then plonk it below a hedge. But I had a life to lead. I couldn't be constantly sitting at home on a state of high alert with a carrot in my hand. Inevitably, there were casualties. A couple of weeks previously I'd cleaned up a particularly messy headless rabbit corpse on the floor of the book room. I don't have the greatest sense of smell but, even though I scrubbed the carpet no less assiduously than a nineteenth-century saloon owner would have scrubbed a stain left from a gunfight, I could not subsequently convince myself I'd entirely got rid of the waft.

I'm very fond of the book room. It's full of books, after all, but it's a cold room with no curtains or double glazing and not somewhere where I spend a lot of time in winter, which is another reason I'd been slow in clocking the strength of this latest smell and only begun to properly investigate it now.

I made a couple of attempts to stop buying books in the distant past but I've since realised it's an absurd denial of who I am as a person. The fact is, books have always been very kind to me, and I can't stand to see them sitting alone in shops, unloved. One day I'll probably trap myself behind a book wall for ever, but the way I look at it is that I'll be reading as I starve to death, so it will be OK. My to-read pile at this point spilt far beyond the shelves themselves and far beyond sense, teetering in higgledy-piggledy piles on tables. Moving the books to shift the shelving units and get behind them – which, I assumed, was where the smell was coming from, having ruled out everywhere else in the room – was a major operation. My initial forensic work uncovered, not too surprisingly, the remains of two dead voles, long since rotted away, but I sensed I was in the middle of a bigger story here, and upon moving the fifth and final bookcase I reached its awful climactic scene.

It was a rabbit, I could discern that immediately. But what it resembled more accurately was a charcoal illustration of a rabbit ghost, drawn by an artist with a bent towards satanism. I felt like I'd stepped inside the missing one of Fiver's nightmares in *Watership Down* that got cut for being too adult. If I blinked, would it vanish? I tried to think of someone close to me who might come and briefly hold me in a tender way, then leave. Parents? Hundreds of miles away. My mate Seventies Pat? No. He lived in

Dudley. The corpse's edges were indistinct, as if surrounded by an evil vapour. I saw maggots writhing where its brain once had been. An impossible black ooze welded it to the wall and oozed with more determined malevolence as I attempted to move it. The smell was intolerable, like a monolithic forecast of every small awfulness you've ever worried would come true. As I went back in for a third time with every bit of cleaning equipment I could find in the house, I genuinely began to wonder what would be easier: carrying on with my attempt to save the carpet or quickly packing a couple of bags and moving to India.

I headed off briskly to the supermarket and returned with more cleaning materials and odour-eliminating paraphernalia suggested by friends and my mum: bicarb of soda, coloured biological washing liquid, Febreze. After four hours I had rid the room of the dark spectre and its innumerable attendant maggots but it had taken out a mortgage on my part-working nose. From above me, a papier-mâché hare, made by my friend Mary for my birthday four and half years earlier and now pinned to the wall, gazed mordantly down at my work.

This is the stuff that's so rarely factored into the time management of a rural self-employed life with cats: the twenty minutes you will fritter away looking for a vole in a cupboard... the half an hour it takes to strip off the spare bed's duvet cover and carefully scrape all the chunky dried puke off it... the six hours twenty minutes you will devote to cleansing your house of an unnameable evil. It was almost 6 p.m. and I had wasted an entire working day. I knew I should make up for it by writing into the

night, but Ru and Claire had asked me along to their natural burial ground for their All Souls Day ritual. It had been too long since I'd seen them, and the potential nostril transfusion the evening promised was too tempting: hilly night air and woodsmoke replacing the writhing shitfires of hell. There aren't many times you find yourself heading to a burial ground to escape the taint of death, but this was one of them. I parked and followed two strangers – or rather the light of the sensible headtorches of two strangers – through a wicker arch and over the brow of a hill to a large fire surrounded by sixty or seventy people. In the distance the lights of the busy seaside towns of Paignton and Brixham twinkled. If you estimated the distance to the sea in hills, which was the tendency here, it somehow seemed closer. 'The sea? That's six hills away.' 'Oh, cool. Thanks. No distance at all!' The blackness of the night added to the sense of its proximity. There is a magic in the air at this darkening time of year, but people in the United Kingdom tend to over-egg it nowadays with show-off pyrotechnics and the fancy dress of pretend Americans. What this gathering proved was that all you really needed to tease it out was a strong orange glow and the magic of naked nocturnal hills, with hot spiced apple juice as an optional extra. As I defrosted my hands beside the Sharpham bonfire I felt another kind of warmth that I had never quite felt before at any traditional ceremony dealing with death: a powerful breaking down of barriers, a removing of a certain ugliness. Not the ugliness that's intrinsic to last rites but an unnecessary one often imposed on top of it.

All Souls Day, also known as the Day of the Dead, is now best known as a Christian ceremony, but its roots go back to European folklore and ancient customs of ancestor veneration. Ru and Claire also see it as an acknowledgement of the fading of the light, the ripeness around us turning into rot and the way the veil seems to thin at this time of year. In a way that felt universal, passionate and not a bit formulaic, Ru talked of the souls we were honouring and autumn's reminder of nature's ability to die over and over again. He also asked everyone gathered around the fire to spare a thought for the refugees who would not make it across the Mediterranean this winter, and whose bodies would never be honoured. Claire and the youngest member of the Green Funeral Company staff, Jennifer, spoke the names of everyone buried on the hillside, and among them I heard a familiar surname that made my chest stop: that of one of my favourite folk musicians. His son. Dead before him, far, far too young.

People were asked to come forward if they wished and speak the name of someone they had lost then throw a pine cone into the fire in their memory. Naturally I had begun by this point to think of my nan. It was only now that I realised that it was once again the sort of anniversary of her death. I became aware that the moisture pouring out of my eyes was not solely the result of smoke and the unfortunate wind direction. I wanted to step forward and pick a cone from the box on the ground and add it to the fire and say something about her amazing kindness, how I'd admired her more every day since I'd lost her, about how she'd lived through war and extreme poverty, then, just as her life was improving, had the love of her life snatched away from her, but something stopped me. Most people were speaking the names of relatives and friends buried on this hillside or nearby. Some had died half a century ago, others, such as a twenty-one-year-old German man someone's son had tried and failed to save from drowning in the sea, only last week. Perhaps it was the strength of these stories combined with a sense of geographical separation – my nan being from so far away and me only being a recent import – that made me hold back. As the ceremony wound down, I began to rue my reticence and found myself oddly reluctant to go home, although not just because of that or the prospect of deceased-rabbit afterstench. Others seemed the same, as if pinned and mesmerised by the flames. Here was the antithesis of LED light: a healthy, primal hypnosis. During a lull in the conversation I noticed two pine cones, one considerably larger than the other. I picked both up and placed them in the embers. Then, pre-emptively clutching my keys, I left.

7

FULL JACKDAW

What you think will stay with you about a house you live in and love for a long time is often not what does stay with you about a house you live in and love for a long time; it is other feelings about the place, unique to it, which set in gradually over a period of several years, whose true uniqueness you will only notice long after you have left. When I think about the house in Norfolk where I lived between 2004 and 2013, which is the house I've got to know more intimately than any other in my adult life, I often think about parties – far more parties than the three or so per year I actually had there between 2009 and 2012, so many parties, an upstairs floor constantly filled with dancing and sleeping people – but what has stayed with me most about the house is a feeling of being in mid-air. Being indoors yet in the sky, sheltered yet right up in the weather, on the sofa or the carpet yet in the treetops.

Suspension, I now realise, was the house's predominant theme. It had been built in the early 1960s – not prettily but thoughtfully, with an upside-down layout – into the side of one of Norfolk's rare steep slopes, overlooking an Ice Age mere which unverified local legend claimed to be bottomless. From the street the house was almost invisible: a single-storey slab of utility concrete with the nonsensical tiling choices of a mind in disarray. This invisibility proved a bonus on a main throughfare on the edge of a town synonymous with minor vandalism. Many other houses nearby regularly had their windows smashed on Friday nights. Around the corner 'JONES MONGS' had been scrawled on one building then scrubbed almost off, then scrawled again, carefully following the ghost lines of the original inscription. The lead flashing was stolen off the front of my house by thugs on speed, but its lone small window remained intact and 'JONES MONGS' was never scrawled on its wall, and for this I still often thank the gods of fortune. On the opposite side the building opened up in a manner many a passer-by would not have suspected: light streamed in from the water and sky through big faulty windows framed with chunky white PVC, and the house hugged the hill like three fat grey steps. On the middle step, where a person felt most suspended and at one with the surrounding foliage, disorientated wood pigeons periodically slammed into the windows, knocking themselves insensible with semi-metallic thuds that reverberated around the building. In the mere, beyond a jetty that rotted off into the water a little more each year, monster catfish – fish of a size mundane British market-town life does not teach us to expect – gorged on the abandoned food of the locality's many fast-food outlets. When I sold the house, insurers had qualms about the building's proximity to the water: qualms that were patently absurd, since the foundations remained seventy yards from the shoreline and dozens of feet above it even after the heaviest rainfall. It would have taken outright apocalypse for the mere to flood the building, and even then there was a feeling that you'd withstand Armageddon were you on the middle floor of the house, where the rooms bored back furthest into the sandy rock. Being in that portion of the house was like hiding in a modest, symmetrical cave – the lair of some very minor James Bond villain perhaps, whose main crime was that he tended to be a bit last minute getting his tax forms in.

There was an astonishing feeling of security in that cave, a quiet walled-off-from-the-world sensation almost unheard of in a building on the edge of a busy East Anglian town. This was in welcome contrast to the lack of security associated on a daily basis with my ownership of the place. The house had been a stretch for me to buy as half of a couple, a bigger stretch for us to renovate, then had continued to be a stretch for me to maintain, alone, at a time when my job security was crumbling. I remember no interim phase between the excitement of being permitted to take out a mortgage on such a captivating and unusual home and the dread of the inevitable day when I would be forced to abandon it. I would walk out of the cave's rear and into the sheltered sky, and feel rapturously suspended, right up in the trees that surrounded the hillside, but simultaneously less pleasantly suspended, floating uncertainly, never able to relax and feel the house was mine or that I could make it fully what it should be. For all the fun I squeezed out of the place, which in the last few years of living there was plenty, much of my residence there had the anxious character of a drawn-out goodbye.

One summer morning during the beginning of the final decisive part of this goodbye I drew back forty-year-old curtains which matched the colour of the sky and saw three men flying through the air thirty yards in front of me at eye level. I had lived in the sky long enough to know that doing so altered a few fundamental laws of gravity, but I was still suprised to see these men bobbing about. Their flight did not appear especially purposeful. It was more like the lazy backstroke you might choose to perform in a roomy swimming pool on a day containing a dearth of pressing appointments. Because it was early in the morning and my eyes had only 70 per cent opened and the sun was shining directly into them, I did not at first notice the ropes attached to the men's waists, nor the chainsaws they held, none of which were yet operational, but I did hear the classical music coming from a neighbour's kitchen window, and all this added to the sensation that I was watching a rare form of aerial ballet. I have had a fear of heights most of my life, but it's a fear with various clauses and contradictory small print written into it. I view planes as an affront to nature and if you plonk me anywhere beyond halfway up the Eiffel

Tower I'll be your worst jelly-legged nightmare, but I can dangle my feet off the edge of the tallest cliffs in the UK and not experience a fragment of nerves, and a large part of my childhood involved getting as far as was feasible up any tree I came across. Observing the flying men, I felt envious of their situation in the branches high above my next-door neighbour's garden, and when their chainsaws started up the envy did not ebb away.

A squirrel tore across my lawn, in flight from the racket.

In such a dry county the hillside in front of the mere was an unusually fertile area of ground. I have never lived anywhere where plants and trees grow nearly as quickly. Two years previously the alders from which the men with the chainsaws hung so balletically had not even been visible from my window, but since then they had shot up the way fourteen-year-old schoolboys do in the summer holidays, running riot in the garden of Deborah and David next door. Mostly invisible to each other due to the raging, fertile hedge line, David and I walked repeatedly in parallel lines from the top of the slope to our bonfires in constant attempts to de-jungle our surroundings from April to October every year. Time-lapse photography of the buddleia below my living-room window filmed merely over the course of an average May would have shown it rising in ominous megalomaniacal fashion towards the cave. Had I not intervened with the loppers, it would have inched in through the gaps in the draughty windows, creeped along my bookshelves and given the back wall of the cave an appealing paisley revamp. Its peers would have followed, and soon my home would have been like a smaller version of the disused Palace Theatre on Union Street in Plymouth, which had a tree growing out of one of its windows. 'That must be the house where the heroin addicts live,' people on the opposite side of the water would say, pointing.

I did not think about trees and shrubs a huge amount during my first couple of years living in the cave, mostly only in the sense that I rather liked them and believed that being kind to them meant not intervening with their whims, but when the pampas grass on one side of the garden had stretched its scratchy fronds in a big permanent yawn and the elders and giant philadelphus on the other side had expanded to the extent that all that remained was a three-yard tunnel of lawn leading to the water, I realised it was time to take action, and I barely stopped taking action for the following seven and a half years – for my sake but mostly for the sake of the potential buyers who would eventually come to look at the house when I was inevitably forced to sell it, who I figured would be less likely to purchase it if its garden looked like a prosaic south Norfolk answer to the Sinharaja Forest Reserve. Sometimes after a day out there my hair would smell so much of bonfire it smelled more strongly of bonfire than my actual bonfires did. One load of shampoo and conditioner was often not enough: the smoky aroma of deceased bark would remain. But that was OK. I liked the smell of bonfires and I had a strong instinct that people who recoiled violently at the smell of bonfire were not My People. In the swimming-pool changing room I often saw young men – and some not so young men – dousing themselves in Lynx deodorant, which never smelled good. 'I think of it as the aroma of masked spunk,' my friend Ellen once told me. I'd never met a female who liked it, yet all over Britain red-blooded heterosexual men in the prime of life continued to blast it flamboyantly into their various crevices. Maybe a bonfire aroma wasn't the best smell to be carrying in a permanent invisible cloud around your person, but it was better than the whiff of Lynx. I liked the smell of bonfires so much that on country walks I'd often take detours to sniff those tended by strangers. Another favourite habit was to leave the curtains of the cave open at night and watch the light from David's conflagrations gradually fade to a tiny orange bulb in an ocean of black. David's bonfires tended to be more carefully arranged and marshalled than mine, but I did always perform the most crucial preliminary procedure before I put a match to the dry foliage: I checked for hedgehogs. I only ever found one, and it was already dead. It was possibly even a twentieth-century hedgehog, a hedgehog that might erroneously have been marketed as 'vintage' by a second-hand shop pushing their luck. A spiky economical bird's nest with the ghost of a ghost of a face.

Bonfires are not permitted in my garden in Devon, but I have a fireplace and take a similar sort of satisfaction in the processes surrounding it. I often get my logs from my dad, who has an arrangement regarding loose wood with the farmer who owns most of the land near him. On other occasions I bulk-order from one of the many woodsmen who lurk on the edges of Dartmoor. My latest batch came from a man called Dan, who collects his wood from the leaf-dense valleys near the moorland village of Holne and is exactly the kind of soft-spoken bearded giant you hope to find working and living in a forest. His logs are a mixture of birch, beech and oak, and burn far, far better than any I've purchased before, especially the ones from my local petrol station, which give off as much efficient sustained warmth as a bag of fifteen lemon-drizzle cakes. This is nothing unique for petrol-station logs. There's something almost impressive about how uniformly and monumentally terrible all firewood from petrol stations turns out to be, as if it goes beyond mere capitalism and is in fact the outcome of a Shit Petrol Station Firewood Constitution drawn up in the middle part of the last century.

After Dan had emptied his superior logs from his Land Rover onto the lane I spent a happy five hours hauling them up the hill to my house and stacking them in a curved formation complimenting the shape of the windows in my porch. The final result probably stands as my life's grandest sculpture, and over the winter I felt a noticeable melancholy as I subtracted from it, ameliorated by the pleasure of watching the blaze in the hole in my living-room wall, not least the timeless thrill of the moment when a burned log fractures and falls, reigniting the wood beneath it: the twist in the plot of a primetime drama on an ancient screenless TV that you know is coming but not quite when. It's hard to imagine a time before electricity, but just how dark must the night world

have been for *Homo erectus* before the invention of fire? That's a whole other realm of dark: a dark that makes your brain ache when you try to picture it, like the end of outer space or the concept of no longer being alive. 'What is the most significant moment in human history so far?' Chris Salisbury asked on a forest skills course which I attended in autumn 2014 a few miles from my house in the dense woodland of the Dartington Estate. 'The invention of the wheel?' said one pupil. 'The printing press?' guessed another. 'No, it was the invention of fire,' said Chris. A protégé of Ray Mears, Chris wears a belt of knives and has the aura of a man who birds will listen to. One of his many good qualities as a teacher is that he has a meditative aura that's just intimidating enough in its strange calmness to make you eager to impress him, which makes you ultimately more likely to remember the wisdom he passes on. Even if you've only spent a day within it, the smoky, somewhat primal universe he presides over is one that you find yourself carrying with you long after you've left, shoehorning terms you've learned such as 'blood bubble' and 'farmer's paint' into regular conversation to the consternation of those closest to you. I did not learn how to fell a tree from Chris but did learn how to coppice, whittle a stick into a sharp rounded point – being careful to keep a wide blood bubble around me, naturally – start a sustainable fire using one match and foraged kindling in blustery conditions on sodden ground, and build a shelter using minimal tools.

An unusually large amount of people depend on trees for their living in this area, and among those I have met

I have noticed a recurring theme: a radiant but non-smug contentment in their own work, often bordering on addiction. 'I get paid for climbing trees,' my tree surgeon friend Dave told me. 'What could be better than that?' As a boy Dave shinned up the oaks in Dartington's North Wood near his childhood home, and now, in his early fifties, he does exactly the same. Sometimes, on my walks, I will look above me and see him dangling from a branch by a rope and feel the same sort of envy I felt at the flying men near my old house in Norfolk. Before he worked here, Dave lived in Australia and Long Island, New York, coppicing and removing trees in the gardens of Jack Nicholson and Billy Joel, among others. He's never been within thirty yards of a gym but hasn't got an ounce of fat on him and looks a decade younger than he is. Often he's up there alone, wielding a chainsaw with one hand, hanging from a limb with the other, yet in the three decades since he received his arboreal qualification he has never come close to being seriously injured. That said, he did once almost render his boss two dimensional when felling a turkey oak that had sheared down the middle of its trunk. On the same occasion, with the force of its descent the turkey oak's trunk managed to take out the hallowed 1930s art deco donkey sculpture in the gardens of Dartington Hall. Dave found the donkey removed from its perch but cradled gently in the fallen oak's branches, almost as if the oak, selfless in its own demise, had wanted to protect it. Trees have not had the easiest run of it at Dartington in recent times. In late 2013 Dave watched from the estate's tiltyard as a train of wind – a rigorously organised wind, a wind with a plan – tore up the river, sending ashes and oaks crashing into the water. Many of these can still be seen in the places they fell. Their sleeping half-submerged torsos look especially enchanting at dawn, smoked by mist, a classic example of the difference between nature making a mess and humans making a mess, which is that in the end nature will always make its mess look attractive. The following summer the two-century-old Monterey pine on the terraces above Dartington's Great Lawn keeled over from old age, leaving a spectacular Jurassic-looking corpse that was subsequently rolled several hundred yards to the tiltyard, chopped up and used by local craftsfolk to make dining tables, lecterns, sculptures and musical instruments.

Two springs later I was encouraged to gaze mindfully at some of the other, intact trees at Dartington as part of a meditative evening walking class I'd enrolled on. It was an excellent time of year and day to appreciate Dartington's gardens, which are full of surprises and retain the messy-neat aesthetic established by the Elmhirsts, the philanthropic millionaires who rescued the estate from near-dereliction in the early 1920s. Oddly, dusk seemed to bring out the reds and pinks and golds more than ever, and there was a soft quietness to the air, which along with the sensitive company gave the impression that the whole world was taking a gentle break from itself. The evening, however, did not pass without incident. At one point I made the error of shoving a holistic scientist into a flower bed. I hadn't intended to shove the holistic scientist into the flower bed; I'd just lost my concentration a bit and not quite got the steering bit of the exercise we were doing quite right. This was a trust exercise, in which the dozen people on the course got into pairs and wordlessly guided their partners around the gardens, using a light hand on the bottom of their spines and showing them objects such as fronds, leaves, grass and other stuff that had taken on interesting hues in the fading light. While being guided in this way, our partners – such as the holistic scientist, who had paired up with me – were required to keep their eyes shut until instructed to open them with a gentle double-tap to the shoulder, enabling them to look at some foliage. With a subsequent identical double-tap we could instruct them to reclose their eyes. It was vital that the whole procedure be conducted in complete silence. With night coming down fast, I wondered about the best way to get the holistic scientist out of the flower bed without speaking to her. In normal circumstances I'd have simply been able to say, 'I'm so sorry, I've inadvertently pushed you into some hydrangeas there,' but that would have been cheating. Instead, I gave the holistic scientist, whose name was Joana, a frantic double-tap on the shoulder. This double-tap had a different meaning to my previous double-taps: less *Gaze at the wonder of this primrose* and more *Quick! Stop right there or you'll hit your head on a branch then possibly fall over!* There was then an awkward moment when Joana realised she was in a flower bed. I flashed her an apologetic look and the two of us tried to conduct a three-point turn on the spot. We then continued on our mindful, peaceful way below a bank of bluebells, remembering at all times to experience the movement of our feet on the dampening ground.

An evening like this, in the countryside, helps you to look up. Big cities condition us to look down. I lived in two big cities back to back for just three years, but it took me at least that long again to get out of the habit of looking down, and I only truly directed my gaze upwards on a regular basis a few years after that when, out of necessity, in that overrun garden in Norfolk I started to get more intimate with trees. Of course, that is what we tree-huggers do: our critics tell us we walk around in a daze, our heads in the clouds, unrealistic about what it means to live. But what is more unrealistic: being aware that trees predate us, that they are both more important than us and crucial to our survival, and celebrating all the joy and magic and additional life they encourage, or viewing a love of them as some kind of ditzy indulgence extraneous to the real business of survival? If you grew up in the eighties, as I did – a time of ruthless corrections to the flaws of the hippy era that were far more destructive than the actual flaws of the hippy era – you'd have often heard 'tree-hugger' being used as a term of derision. But there is nothing wrong with being a tree-hugger. Hugging trees is great. Even better is waking up the next day in a tree's arms and telling it your dreams. I haven't actually slept in a tree but I have climbed several over the last few years. I prefer the ones with moss on them, but it's not a deal-breaker if they don't have any. There is no left-brain thinking going on when I climb a tree. I am not at any point saying to myself, *This branch looks a little weak; I'd better not stand on it.* It all happens instinctively – probably because I have hundreds of ancestors who also liked to climb trees. Standing on the top step of a ladder and pruning my hedge, I am only semi-confident, a little untrustworthy of the metal rungs even though they've been built specifically to support me, but when I am twice as high as that, spread out along the branch of a mossy oak, high above the Dart gorge on Dartmoor, I feel entirely relaxed and secure.

Because I look up more now, I am also more aware of the small soap operas being acted out in the branches above me. For a long time I was conscious of the deficiencies in my knowledge of birds and would say to myself, *You really need to make an effort to take more of an interest in birds*, but when I finally got around to taking more of an interest in birds it was less because I told myself, *You really need to make an effort to take more of an interest in birds*, and more because a greater interest in trees is a sensitising experience that leads organically to a greater appreciation of birds. I definitely do not exempt the more common birds from this appreciation: the wood pigeons who sexwrestle in the branches of the hawthorn beyond my garden hedge for example, or the jackdaws and gulls who helpfully hoover up the food that my cats are too spoilt to finish. Two beady-eyed gulls circle above my chimney every morning, watching for the scraps I put out. Their surveillance is done from an almost inconceivable height, twice as high as the highest jackdaw flight path and probably a dozen times the height of my house. They probably think they're doing very well out of me, but in reality they're doing me a favour. I can put any kind of food waste outside my back door, return moments later, and it will be gone. Chicken bones gnawed bare by the cats, stale quarter-loaves, beansprouts, old jalapenos: you name it, they're totally into it. I have the notion that, when the time comes for my ailing, sluggish laptop to finally die, all I will have to do is leave it on my back doorstep for five minutes and never have to think about it again.

If the gulls don't get the scraps, the jackdaws do. Since I moved here, a family of them have lived at the top of my chimney. I have had a cage installed on the chimney now to protect them, but for a while their situation was a worry. In 2014 a fledgling dropped down into the empty grate then sat happily on my arm for an afternoon before I climbed onto the roof and placed him near his family, only for him to be annihilated by a sparrowhawk. Then there was the adult who fell into a roaring conflagration of my dad's best logs two years later. I was in the kitchen making a cup of tea at the time, but my friends Rachel and Seventies Pat saw the jackdaw fall into the flames.

'Tom! Tom! Get in here! Quick!' shouted Rachel and Seventies Pat, who did not have fires, or jackdaws, in their houses. I rushed into the room, half-expecting to find the room ablaze, but instead found a confused bird flapping around the room's perimeter. I dived and caught it then took the jackdaw outside, where it hopped around looking dazed for twenty seconds, before flying up into the boughs of the Scots pine in the garden. The situation could have been much worse, and everyone felt relieved – not least the jackdaw, I imagine.

'Do you think it's OK?' asked Rachel.

'Yeah, it seems to be pretty much still a full jackdaw,' I replied.

'Full jackdaw,' said Rachel. 'Thank God.'

We drank a little too much wine that night, and the next morning I asked Seventies Pat how he was feeling.

'Surprisingly fine,' he replied. 'Pretty much full jackdaw.'

The three of us were up before dawn the day after that, which was 1 May, to watch the morris dancers at Totnes Castle and the sun coming up over the hills near Brixham: the light, accompanying the singing of 'Hal-an-Tow', the old Helston May Day song, could hardly have been more perfect.

'That was great,' said Rachel. 'Full jackdaw!'

Later, the three of us planned a walk beside the river, where the footpaths were still muddy after heavy April rainfall, and I asked Seventies Pat – who is never out of 1971 dandy uniform – if he had brought any proper walking boots.

'I've bought my walking cowboy boots,' said Seventies Pat. 'Does that count?'

I let out a sigh.

'Don't worry about me,' he reassured me. 'I'm full jackdaw.'

Jackdaws are often written off as ruffians or villains, with their old-fashioned burglar cartoon masks and egg-stealing habit, but in flight they're no less serene or beautiful than any other bird. They will dive-bomb down my chimney pot towards my lawn then flip and turn at right angles for the trees behind the hedge; air

poetry delivered at speed. The collective noun for them
is a clattering, which goes a fair way to summing up the
busy, almost metallic sound they often make in full gang
mode. When I was asleep last summer with my bedroom
window wide open and one landed on the sill behind
my head and squawked, the effect was not dissimilar to
someone sneaking up behind me and clanging two iron
poles together as a practical joke. Jackdaws are rarely
alone, though. Not for them the spontaneous bohemian
life of the unshackled blackbird. Their existence is centred
around punctilious, community-based organisation.
Groups are frequently known to fly into farmland, each
pick an individual sheep to land on and delouse, then
leave. Sheep are rarely heard to complain about this. When
I round the corner of my house and startle three or four

jackdaws eating the food I've left out for them they still make the effort to take off in formation, as if the allotted leader among them has said, 'One, two, three...go!' They also mate for life, even when they're unhappy with each other or struggling to have children together, a trait that seems both admirable and a bit self-defeatingly 1950s of them. When I looked into the eyes of that fledgling I briefly befriended I saw a human intelligence that I've not seen in the eyes of any other bird with the possible exception of two or three particularly lugubrious parrots.

A Scottish man called Norman who I met at an owl club in Torbay told me that in his 1950s boyhood on the edge of the Cairngorms he and his friends would often foster various types of orphan crows. The jackdaws were always the most responsive and bright of the lot. 'One boy had a jackdaw who'd follow him to school, then wait on the roof for him until lessons were over,' Norman said. Bending to kiss the beak of his African spotted eagle owl Ellie, he told me he now preferred to spend time around owls, and that doing so had aided his recovery after suffering a stroke a few years ago. I had been invited to owl club by Pete, who I first met in Totnes when he was walking around town with an owl called Wizard from the local rare breeds farm. Pete is one of two men regularly seen around Totnes walking owls, but it is genuinely perceived that he is the more authentic, since he was the first to take owls around the town, and the other man's owls are smaller. Being invited to owl club felt like a privilege, especially as I was to be the sole person in attendance who didn't have their own owl, so I thought it was the least I could do to wear my best shoes. Within a matter of seconds, however, the shoes were in jeopardy. An owl had defecated very close to the entrance to owl club, and I found myself weaving, last minute, to dodge the owl poo, swivelling and swerving in a move arguably more impressive than any I'd pulled while trying to mimic some of the nascent disco moves from early 1970s episodes of *Soul Train*.

'I'll just get that,' said Pete, diving in with some kitchen roll to clean up the owl faeces. 'Ooh, who's THIS then?' I asked, gesturing at the great grey owl a few feet away, but Pete's head was dipped and he assumed I was referring to a tall pensioner in front of me. 'This is Alby,' Pete answered. 'He's our chairman.' I'm not the kind of person who'd say 'Ooh, who's THIS then?' to open a conversation with a stranger in his early seventies, but it was novel to be briefly mistaken for one. 'Hello,' said Alby. 'I don't have my owl with me today because I'm undergoing chemotherapy and cannot afford to get scratched.' Behind him, an African spotted eagle owl baited excitably at a ringtone of the opening riff from the Who's 'Baba O'Riley'. I'd been at owl club all of two minutes and already there was drama everywhere. A rumour circulated that, soon, flapjacks were to be served.

Owl club – or Torbay Owls and Company, as it's more formally known – is a splinter owl club from a bigger owl club. 'We started our own because there was lots of backbiting at the other one,' I was told by Norman, who with his wife Jan owns two other owls in addition to Ellie the African spotted eagle owl. Alby reassured prospective members of owl club that they wouldn't get 'any of that "My owl's better than your owl" stuff here'. These possible members included Jamie, who'd brought his European eagle owl Boo along to owl club. Although only eight weeks old, Boo already weighed sixteen pounds and would eventually grow to twice her size. That is, if she did turn out to be a she. Many owls, I was informed, are 'very hard to sex' when they're young, although one man sitting near me said he could do it with a 95 per cent success rate using magnets. Something made me stop short of asking how.

Not everyone at owl club had brought their owls with them. Some had just come for owl advice. This was given by Alby and included 'Never approach an owl from behind,' the dangers of being 'footed' by an owl and food tips such as 'Always have a plastic bag with you in case you see a car hit a pheasant.' Alby explained he had been on steroids recently, which made him 'feel like he could break into Paignton Zoo and feed the lions by hand'. He stopped short of demonstrating, but produced some large frozen rats from a cool box to feed to tonight's owls. Authoritatively, he explained how to tie a falconer's knot – 'my way, the good way, not the way you see on YouTube' – and that stroking an owl's back feathers is bad, as it removes the natural oil from them.

I was reassured that all the owls of owl club lived in spacious aviaries in the Torbay area, but I decided that my visit to owl club would be a one-off and that the owls I observed in future would be wild ones. Plenty of these were available in the trees beyond my garden, after all.

'Are there any owls around?' I would sometimes say to these wild owls and, usually within under a minute, one would reply in the affirmative. Contrary to what a lot of people will have you believe, no self-respecting individual owl actually says,'T'wit t'woo.' It is a statement that, to be delivered with authenticity, requires two owls. The high-pitched female tawnies say, 'T'wit' – which is really more like 'Toooo-WEEEEEET' – and the more bassy and insouciant male tawnies answer, if they're in the mood, with 'T'woo.' The spinney immediately to the west of my house seems to be very female-dominated, sometimes apparently stiflingly so for its residents. Several lady tawnies will screech in the early hours, kind of casually at first, then with a growing hen-party intensity, until finally after an hour or so a lothario manowl will chime in with a low-key yet confident 'Woo' like the Owl Fonz quietly entering a room full of leather-clad rock and roll girls. 'Do not panic,' Owl Fonz appears to be saying at these junctures. 'As you will soon discover, there is more than enough of me to go around.' The owls here are especially vocal in early spring and early autumn, but they're tough-nut all-year-rounders, like the jackdaws and the gulls. The most eager of the seasonal birds to get to work are the greater spotted woodpeckers, in late January. The sound these make is uncannily similar to the one the creaky wooden gate to my garden makes upon being opened by my postman. *Ooh, I have mail*, I will sometimes think, when in reality I just have woodpecker.

It was once popularly believed that woodpeckers were bad for trees. In fact, the work they do is another kind of tree-hugging, their true agenda being not destruction but to contribute to arboreal health: they bore into decaying timber, feeding on the grubs of bark-munching beetles. In this way they are the antithesis of grey squirrels, whose cuddling of trees masks a true agenda of rampant nihilism. Dave has had terrible trouble with the greys at Dartington, who have chronically weakened many of his beeches and sycamores. 'A lot of it is about sexual frustration,' he told me. 'The male squirrels get horny, and they can't find a mate, so they attack some bark.' Everyone I know who regularly walks in the Dartington area seems to have had a horny squirrel trash-talk to them at some point. It is a shocking noise when you first hear it coming from the branches of a nearby tree: birdlike, but tongue-flicking and not at all fluffy. I am sure one of the grey's smaller, less destructive

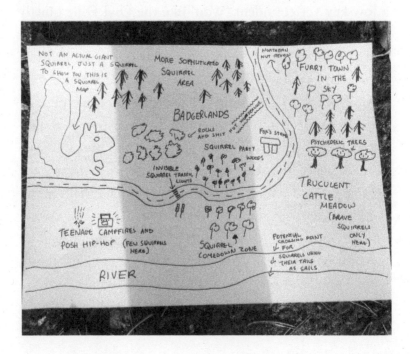

red counterparts would never be so uncouth. October to November tends to be the most high-spirited time for the grey squirrels of south Devon. They fling themselves about like flouncy teenagers with too much energy and dance across the canopy, sometimes appearing to balance dozens of feet above the earth on nothing but a gossamer sycamore leaf. Some have been seen riding on the back of sheep, although despite carefully studying them and even drawing a rough map of squirrel activity in my area, I have never witnessed this myself, and I sense the motive for doing so might be less altruistic than that of jackdaws. I don't have a horse chestnut tree in or near my garden, but in October I often find numerous spiky, half-opened conker shells on the lawn, which I have realised is the work of picnicking squirrels. An especially bold one will sometimes barrel down the middle of the lane, creating a queue of cars behind, like a tiny furry tractor. Only a day of strong winds seems to slow down their autumnal high. Squirrels have, however, allegedly found ingenious uses for wind. In his 1607 book *History Of Foure-Footed Beastes* Edward Topsell writes of the squirrel, 'for when hunger or some convenient prey of meat constraineth her to pass over a river, she seeketh out some rinde or small bark of a tree, which she setteth upon the water or goeth into it, and holding her tail like a sail letteth the wind drive her to the other side.' This is a pleasing image but one which striketh me as bullshit.

I have stood in the dense steep copses near my house in November storms and heard the fearsome creak of bending trunks above me, a far more fearsome sound, surely, if you are a foot and a bit long and covered in fur. A red oak ripped itself out of the ground on the hillside above the house during my first autumn here with a noise beyond thunder. In another storm, a holm oak behind my garden – a vast elevated maze of a tree over three hundred years old – came down on my phone line. Sometimes, when the leaves seem to be holding on a little too long, these storms apparently come along to do a kind of necessary industrial clean to hurry winter along. But the final deleafing of trees will often take place on the most windless of days, the pressure of icy still air sending the last crinkled brown survivors gently to the ground, defeated. There are long bony months ahead but it's still a good time to be heavily into wood. Summer's the big party season for trees, but winter is when you really get to know them as people. It's when you see behind the green curtain to the detailed architecture of the branches of an elm or a maple. It's when you see ivy's roots stretching up a trunk like veins on the tensed ageing wrist of an arm-wrestler. Last winter I kept watch on a solitary, huge, two-century-old oak on the hillside near me – a wise but not wizened tree, confident in its loner status – and photographed it every few days, yet even in its barest months its moods still palpably swung. On a Wednesday it might be cloud-whipped and cantankerous, then sheep-sniffed, sun-kissed and soporific on Friday then greyly ice-glazed and impenetrable on Saturday. You could argue that late autumn and early winter are the most tree-dominated seasons of all in rural Devon as it's when their aroma is most prevalent: the time of woodsmoke's primal reminder of the woodier place we all come from. There's nothing quite like the way woodsmoke cuts through cold country air, and even if you're like me and seek it out and delight in it, summer is always enough to make you forget just how heady its aroma is. I climbed to the top of my favourite local mystic hill, Yarner Beacon, last December and caught a strong whiff of it: an invisible cloud of promise in the dead chill. The smell was initially confusing, as there is no house within a quarter of a mile of Yarner Beacon's summit, and it took me a few moments to realise that it was in fact coming from one of the bandsaws in the woodyard at the foot of the hill.

I'd walked past the woodyard numerous times and was dying to find out what went on in there. I only had to look through the gates at the giant logpiles and headlightless old vans to want to write a vast, epic work

of fiction set within its boundaries. But you never know with a woodyard: you could pop your head inside and get a cheery welcome in a cloud of sawdust, or it could contain a dog who will bite off one or both of your testicles. Fortunately, when I finally got the chance to visit this one – through Dave, who in a bit of serendipity or perhaps mere logic in a world where woodsmen tend to stick together, was friends with its owner, Alan – in March 2017 it turned out to be delightful. Alan is seventy but says he will continue working with wood 'until I drop dead'. He leaves the actual tree surgery to his son and grandson now but is on the receiving end of a relentless campaign from his new partner to get him to spend less time at the yard. 'She won't win,' he told me. I asked him what it was he did there on an average day. 'Just playworking, really,' he replied, grinning from ear to ear. 'I love it.' When I arrived, he was standing on top of his tallest logpile, doing something I assumed to be very important and which I worried about interrupting. Now it occurred to me he was probably just enjoying the unalloyed pleasure of picking up and holding logs, as men have done since time immemorial for reasons they can't fully explain.

When Alan used to get home from the woodyard, his wife, who passed away six years ago, was able to take one sniff of him and detect exactly which kinds of trees he'd been working with. 'Douglas fir was always a dead giveaway,' he said. When she worked in the office, she'd chuckle to herself watching Alan on the security camera as he wandered out into the woodyard and walked in circles, trying to recall what precisely he'd gone out there to do. His stocky smiliness and combination of being dozy yet very good with tools reminded me of my late wood-loving granddad Ted. Alan's first tree jobs had been straight after school, when he worked for what he called 'a hard, deaf bugger'. In those days there were no Kevlar-stuffed chainsaw trousers or gloves, and when the first helmets came into use in the trade his boss would call anyone he saw wearing one a 'puff'. Despite his absent-mindedness, safety-scorning guru and lack of protective clothing, Alan, like Dave, has never been seriously injured, although his son suffered multiple fractures of the pelvis and a collapsed lung when working on a beech at Totnes Showground. Alan's most dramatic tree experience was the time the branch of a fallen elm that had been wedged up against a concrete kerb twanged him dozens of feet through the air. 'They told me that when I landed, my feet and nose were half-buried in the ground, but I can't remember any of it,' he said. He offered me a cup of tea. 'I've saved you the clean mug,' he said. 'You don't want this one,' he added, showing me another mug, white but stained totally black inside with the remnants of a thousand dark drinks. 'That's what my boys drink out of. Never wash it. They don't care.'

Alan told me I had to keep an eye on the time for him as he was scheduled to go what he called 'rock 'n' rolling' that night in Newton Abbot. He said he was not good with time, did not let the concept of it trouble him much, an attitude which had historically made him a deficient capitalist but been beneficial to his stress levels. As he showed me around the yard he looked a little wobbly around the shoulders, but I sensed that if you ran at him from a great distance, he'd stay vertical on impact: solid, immovable. All these qualities, I thought, were very treelike. 'You're a tree,' I told Alan. 'I'm a tree,' he confirmed. I'd witnessed a few of the modern biodynamic hippy farmers in the area chuckling in the village pub about Alan's no-nonsense approach to felling, but he clearly cared deeply about his leafy patients. A few years ago a bloke from Torquay had asked him to come over and remove a walnut tree from his garden. Alan examined the walnut, which he found to be in rude health, and asked why the bloke wanted it removed. 'It's casting a shadow over my barbecue,' he replied. Alan told him there was nothing wrong with the tree and refused to take it out. 'A few months later I drove past the house and saw it was gone,' said Alan. 'Broke my heart, that did.'

The woodyard sits in a cool dell, and Alan loves the wildlife there, which proliferates but quietens down after heavy rainfall, when water gushes down the beacon and the area floods. 'Lots of badgers and deer and rabbits and squirrels here,' he said. He shook his head with a woodsman's ruefulness. 'Bloody squirrels. Tree's worst enemies.' We walked to the gate, and I admired a 1950s Airstream van with a few vital components missing from it. 'That project's been on hold for a while,' said Alan. 'Before my wife died I'd been meaning to sort it out, take it down to Portugal, see the proper old country there. Maybe I still will.' I asked him what it was about that area that appealed to him.

'The sawmills, I suppose,' he said.

On the way back from Alan's I passed the remains of the holm oak that had come down on my phone line. It had been so vast that although a fair portion of its stump still stood, its demise had changed the shape and angles of everything: the surrounding, smaller trees, the tall hills in the background, a formerly reticent allotment wall, now bolshie. Dave had told me that when a big tree like this comes down in a storm, it's often not just the work of the wind. In this case there had been several other factors: the build-up of catkins at the top of the tree, several days of heavy rainfall leading to accumulated moisture and heaviness in the catkins. An hour or so after the holm oak fell, just as I was becoming cognizant of the fact that it had taken out all the modern forms of communication available to me, a policeman knocked on my front door to say a 999 call from my property had been recorded. I said that was impossible, as I had no working phone, but he asked to come in anyway, presumably just to check I didn't have anyone tied up at gunpoint in my cellar. He seemed satisfied, especially after realising I don't have a cellar. When he left, I walked to my garden gate, passing the spot on the concrete path where, earlier that morning, my cat Ralph had deposited some vomit which had since been eaten by a gull. I opened the gate and walked to the top of the hill past the tree and called BT from my mobile. What ensued was the following conversation.

ME: A tree's come down on my phone line.

BT: OK. First we have to check if there's a fault on the line.

ME: There is. It has a huge tree on it.

As can so often happen when you're dealing with telephone and Internet companies, I soon became trapped in a labyrinth of bureaucratic computer-says-no nonsense, and a farce developed, raging on for a lengthy and precious period of my life. I was informed on a couple of occasions by BT that their engineer was on site fixing the problem but, being on site myself, I was able to confirm that this was untrue. I wandered back up to where the holm oak had crashed down and parted some large nettles and fronds surrounding it but did not find the BT engineer beneath them. With each succeeding call, I started to get a stronger sense that I was experiencing a classic example of linesplaining. With no mobile phone signal to be found in most of my house and garden, I spent several not unpleasant days cut off in every technological sense. One morning I also ate an apple. I felt like I was getting a very minor insight into what it would be like to live as a horse.

When an engineer finally arrived I told him about the police incident. He seemed unsurprised. The engineer said that when phone lines earth, they often automatically send a call to the emergency services. I could not help dwelling on the image: the holm oak had lived a grand life, through the Napoleonic Wars, the Industrial Revolution and series one to twelve of *The X Factor*, and must have known its time was nigh, but as it breathed its last it was still desperate enough to call the emergency services for help.

'Maybe it was trying to get hold of Special Branch,' said the engineer. He told me that the damage the tree had done to the line was now repaired and my phone and broadband were once again functioning. 'Anyway,' he continued. 'It's all a bit of a moot point.'

'Oh really? Why's that?' I asked.

'Your line was already more or less buggered. It had been chewed to ribbons by all these squirrels around here.'

8

BOATS AGAINST THE CURRENT

The small lido where I swim during the summer months is unheated and when I arrive is often empty. When I first used to get in I'd lower my torso into the water very gingerly and wince a bit, but in more recent times being semi-naked and immersed in cold water has become such a normal state for me I throw fuck to the wind and hurl myself right in, barely noticing the chill. I take a little while to get going, not just because I'm warming up but because my first couple of lengths necessitate several detours, as I rescue the handful of bumblebees that are invariably flailing about upside down on the pool's surface. If the bees are near the edge of the pool I do this with a cupped hand beneath the water and a gentle scooping motion that I hope will not hurt the bee or result in a sting, but sometimes when the bee is more centrally located I will return to my clothes pile and fetch an espadrille or a flip-flop, hold it aloft while swimming one-armed, then use it to lift the bee out of the water onto the concrete slabs at the side. If anyone who lives in the flats near the pool is watching me from their window, this must look very strange. *This man is very committed to his latest piece of performance art*, I can imagine them thinking. *He believes he is all alone, unobserved, but he still goes through with it in such a serious manner. It is sad yet kind of admirable.*

A lot of people might think it slightly unhygienic to swim around in the company of insects, but I regularly push the envelope of my aquatic interspecies social life into far more perilous bacterial territory. Last summer, on the hottest day of the year, I swam in the River Dart with my friends James, Bea, Monika and Helen. 'Wow, this is amazing!' we said to each other as we bobbed about in water much warmer than the lido, the smell of a barbecue drifting over from the shore and an early-evening sun winking through the boughs of the oaks overhanging the bank. Then we got out, towelled ourselves dry and watched in silence as a Jersey heifer lowered itself into the shallows and released a huge, hot jet of piss into an area only a few feet from where we had just been doing breaststroke.

I generally prefer to swim further upstream than this in the Dart, beyond the South Hams towns of Totnes and Buckfastleigh and their sewage plants, where it's easier to convince yourself that the water is clear and pure and blank out the fact that there might be a decomposing ram wedged between two algae-shined rocks just seven or eight hundred yards around the corner. I have given more

thought to these issues since my first year in Devon, when, as an almost certain result of overzealous river swimming, I developed a urinary tract infection right out of the top drawer of Satan's tallboy, which subsequently degenerated into full-blown prostatitis. Early on a Saturday last July I traipsed a couple of miles north from the moor's edge along rocky banks, past half a dozen canoeists, an elderly hippy couple sitting on the bank hand in hand and a lanky Rapunzel-haired girl with a feed bucket calling to three ponies, until finally I was alone next to a deep clear pool of black-gold water. I stood on a natural granite platform around twenty feet above the pool's surface and envisaged the hidden jagged underwater rock that would slice mercilessly through my thigh muscle, leaving me stranded and bleeding as the cold, unforgiving moorland night thundered down. Then I thought, *Ah, to hell with it!* and jumped in anyway. In my defence I had previously done a reconnoitre of water depth and underwater rock location because, contrary to what some of my recent swimming missions might have suggested from a distance, I largely enjoy my life and do not actually wish to die before my time.

The current in the pool was benign, but when I swam up to the waterfall at the top end I realised that I was no longer moving forward and got a sense of what a formidable monster its force could be on a harsher day after some customarily heavy Devonian rainfall. As I walked back to the car and dripped dry in the sun and breeze I felt a cold electricity in my fingertips, and my entire body seemed to have a coating of dark, magic renewal, as if it had found something in the water that reminded my body what it really was, before all this distraction we tentatively call being a person. I returned home, faffed for a while in a delusional attempt to work, then got in the car and headed to the sea to swim some more. A mild but spectacular fret came in over the cliffs as I arrived, giving the Gammon Head rock the appearance of a smoky sea volcano. A sensible person might have turned back, but I have done various bits of research into being a sensible person over the last couple of decades and decided it's not for me.

Over the last year or two I have become slightly addicted to swimming, and nobody is more surprised about this than I am. The last time I was addicted to swimming was between the ages of six and nine, when, over summer weeks that take on a quality of endlessness in my memory, I would dive repeatedly into an Italian swimming pool under a fierce sun and transform with

great alacrity into a small sinewy human Brazil nut. My dad, reliving a Mediterranean childhood he'd never had, would dive beside me, no less boisterously, then play energetic games of table tennis against Germans and Italians and Austrians on a table down some steps behind the pool. 'OOH, YOU BASTARD,' I'd hear my dad saying to Germans and Italians and Austrians, as I got ready to dive into the pool again. 'GOOD SHOT.' These Italian holidays are such a large, powerful part of me that, any time I'm now in the lido and I get water up my nose, I am dizzied by a time travel stronger than that evoked by any smell. With this arrives a dramatic feeling of ambivalence. On the one hand, I have swimming-pool water up my nose, which is never pleasant; on the other, it's 1983, I am back in Tuscany, nobody's ever expressed an emotion via a GIF, I've spent the morning listening to *Remain in Light* by Talking Heads and I am about to eat earth's greatest pizza for less than what you would now pay for a pencil. All people have years when they are more them than they are in other years, and 1982, 1983 and 1984 were all years when I was very me. This is probably a big reason why I swim. I also like the way it has changed my body, without me having to go within a mile of a gym, which is something I would rather pan-fry one of my own internal organs than do.

You have to be careful about saying this stuff nowadays, when technology has opened up whole new virtual corridors for fitness boasters to strut down, flexing their biceps and sticking their squat-toned rears in your face. People nowadays want to hear that you are abandoning your responsibilities to your body and bingeing on doughnuts and a six-pack of extra-strength budget lager. They do not want to hear that you are getting fitter than you have been for years, and they especially do not want to see a blow-by-blow record of it. So I will leave my fitness bragging at this: I feel better as the skinny slightly wiry person I've been since swimming a lot than the slightly skinny not all that wiry person I was before. I don't think it's for everybody, and I don't even find skinny slightly wiry people especially attractive myself. Do whatever you want to do and don't let a stranger dictate how you live your life. Eat some fried stuff with cheese, maybe? It's nice.

I hesitate to call what I do wild swimming because I've always thought that's a bit like calling lawn mowing 'wild vacuuming', but I do sometimes call it wild swimming because lots of people do, and joining in makes communication easier, and I think it would be needlessly intransigent of me to completely boycott the term 'wild swimming'. Like a lot of people, I first attempted some more adventurous swimming in earnest after reading the inspiring book *Waterlog* by Roger Deakin, the late nature writer who lived only a couple of miles up the road from my house, across the border from Norfolk into Suffolk. Deakin won me over with the freedom of his writing and lifestyle, describing muzak as 'chlorinated music', and by being the first person apart from me I had come across who used the word 'endolphins' instead of 'endorphins'. But perusing the excerpts from my diaries in 2010 and 2011 that centred around the indoor pool where I had been swimming; however, I can see that there might have been more than just Deakin's prose nudging me out into open water.

1 August 2010
I'm like most people when I'm getting changed in a public area: I keep my eyes down, myself to myself and my turning circle tight. But when, as was the case today, a man is standing in front of me, meticulously drying his pubic hair with a hairdryer, it is very hard not to notice.

4 August 2010
They played that awful Duffy song at the pool today and I hid underwater until it was over.

29 September 2010
No sign of Guy Who Blowdries His Pubes at the

pool today but it was quite busy and Man Who Swims Like His Body Is His Large New BMW, Farting Chinese Guy and Mr Zorro Towel were all there. I also note that the new NO COMPARING TATTOOS THEN DUCKING EACH OTHER sign doesn't seem to be having much effect.

3 October 2010
Conversation in changing room. YOUTH ONE: 'All right, Rob? What you here for today, mate? Kick-boxing?' YOUTH TWO: 'Nah, most times I just come here to 'ave a wash these days, to be honest.'

20 October 2010
Dear man standing in the shower cubicle next to me when my bottle of conditioner exploded: I'm sorry if you thought the white rain falling on your head was semen.

17 December 2010
I love the way that when I'm swimming at the pool in low sunlight the rays will softly illuminate the ripples and the used plaster that floats by on them.

3 January 2011
Awkward conversation witnessed in the steam room today between two men in their fifties, largely revolving around one of them's desire to

have rough, uninhibited sex with his son's new girlfriend. 'I can't help it,' he said as his friend shifted uncomfortably on the slimy porcelain ledge beside him. 'Every time I see her I can't stop thinking about taking her from behind.'

17 March 2011

The pool seem to be having a crackdown on the condition of 'dirt leg' among their regulars. At least, I can only assume that that's why a cleaner sprayed my shins powerfully with his hose through the gap under the door as I was having a shower this afternoon. Still, it is reassuring to know that the facilities are being kept clean, especially with the realisation that there are many out there who view shower-based urination as exercise salad's essential accompanying vinaigrette.

I enjoyed swimming in the sea in Norfolk and Suffolk, but my excursions to rivers, largely the slow-flowing Waveney not far from my house, were poorly planned and characterised by a half-commitment to the task in hand. I climbed apprehensively into the water from small vertical banks thick with bulrushes, breaststroked fifty or so yards upstream with the air of someone who'd broken illegally into a private complex, came face to face with an obstacle or something I'd convinced myself was an obstacle – Did that Egyptian goose look a bit handy? – then breaststroked back and got out, silty-toed and unsure of my role in society. But in 2014, when I moved to Devon, I found that its rivers were much more inviting: clearer and faster-flowing, their rocky banks dotted with enticing launching points. The sea down here is warmer too – not on the whole *warm* warm, but between May and October it generally doesn't make you shriek or pull a face like you're sucking a lemon when you get in, which was previously the norm for me.

I posted a few photos on Twitter and Instagram of the swimming challenges I set myself in Devon last summer, which probably look far more spectacular and brave than they were. What I forgot when I did this was that my dad, who is always on a determined search for the cloud in every silver lining, stalks my social network accounts with the zeal of a private detective. Pretty soon the emails started to roll in: three, sometimes four, every day. 'TWO DIE IN RIP TIDE OFF THE COAST OF NORFOLK,' announced the subject heading of one. 'SEARCH FOR CURLY-HAIRED MAN, 41, FEARED DROWNED, CONTINUES,' said another. After about fourteen links to modern news stories, tales of a more retrospective kind of maritime horror began to appear. One dated from as far back as June 1956.

With hindsight I admit that the first swimming challenge I set myself was quite bold. I hadn't even thought of setting myself swimming challenges before that. I was splashing about in my favourite cove in a dreamy way, and as I was I got to thinking about the cove around the corner, which I had visited on holiday when I was little, and I thought it would be quite fun to

swim around the corner to revisit it, so I set about doing just that. Swimming to this cove from my favourite cove didn't seem a huge deal, as when you start you are close to the shore and the water is clear beneath you, but as I rounded the corner everything was very different: I was fairly far out in open water, the waves were bigger and stronger, and I got a small but genuine sense of what an unsympathetic bastard the sea could be. The swim was around a mile in total, and I was tired when I returned to the beach of the original cove, so much so that I staggered a bit like someone who'd escaped from a shipwreck. I also couldn't see from getting so much saltwater in my eyes, which probably made it look like I was crying, perhaps owing to having lost a loved one in the same shipwreck. When I fully regained my sight I noticed both of my kneecaps were streaming blood and that a devastatingly beautiful woman had appeared on the beach not far from my towel and bag, as devastatingly beautiful people have an annoying habit of doing when you are looking your least dignified. On the plus side, I knew that my hair would feel great in an hour or so in that excellent crunchy way it does when you've been in the sea.

'YOUR KNEES WERE BLEEDING BECAUSE YOU SMASHED THEM AGAINST SOME ROCKS,' my dad told me later that week on the phone. 'I ASKED MALCOLM AND HE TOLD ME. I SHOWED HIM YOUR PICTURE TOO AND HE SAYS YOU'RE AN IDIOT. HIS BROTHERS HAVE SWUM THE CHANNEL AND HE'S REALLY STRONG AND GOOD AT SWIMMING. HE'S SEVENTY NOW BUT HE CAN

STILL PICK ME UP AND TURN ME UPSIDE DOWN
IN THE WATER AT THE LOCAL POOL. DON'T DO
SWIMS LIKE THAT ON YOUR OWN. AND WATCH
OUT FOR FOOKWITS, LOONIES AND JELLYFISH.'

My second swimming challenge – to cross the mouth
of the River Erme at Mothecombe – looked quite brave
from the photo I took, but didn't feel particularly brave
at the time. It was a first for me in that it involved
swimming in the rain, which was much more pleasant
than I expected. I'd watched the temperature gauge in
the car drop as I'd driven south-west to the beach from
home – 22 degrees, 21, 20, 19, 18 – and worried about
getting a chill, but the water was shallow and pleasant.
Only when I crossed the little invisible barrier separating
river mouth from sea did I notice a shift in temperature:
a hint of something breathtakingly cold and epically
devoid of remorse that you knew was not far away. As
I swam, gentle inquisitive seaweed grabbed for my legs
like a thousand face flannels gone sentient. The sea was
murkier than it had been ten miles away, at my favourite
cove, but kinder. This is something I love about the south
Devon coastline: its erratic shifts in personality, its high
standards of experimental cliffing and inability to settle
for the three or four types of flooring that many other
coastlines do.

A couple of days after that a softish package arrived in
the post. I opened it with fevered excitement, expecting
it to be the Linda Ronstadt T-shirt I had ordered from
an American website. Instead, I found a fluorescent
item – not, as I first assumed, a high-visibility tabard, but

something harder and more rubbery in character. OPEN WATER SWIM BUOY, announced its packaging, which also included a strap and buckle. BE BRIGHT. BE SEEN.

That afternoon an email popped through from my dad. 'NOW FUCKING USE IT,' instructed the email, which contained no subject heading or preamble.

It is curious how during a period of your life you will find yourself drawn to some music in what you believe is an entirely arbitrary way but later see a correlation between the character of the music and what you are doing in that period of your life. During my addictive summer of outdoor swimming I had been listening obsessively to the first four albums by the Californian psychedelic rock band Spirit. I had listened to these a fair bit during the late nineties, then moved on to Spirit's less well known, floatier mid-seventies period, and had recently felt like I needed to give their early work more time. Spirit sold a fraction of the units that their similarly jazz-tinged LA contemporaries the Doors did, but they were a much braver band, although their bravery is far less showy so sometimes people don't notice it, and their story is more tragic and weird. Another thing that makes Spirit cooler than the Doors is that they were formed by a teenager – the group's songwriting mainstay Randy California – and his bald, middle-aged uncle. Jim Morrison, you sense, would have thought himself too cool to form a band with his bald, middle-aged uncle, which is of course one of the precise reasons he is in reality more uncool. Spirit are brilliant and weird and perfect for a green summer day, and this was at least part of why I could not stop listening to them.

But there is something very watery about Spirit too: a bubbling quality to their far-out yet understated songs. California was a strong, obsessive swimmer, an athletic hippy who, already a Hendrix-approved guitar prodigy, was only sixteen when Spirit recorded 'Water Woman' and the other songs on their visionary 1968 debut album. In 1973, while living in west London, he infamously swam out into a choppy, violent Thames while tripping on LSD as a crowd watched, fearing for his life. He made it back to the shore that time, but, swimming off the coast of Molokai in Hawaii in 1997, California and his twelve-year-old son were caught in a rip tide. His son, with California's and a lifeguard's help, survived, but California did not.

On a Friday in August I was walking to the pub listening to Spirit's most famous song, 'I Got a Line on You'. The track opens with California singing of taking someone down to the riverbed and giving them something that will 'go right to' their 'head'. It was as I listened to these exact words that some teenagers called and waved to me from the riverbank. I removed my headphones to hear what they were saying. 'This might sound like a strange question, but have you seen a naked boy running around by any chance?' one of them asked. I said that I had not. It didn't, in all honesty, seem that strange a question in this area, where on a warm day skinny-dippers are as rife as moorhens.

I did not give the question much more thought until my friend Sarah and I were walking back from the pub and saw men in orange jackets wading in the river, shining torches into the water. Five minutes later a police car stopped beside us and its driver made the same enquiry:

had we seen a naked teenager anywhere in the vicinity? We said we hadn't. The next morning I woke to the sound of circling helicopters. A sixteen-year-old boy had been spotted on Friday evening, running towards the water, naked, under the influence of a legal high named N Bomb, and nobody had seen him since. On Sunday his body was found in the river by divers.

Throughout most of July the stretch of the Dart between the moor and the estuary had seemed amazingly tranquil and shallow: the ethereal and unthreatening nature of most of the people in it only adding to the ethereal and unthreatening nature of the water. It looked trustworthy: a place that repelled dark events. I challenged myself to swim from the mellow stretch of the river near Dartington Hall to Staverton, just over a mile away, but gave up after progressing barely a quarter of the way because for a while the river became so shallow that my chest and legs were in danger of scraping on the pebbles on the bottom. This was comical, but a river is not comical, or at least it is only comical in the way that all the most serious things are also comical. A river should also not be mistaken for being only one thing. It can be many things on the same day, and many, many more things over the course of a year. It should not on any account be messed with, as something linking directly to the Mother of All Things That Should Not Be Messed With: the sea.

Later in August I left Devon to complete a short spoken-word tour. After an event in the north Pennines, I stayed in a farmhouse B & B under the grey ridge of the nearby moor and ate a hearty breakfast consisting of eggs from the farmhouse's chickens, although not the eggs of one particularly bold chicken, who had recently left the farmyard to live as a nomad. 'We still sometimes see her, up over there, wandering along the ridge, alone, as the sun is setting,' said Michelle, the B & B's owner. Fortified by these more homely eggs I set off with my conservationist friend Chris along the Pennine Way to High Force, the waterfall which, when in full spate, has the largest volume of water of any in England. 'Shall I bring my trunks?' I asked Chris, who knows this area better than I know the contours of my own knuckles. 'I wouldn't advise it,' he replied.

After passing the whitewashed cottages of Lord

Barnard's estate and admiring the aerial ballet of an enormous late flock of golden plover, we proceeded a few miles along the way and stood on the unprotected southern bank on wet rocks within inches of the precipice of the waterfall, where the torrent makes its uninterrupted ninety-eight-foot plunge to the pool below. Its elemental power was like nothing I had known. No photograph I've seen of High Force comes anywhere near capturing it, although Joseph Turner's sketches of the waterfall from the early 1800s do come a little closer. The roar tumbled me into its epicentre, and I was inside the wet whirlwind even without taking the fatal single step forward, my bones crushed by its spate like so many matches before I'd even hit the bottom. I was pinned to the spot, and my future and past and even a great deal of my present receded to a unimportant fog beyond the race of a gazillion droplets of good cold northern water. Nothing could be more opposite than this to any of the vicarious, part-lived lives we sometimes live, and for a split second it felt like it would be worth perishing just to entirely embrace that oppositeness, but only for a split second. Chris had been right: there'd been no need to bring my trunks.

I had been touched when I completed my first few swimming challenges and people expressed worry over me, but I also chuckled inwardly. Sure, I was alone when I did them, but how could there be anything to worry about? I was, after all, me. I am outdoorsy, but I often feel that I define being so in a different way to many. I am not a daredevil or an adrenaline junkie. I am not one of those youths who dive from a height of over twenty feet into the Tees from the wobbly suspension footbridge two miles downstream from High Force, close to the waterfall's still quite intimidating little brother, Low Force. I am not even one of the fourteen-year-olds who strip off and push each other into the Dart near Totnes weir in January when the thermometer says one degree. *Look at all the other risky, wild challenges properly adventurous people set themselves every day*, I thought when people expressed reservations about my swimming adventures. *Why focus on a frivolous not very brave person like me, with my silly half-adventures?* But if I am truly honest with myself, a small element of risk *has* been part of the driving force behind my swimming. I have a positive view of risk and doing the opposite of what most people tell me to do since I associate risk and doing the opposite of what most people have told me to do with all the most positive turning points in my life. Then there was the fact that I had hoped to complete at least one of the two books I was writing, and due to various factors – losing a vast chunk of one in a data disaster, making the greedy decision to also have a life – I had not done so, and this had left me dissatisfied with myself. I wanted the sense of achievement that goes with getting my writing out of my system and, sometimes, into a small public sphere. Deciding to do a small outdoor swimming task then completing that small outdoor swimming task filled some of the holes where that sense of achievement should have been.

I avoided the Dart during the couple of weeks following the boy's death not because I was scared to swim in it or didn't plan to again, but to avoid it seemed somehow respectful. Part of this was perhaps out of respect for the river too. Can you respect the landscape too much? I don't think so. I love the landscape of Britain's Deep South West so fervently that I have chosen it ahead of an arguably more straightforward life closer to many people I love. It is more life-enhancing than any other terrain I've lived amid, but I hear more stories of tragedy associated with it than any other landscape I've lived in, and I cannot help but believe these two facts are inseparable. I think I have as much respect for this coastline, these rushing rivers, these hills, these moors, as it's possible to have, but it turns out there is always more to be had. Perhaps that moment when I swam around the bend from my favourite cove and an unsuspected tide did a sleepy quarter-roar at me like a grumpy lion rudely half-woken from an afternoon sleep and unseen rocks clawed at my knees, and maybe even that other moment when I went beyond the line of the bay at the mouth of the Erme and the temperature dramatically dropped with its suggestion of power and violence, were examples of me not showing the necessary amount of respect.

I'd had my eye on another swimming challenge: a more ambitious one but one I still viewed as very manageable. This was to swim around Burgh Island, a rocky mound off the mainland near the village of Bigbury on Sea, with its own pub and art deco hotel. I chose a Saturday for my mission, which wasn't ideal in parking terms. Having found the main car park at Bigbury on Sea full, I left my car up the road in the memorably named Economy Beach Car Park. This cost me four pounds, although it had only been a pound back in January, when it was the subject of possibly

the most forlorn photograph I have ever taken of the British seaside. It is not just the economy beach car park sign, the advertised one-pound fee and the bleak hillside beyond that make this photo, but the centrally framed bin and clump of pampas grass. 'Hey! Married couples! Come and do your swinging here!' it seems to say. 'But please take care to dispose of all rubbish afterwards.' That said, it is not my favourite photo out of those I took at Bigbury on Sea during my winter walk there. My favourite photo out of those I took at Bigbury on Sea during my winter walk there is of a lone windswept sheep on the bare hillside above the village, gazing off towards the art deco hotel on Burgh Island as if dreaming of one day staying in its plushest suite.

Now, seven months later, with the island in my sights, I walked down the hill to Bigbury Beach from the car park, then across the tidal causeway, dodging numerous sandcastles and selfie-takers, but by the time I'd waded out

to the island I was alone save for a rockpooling father and his two teenage sons. I removed my T-shirt and reached in my bag for the float my dad had bought me and realised it was still in the car. *That's a shame*, I thought only two-thirds sarcastically. I placed my bag on a rock and swam out eighty yards through gaps in the rocks in a pungent, fishy sea. The tide was coming in and the waves were medium-big, but my front crawl felt strong and effortless and I could sense a solidity and sureness to my shoulder muscles that I had not had the previous summer. But as I rounded the corner to the part of the island furthest from the mainland, I felt an abrupt solitude, and paused. I'd had a lacklustre morning of writing and badly wanted to get round that bend and that other bend beyond it, and feel the sense of accomplishment that went with it, but something was not right.

Here I was again: frivolous me, a non-daredevil non-wetsuit-owning person in five-pound supermarket trunks, but the water didn't give a crud who I was, just like the water didn't give a crud who Jeff Buckley was when he swam into the Mississippi in 1997 in an apparently carefree mood, singing a Led Zeppelin song. What was the difference between being Randy California, the strong swimmer in the Pacific with his son, and Randy California, the tragic, drowned singer? What was the difference between being J. G. Farrell, the comic novelist sitting on a rock on the Irish coast fishing, and J. G. Farrell, the tragic novelist dead before his time? The difference was a tiny moment. Terrible sea stuff didn't just happen far out in open water. My uncle Paul swam less far out on the north

Cornish coast than I was now and got swept away by the tide, and would almost certainly not be still with us had a surfer not spotted him and come to his rescue.

I turned round. I swam back past the rockpooling family and clambered out of the water over slimy, limpet-covered rocks. I walked purposefully across the beach and up the hill. I got into my car, painfully aware I had not wrung anywhere near my money's worth out of the Economy Beach Car Park. I drove away. The interior of the car smelled of damp and crisps, which was entirely logical since when I was in it I was very often damp and eating crisps. Still in my trunks, I went directly to the lido, which like all lidos was originally built to take the place of swimming in seas and rivers and lakes for several reasons, many of which remain valid to this day. I swam forty-six lengths. I didn't feel closer to the earth or my primal self, but I felt good and alive. I noticed a bumblebee on the far side of the deep end. I must have missed it when I got in. I transferred it to dry land, where it shook itself and staggered away. It was a quite large and beautifully furry one – almost fluffy in fact. It had probably been drawn to the water by the glint of the sun on the surface, but it did not have a sense of its own limits.

9

BLACK DOG

Fur and Sherbet

It was a thankless winter's day, a nagging wind was shaking the last stalwart leaves from the trees, and I was trying to find some picture hooks so I could hang a couple of bits and bobs on the walls and make the place feel a bit warmer. I wasn't having any success in the house so I decided to have a look in the garage instead. I hadn't been in my garage for several weeks and, in opening its heavy up-and-over door, managed to disturb a sleeping cat. I'm not sure who was more surprised, me or the cat. We both did a little jump, and the cat escaped through a hole in the back wall. I hadn't been aware that my garage had a hole in its back wall, nor that it had a cat living in it, and both these things made me think I should make an effort to get to know my garage better.

The cat was not one of the four who each sublet a room from me for a non-existent payment delivered on the first of every month but an enormous tabby stray who'd been hanging around in and near my garden for the last few months, spitting cusswords at my three male cats and periodically trying to mount the female one. Going on his tumble-dryer-soft fur and athletic good looks, I'd at first assumed that he was what those who know felines well tentatively call 'owned', but time had proved otherwise: none of my neighbours knew who he was and, as the weeks passed, his 3 a.m. meowing sessions outside my bedroom window had become more keening and forlorn. Despite a vertical white warpaint stripe on his nose he was almost approachable when I first met him, but, mistaking him for a spoilt thug, I'd chased him off a few times, waving the bill for the damage he'd caused to the nose of my own tabby, Ralph. Since then he'd become less sociable but no less ubiquitous.

You can live a relatively lavish life in summer and autumn in this somewhat utopian part of rural Devon if you're a stray cat with a modicum of resourcefulness. After you've picked off one of the endless supply of unsuspecting local rabbits you can wash its innards down with some fresh stream water then conk out for a few hours under a hibiscus while a person clad in sackcloth soothes you to sleep with their biweekly flute practice. But now it was early December. With the temperature dropping and the wind raging, I was glad my feline intruder had found a sheltered place to sleep among rusting golf clubs, old magazines and hardware.

Even at its worst, the wind in the South West never makes your eyes, cheeks and chin sting in that way a winter wind on Britain's east coast will. That said, it had been blowing with the breath of a hundred-headed Celtic demon recently. Branches tapped furiously on my dark office window as I wrote, and the thick granite walls of my draughty single-glazed hilltop house seemed to be all that was stopping it from being whipped up from its foundations and blown over the valley towards Newton Abbot. In the midst of this cacophony, a small alien meow could have the effect of a tiny person sitting in your ear, playing one of history's saddest melodies on the planet's smallest harp.

On the morning that I opened my garage and discovered the stray cat – to whom I'd given the draft name of Uncle Fuckykins, because there was nobody around to stop me and, since he was unlikely to ever be mine, I probably wouldn't be forced to live with the long-term ramifications – the wind was at its most heinous. It was the kind of undignifying wind that makes you hope that nobody you admire sees you while you are standing in it. Only a total idiot would spend any time in such a wind that wasn't totally necessary. So, having left a bowl of food in the garage for Uncle Fuckykins, I got in the car, collected my friend's dog and embarked on an eight-and-a-half-mile walk on a particularly exposed part of the moor. I'd read a bit about the section of the moor in question the night before in a nineteenth-century book. 'This area is sometimes referred to as the Valley of the Thunderstorms,' it announced. *Brilliant!* I thought. *Let's go.*

I had first met my friend's dog, who is called Billy

but sometimes referred to as the Blackberry due to his resemblance to a blackberry, a couple of years earlier on the Internet, which in our amazing modern world is now often the way that dogless men looking to borrow dogs and dogs looking to be borrowed find it convenient to meet. This had been made possible by a site called BorrowMyDoggy. It had taken me a little while to be totally comfortable about admitting I had met my part-time dog on the Internet, but I was OK with it now, and so was Billy. Of course others might have a problem when they found out how we got together, but in the end it was their problem, not ours. Back during the previous decade I'd borrowed dogs from people I had met in real life. There was Nouster, a proud birthday-card Border collie who lived with my landlord and who I'd walk around the two broads near my house in Norfolk. Then there was Henry, my neighbour's cocker spaniel, who liked to roll around in pheasant carcasses and steal chips. But that was a different era and a different universe. Since then the lives of humans and dogs had become more virtual, and different ways to meet dogs had become more acceptable. Every Tuesday I picked Billy up from his owner Susie's eighteenth-century cottage on the edge of the moor. Turning the back-door handle of the cottage was like a trigger that operated an invisible piece of elastic connected to Billy, who would twang towards me from wherever he was in the building, making a series of noises that shouldn't by rights emerge from any animal not made out of rubber by a large corporation. Sometimes two more dogs were there with Billy. These belonged to Susie's daughter Syd, and were older, dignified, sad-eyed hounds of great scruffy beauty, only unnerving to be around for the fact that – despite being unrelated by blood – they looked like tiny and massive versions of exactly the same dog. *We'd quite like it if you walked us too, but we know you can't, and we completely understand,* the been-around-the-block eyes of the calm, wise scruffy dogs said as Billy pogoed the length of my body and yipped like a creature who was shortly about to explode from unalloyed joy and leave nothing but a small pile of fur and sherbet on the cottage's irregular two-hundred-and-fifty-year-old flagstones.

It's not that I wasn't flattered by this yipping and squeaking, which could go on for up to a quarter of an hour. I did feel, however, that it was a little fawning and unearned. My cats curled up on my lap, played inspired paw piano on my chest and headbutted my knuckles affectionately, but that was the result of my willingness to make myself an annexe of their personalities, plus the years of research I'd done into their likes and dislikes: what food to buy them, when to stop buying it and purchase a more expensive kind instead, which knitwear to donate to them as bedding, where exactly behind their ears to scratch them and at what time of day. All I did with Billy was allow him to accompany me on long walks across moors and cliff tops. I'd have been doing the walks anyway, even if he didn't come along, so it was honestly no big deal.

Dartmoor is the only place in Devon where the bite of the wind can almost match its east coast counterpart. As

I climbed past the Nutcracker, a logan stone near Britain's loneliest Christmas tree, to the summit of Rippon Tor, the breeze spun me in a quarter-circle and turned my hair into old, useless bindweed. Beside me Billy sulked slightly, having been put on his lead for the benefit of sixteen semi-wild cattle. Once we were over the brow of the tor I let him off and threw a stick to appease him. He fetched it then guarded it jealously from me in his customary fashion. I seldom put rotting wood between my teeth and had never given Billy any concrete reason to believe that I would steal one of his sticks, but even after knowing me a couple of years, he remained suspicious of my motives when he had one in his mouth. Billy is a black dog, an apt shade for Dartmoor, which is so full

of demon hound legends they sometimes slosh over its sides, but ghoulishness is not really his area of expertise. A toy–miniature poodle cross, he is scarcely bigger than Uncle Fuckykins and possibly a degree smaller when his black curls are slicked down with upland rain. Susie had recently had a terrible infestation of rats, who'd chewed through the bathroom pipes and electrical cables in her cottage. A few weeks ago she'd gone into her kitchen and an especially big one had hurtled straight at her. 'I jumped on a chair and screamed,' she told me. 'I was hoping Billy might come to my rescue but he just jumped on the chair with me and started screaming too.'

As my borrowed black dog and I turned west for Top Tor and Pil Tor, I mentally listed the dark and mysterious moorland legends he might inspire. The best I could come up with were the following.

1. The dark and mysterious legend of how he ran after a cyclist on a path near Ivybridge but then got spooked by some rainbow-jumpered hippy kids listening to dubstep under some trees.
2. The dark and mysterious legend of how he ran away from me and my birdwatcher friend Roy down a deep ravine near Venford Reservoir, yip-squeaking after seeing what he thought was a sheep, and didn't come back for thirteen minutes.
3. The dark and mysterious legend of how a post office receipt fell out of my wallet, and he ran off with it then barked and chewed it when I ran after him and asked for it back.

4. The dark and mysterious legend of how he wove through the legs of three cows in a water meadow, like a tiny idiot.
5. The dark and mysterious legend of how he ran after a black Labrador into a river then thought better of it.
6. The dark and mysterious legend of how he got miffed with me when I dropped him off at home an hour earlier than usual.

Above us, further west, a celestial hole opened up in the clouds, shooting rays down over the ancient stone rows of Fernworthy Forest: as good a spot for a bucolic alien landing as there could be in England. In the valley below, just over a mile away, I spotted the unusually tall, damaged spire of Widecombe church and abandoned my route to turn half-right towards it, remembering the story Mike, a veteran member of the Dartmoor Search and Rescue Team, had told me about Jan Reynolds selling his soul to the Devil there in the autumn of 1638. One of the many commendable facets of selling your soul to the Devil in the seventeenth century was that you'd invariably have to go to a tract of bleak and windswept land to do it properly. Nowadays you can accomplish it far less romantically from the comfort of your own home just by running a corrupt property developing enterprise or writing a hateful column about immigrants or homosexuals for a tabloid newspaper. The Reynolds story is a West Country equivalent of Suffolk's legend of Black Shuck and Blythburgh's Cathedral of the Marshes, in which a real-life violent storm caused damage to the house of God and was blamed on demonic activity. In Widecombe the damage was not caused by a black dog, but by the Devil and his flying horse, who wrecked the church during their journey to claim the soul of Reynolds, a well-known local gambler and church-dodger. As Reynolds was carried off over Birch Tor, he dropped the playing cards he'd been holding, which allegedly left giant imprints on the moor in the shape of the symbols on the cards. Mike has been on the rescue team for a long time, but not long enough to have been actually involved in the attempt to rescue Reynolds from the Devil.

Widecombe-in-the-Moor is even more famous for the folk song 'Widecombe Fair', which is also equine-themed: a tale of a horse theft in the area, along with a list of people going to the fair in question. An argument could be made against the necessity of the list's length. The early-music-influenced psychedelic folk band Renaissance and trippy displaced garage rockers the Nashville Teens both made the song their own in phantasmagorical ways in the early seventies, but the lyrics remain a bit like an old-time folk version of one of those tedious conversations you overhear on a train in which a cocksure young man is speaking into his mobile phone to another cocksure young man and listing all the people he has secured to join them for a night out ('Tom Cobley's confirmed now, and his grey mare – it's going to be sick!'). Behind me where I sat and ate a plate of chips smeared with melted cheese in Widecombe's extremely welcoming Rugglestone Inn were some original 1800s illustrations detailing events at the fair. These were enchanting, although conveyed a strong ambience of 'several people taking advantage of the hubbub elsewhere by sneaking off to have sex with people they shouldn't'.

While I ate my chips I read more about Widecombe in Sabine Baring-Gould's collection of Dartmoor essays *A Book About Dartmoor*. It could be argued that the title of this is similarly overlong. A simple *Dartmoor* would have got the same point across adequately. Nonetheless, I decided to let that go at the time of purchase, as my local branch of Scope had been only asking £2.50 for it. Baring-Gould describes Widecombe as a village 'walled off from the world', but when I climbed one of these steep green walls twenty minutes later all I could see was that hole in the sky and beneath it heather, dead bracken, tussocky grass and large prehistoric boulders: a debatable definition of 'world' but one I was very comfortable with. There was room to imagine so much into existence here. Ascending Buckland Beacon beside a dog apparently made entirely out of knitting material, with that glowing crack in the clouds above and not another human in sight, it was not hard to look back and picture woolly rhino and mammoths trudging across the valley below.

I like to imagine that there was a time when all animals were woolly, not just rhinos and mammoths.

'That snake over there looks exceptionally warm.'

'Yes. That's because it's a woolly snake.'

The colour of the dusk as the walk ended reminded me of the dusk in *An American Werewolf in London* when David and Jack come down off the moor to visit the Slaughtered Lamb pub in East Proctor: smudgy granular

purple-green. As a fourteen-year-old, I recorded some
evening golf highlights on BBC2 and let the VHS tape run
on so it also recorded the first thirty-five minutes of the
film when Alex Cox showed it on the *Moviedrome* series.
Over the next year I watched those thirty-five minutes
more than a dozen times. When I finally saw the rest
of the film, as an adult, I enjoyed it but felt slightly let
down, particularly by its gory ending. I like my horror
to be about the power of suggestion, not blood – another
factor, quite probably, behind my love of Dartmoor. I
amped up that power of suggestion on the way back by
ignoring the classic *American Werewolf* advice to stick
to the path, although this wasn't the most swashbuckling
move, as I remained thoroughly aware of where the
path was the entire time. As a result, every bit of me up
to shoulder height – and a few bits beyond – was mud-
spattered, but that had been very much part of the plan at
the day's beginning. Where is the pleasure in being clean if
you have never got dirty?

A lone set of headlights winked around Rippon Tor in
the distance, and the temperature underwent a drop that
felt like a small old cushion being pulled from beneath
us. We'd done almost nine miles, my hip clicked, my
calves ached, and Billy limped a little on his back left
side. We jumped peaty puddles in unison as if tiredly
choreographed. Multiple gorse perforations incurred on
the climb to Buckland Beacon gave me shin burn. Half
an hour earlier I had been stroking the head of a cheerful
storybook sheep in daylight; now it was abruptly apparent
that this upland was not just the setting for the unwritten

ghost stories in my head, but a place where, if you were tired enough and cold enough and lost enough, you would probably not take long to perish. I was glad to reach the car, to drop Billy off and to fantasise about the hot bath I'd soon plunge into. I nagged myself into making a quick stop at the supermarket on the way home – partly for me, but primarily to get some food of a slightly better quality than normal for my cats, due to the stab of guilt I felt for feeding some of theirs to Uncle Fuckykins. If feeding him was to be a regular event, some prandial hierarchy needed to be imposed. While queuing to pay I checked my phone: there was a message from my dad, who'd found out I was walking today. 'DON'T STAND ON TOP OF ANY CLIFFS IN THE WIND,' he said. 'AND WATCH OUT FOR FOOKWITS AND LOONIES!' I returned the phone to my rucksack. 'Surprising item on the bagging scale,' said a robot a couple of aisles away, calm yet intrigued. In front of me at the human checkout a woman was purchasing a jet-black eel, wrapped in cling film. I was not aware that any supermarket fish counter sold a creature of such size. It was longer than my arm and probably thicker. I felt very unadventurous with my blueberries, crisps and chicken slices.

'Wow!' said the checkout operator to the woman with the eel. 'Is it the cat's birthday?'

'No,' replied the woman.

Terrorist Canoes

That night, after devouring several of the chicken slices, my female cat Roscoe slept on my bed, burrowing purposefully into my side. She'd been doing this a lot since the arrival of Uncle Fuckykins: a period when she'd become a noticeably more clingy indoor being and a noticeably more distant outdoor one. On our way back home to Norfolk in spring 2012, after picking up our new kitten from west London, my girlfriend and I listened to the song 'Roscoe' by the bucolic, 1800s obsessed rock band Midlake. We decided to name the kitten in honour of it. It also seemed vaguely fitting: early signs suggested that the kitten, who had the appearance of a cartoon masked feline supervillain, boasted a scrappy tomboy character, and, having adopted a couple of male cats with female names in the past, it seemed only fair for me to even the score. But it had turned out to be more apt than I could have ever imagined. In the song, Midlake talk about what

a 'productive' name Roscoe is, and Roscoe soon turned into the most industrious of cats: an animal who, when not asleep, had a permanently businesslike air about her, always seemingly involved in some important hedgerow admin or undergrowth-based clerical work. When I was lucky enough to be greeted by her in the garden, her white paws gave the impression that I was talking to someone very industrious who wore running shoes in order to move more quickly to and from meetings. When in the house, during periods when my clothes were drying on radiators, she would go around the upstairs rooms, efficiently pulling each item onto the floor with her stretched-out paws until she found a garment that she deemed sufficiently comfortable to sleep on.

The first six months of our new life in Devon had been a tough time for Roscoe. A dumb, sunny, ginger stray called George, who I took pity on, divesting him of his testicles through a third party and allowing him to live with us, made it his devout mission to dry-hump her at every available opportunity. Horrified, Roscoe – renowned in the past for her take-no-shit attitude with male cats almost twice her size – began to make a series of uncharacteristic escapes. I knew matters had reached crisis point when, one day outside the local pub, my girlfriend and I saw her sitting at one of the other tables, ignoring us and socialising with some rough-looking strangers. George was shipped off to live a life of room-service bliss with my parents that autumn, and a ten-month period followed in which Roscoe really got back on top of her work, cuffing my much larger male cat Shipley into line, crunching on mouse skulls in a practical, unshowy way and patrolling the perimeters of the garden in a manner that couldn't have looked more systematic and industrious if she'd had a tiny carpenter's pencil behind her ear. But since the beginning of the reign of Uncle Fuckykins she'd been nervous and unsettled – even more so perhaps than when George lived here. The only room she was any longer comfortable in was my bedroom. She now appeared to have two modes: asleep next to me or as far from home as possible. Returning from a party on Halloween, I'd been startled to hear a familiar meow behind me on the river path over a mile from my front door and turned to see her scuttling out of the bushes in pursuit of me. Roscoe had always had an unmistakable, panicky sort of meow, which seemed to have never quite fully developed. Here, so far from her usual territory, near main roads and Devonshire techno hippies, the meow seemed doubly insufficient. Shaken to see her in this foreign area, I picked her up, held her tight inside my coat and walked her back to my house, moving off the lane a couple of times to hide in the undergrowth when Halloween revellers came the other way, lest she freak out and escape back towards town.

Something had to be done. But what? Uncle Fuckykins had become just the wrong combination of elusive and ubiquitous: I could no longer get near him, yet he was always around. Ralph, the most alpha of my cats, had chased off other intruders in the past, but he was in early old age now and knew better than to mess with a young hooligan, particularly after that nose injury. As he and I sat on the porch step one day and watched Uncle Fuckykins nonchalantly cleaning a paw beside the garden gate, a sense of helplessness set in, as if all that was left to do was for one of us to call the police. Twice in the four days after my walk on the moor with Billy I had heard Roscoe's anguished alarm cry in the bushes behind the house and found her pinned against walls and fences by the marauding Fuckykins. As she ate, she looked nervously over her shoulder in the direction of the back door, before retreating to my room for periods of up to thirteen hours.

The following morning I was in the living room cleaning up the spleen of a vole killed by Ralph when I heard the bang of the cat flap and saw Roscoe hurry past me and up the stairs. Like many of us, Roscoe yo-yos in weight between the seasons: she's svelte in summer, but in winter takes on the appearance of a black and white bowling skittle, waddling a touch when she picks up speed. But she was moving more awkwardly than usual and I noticed she was drenched, which was odd as, although the ground was wet, it hadn't rained for several hours. I deposited the vole's spleen outside, where it would be soon devoured by jackdaws, and went upstairs, where I found Roscoe beneath the bed in the spare room. I did not look at the large wound on her left side for long, but what I saw was enough to propel me to the cupboard where I stored a couple of large plastic cat carriers, bundle her into one of them and drive to the vets' as fast as possible. In the surgery a junior vet shone a torch into the gash, which I now realised was extremely deep. Roscoe appeared calm, but the junior vet asked me to leave her at the surgery so one of the senior members of the practice could investigate whether there'd been any damage caused to her abdominal wall. Further investigation revealed two more wounds, closer to her tail.

Returning home, I blamed myself. By not acting decisively and trapping Uncle Fuckykins, I had permitted this to happen. I stamped out furiously to the garage, where I found that both of the bowls of food I'd put out were empty, but there was no Fuckykins. Just over an hour later, one of the senior vets at the surgery, Trevor, called. Roscoe's abdominal wall had been severely damaged, and an operation would be needed to repair it. When I told him about Uncle Fuckykins, he sounded doubtful. 'The main wound has all the hallmarks of a bite, probably by a large dog,' he said. 'I don't think even a very big cat could have caused this much damage.' As Trevor said these words, a memory – strangely repressed until now – returned: me waking that morning to the thump of fast, heavy footsteps and a man's impotent, frantic voice behind my garden hedge. 'Oscar! Oscar!' the man had been shouting breathlessly. The meadow beside my house is one where dogs are not permitted, let alone permitted to roam off the lead: an instruction very clearly signposted. I had not connected the two events before but now they seemed too much of a coincidence: the extent of the injury, the wet fur. My undersized, sweet cat had been dragged through the grass in the jaws of a dog belonging to an irresponsible owner. An irresponsible owner too cowardly to come forward and admit what his dog had done. A hit-and-run. How on earth could I find him? I didn't even know what he looked like. And what if I did? How could I prove what his dog had done?

The following day I waited for the results of Roscoe's surgery in a state of total helplessness. Going into the spare room for the first time since I'd taken her to the vet, I saw what I'd not had time to see before: a large bloodstain on the bedding, where she had clearly sat before retreating under the bed. My clothes dried on the radiators in the other upstairs rooms, unvandalised. I set off down towards the river and walked a few miles through the countryside, not knowing what else to do. Late in the afternoon I received a call to say Roscoe had made it through the surgery and was just coming round from the anaesthetic. Now it was a matter of waiting to see if the operation had been a success.

There was one decisive thing I could do while I waited. If Roscoe was going to recover and return home, I wanted to ensure her life was as stress-free as possible when she did. After a few phone enquiries, I drove to Newton Abbot and borrowed a metal cat trap from a lady who worked for Cats Protection. A couple of days later, using some of the brand of cat food I think of as Posh But Stinky, I managed to lure a frantically meowing Uncle Fuckykins into this knee-high prison and transport him to the vets'. Up close he was even more impressive: two thirds tabby, one third tiger. I had never met a more solidly built cat. Upon seeing him, even Sarah, one of the receptionists at the vets', who saw hundreds of cats over the course of the year, was visibly taken aback. In the examining room Fuckykins jumped on my lap and the nurse ran a scanner over him. No price

flashed up for him as she did, but I sensed that, if it had, it would have been extortionate. The surprising news that came back from the scan was that his home was eight miles away, in the seaside town of Paignton.

'He's called Mittens,' announced the nurse.

'You're kidding,' I said.

'Nope. Well, that was his original name, and what we have him down as. But he went to live with a neighbour, and she renamed him Mogs. He's been missing since May. She's had posters up all over the neighbourhood and had just about given up hope.'

Uncle Fuckmittens, as I had now already begun to think of him, was of course by no means unusual in being apparently quite young yet already having had several

300

names. That happened a lot with cats, I found, even when the cat didn't get passed between multiple humans. Cat names have a tendency to evolve like avant-garde jazz. It is unlikely that, by the time of its fifth birthday, the name by which a cat is most regularly known will have any resemblance to its original name. The proud white cat I lived with during my adolescence was called Monty, which begat Ponsenby, which begat the Ponce, which begat Pompous Cat, which begat the Pompidou Centre. Similarly, Roscoe, who was still only three, had become Rosc, then Roscins, then Ruskin, and had often recently been addressed as Anglia Ruskin College. I'm sure Fuckmittens would not have remained Uncle Fuckykins had I adopted him, and I had to admit, as I listened to his traction-engine purr and he padded my thighs, as if trying to extract seven months of missing love from them, I did briefly picture a scenario in which I had and fantasised about some of the new names that might emerge from such a union. It was pure fantasy now, though. He would be incarcerated here for the night before his original owner came to collect him, then, unless he regained his wanderlust, I would never see him again. Thoughtfully, Steph the nurse housed him on the opposite side of the building to Roscoe, who was in no state to be reunited with her former tormentor, even in a purely aural and olfactory fashion.

After I'd said bye to Fuckmittens, I was taken by Steph to say hello to Roscoe in the cage where she was recovering. I'd prepared myself to be shocked by her state, so my shock at seeing the mess her side and rear were in, no longer protected by all that fur, was a fortified kind of shock, but it was still shock. Steph told me the vets were happy with her recovery so far, and I might even be able to take her home in a couple of days. As if to confirm this, a druggy-eyed Roscoe staggered over to me and nutted my knuckle like a loving but essentially violent wino. Two days later, armed with a bag full of cooked chicken slices and a small hospital's worth of medication, I transported her back home, the two drains the vet had placed in her side to take the fluids from her wound still present. I was glad and slightly amazed to have her back in the house, but something didn't feel right. She still seemed like a very ill cat and overnight refused the food I put out for her, sitting plaintively inert beneath the chest of drawers in my bedroom. In the morning I took her back to the surgery, and another vet, Dermot, found that her temperature was very high and the infection had re-entered her abdomen. She would need a repeat operation, and it would be expensive, costing significantly more money than I had in my bank account. Was I sure I wanted to go ahead? Of course I was sure. I would find a way to cover the cost, no matter what it meant for my own future.

What do you do while you are waiting for a phone call to tell you whether an operation to save your cat's life has been successful? I certainly wasn't going to get any work done, so, as before, I walked. It was no sane weather to be out on Dartmoor, but going there felt like the right thing to do. I plotted a route hastily on an OS map still dog-eared and a little soggy from my last walk: six and a half miles, rising steeply from the flat land, past the appealingly named village of Owley, then around the back of the desolate expanse of Ugborough Beacon, returning over its peak. A short hike by my standards, but by no means an easy one.

I entered the edgelands of the moor via one of its most Gothic gateways, beneath the tall Victorian railway arches supporting the London-to-Plymouth line. By my reckoning, by the time I returned the surgery would be finished, and the vet would be due to call. Ahead of me the Beacon was hidden in plumes of occult-looking cloud. Gloopy churned mud slowed my progress, arable winter Devon encapsulated in each footstep. I looked forward to getting onto the high part of the moor, which though much wetter would have better drainage that would make the going easier underfoot.

My phone rang when I was barely halfway to the summit, before I reached the part of the moor where the signal provided by the network became merely a figment of a new planet's imagination. Dermot the vet was on the other end of the line. He was part-way through surgery and wanted to tell me that the infection from the dog bite and the resulting internal damage was even worse than he'd suspected. He felt it best to warn me now, due to the risks involved and the even greater expense. I listened carefully, learning even more about the inside of Roscoe than I had already since last Monday, which was a lot. As I heard about all the damage done to my small sweet cat by the large jaws of a dog let off its lead by a thoughtless owner in a place where it wasn't permitted to be, the rain rat-a-tatted more heavily on my anorak. The two largest segments of darkness in the sky looked like a pair of bullies edging in on what pathetic slither of daylight there was. I looked up towards the moor, two fat droplets of rain ran down my cheeks and I felt like I was in a film scene put together solely to labour the point of what a relentless, remorseless monster winter can be.

I am someone who sometimes struggles with the lack of light in winter, and the more rural you get, the more that lack of light can overwhelm the senses. For many people the tough time is January and February. I can see why: January can feel like fumbling about for comfort in a big unlit hall and feeling only bones, and February tends to come across as an unnecessary extra encore that winter does to please its hardcore fans. But for me it's always December that's been toughest: that sensation, growing more acute as the solstice approaches, of nature locking itself up, of each day being a narrowing wedge carved out of cold black slabs of nothing. This is why we invented Christmas, but Christmas has its limitations as an anti-depressant. I am fond enough of the day itself but am not a fan of forced jollity or environmentally harmful gluttony, which doesn't make me especially well disposed to the build-up to it. Once New Year arrives my spirits begin to turn gradually in a better direction, all the way to April and May, by which point I'm so giddy in the sweet humming air that I want to climb every tree and kiss every bumblebee I lay eyes upon. I've been the same all my adult life, although it took me a while to properly recognise it. I was perhaps more aware than ever of the darkness approaching this year, more conscious of my need to look after myself at the end of a tough year. I'd not been doing too badly until Roscoe was attacked, but the incident spun and tumbled into my recent past and knocked loose a few other bits of pain that I'd tightened up. It is at times like this that you realise just how precarious you are in the depth of winter. What if several other awful incidents happened too? Who was to say they wouldn't? How do people survive through that?

At the end of autumn when these dark wet days were first flexing their limbs I'd visited a pub on Dartmoor with a friend and, apropos of nothing, a man had inflicted upon us an offensive impromptu lecture about the UK's current terrorist threat. We listened to his tiny misinformed viewpoint about the Muslim faith and what he repeatedly referred to as his 'Christian Country' and did our best to change the subject, realising that saying what we actually thought – that he was a dicksplash of medium-large proportions, for instance – would change nothing for the better. I wondered what had made the man obsess about Muslim terrorists on one of the highest parts of the South West Peninsula, surrounded almost entirely by sheep, ponies and moss. Was it those Muslim terrorists you often witnessed sitting about looking shifty in the Bronze Age hut circles at Grimspound, plotting the downfall of Western civilisation? Or perhaps it was the Muslim terrorists you constantly saw paddling down the River Dart these days, in their terrorist canoes, from the river's hard-to-locate source at Cranmere Pool? It was clear that it was the man's very insulation and separation from terrorist attacks that had made him so irrational and fearful. I could not relate specifically to this, but I could in the sole sense that I do often fear winter more irrationally when I'm slightly insulated from it. When I'm at home, protected from winter by a roof and central heating, it seems much more frightening, plays on my mind far more malevolently. This is part of why my method of conquering it is to face it head on. I walk through its gaping jaws, voluntarily, spontaneously, when I should be doing other stuff. When I do, the rain and wind somehow don't seem as scary as they do when they're hammering on my bedroom window at night.

Some might argue that today I had chosen to look winter a little too squarely in the face. Leaving farmland behind and approaching the Beacon, what I saw ahead of me was a dreary, drenched otherwordly landscape of gradually fading visibility. This was by no means the highest, most remote bit of Dartmoor, but when hard-bitten veterans of the national park told me that there was a certain kind of weather you shouldn't be out on your own up here in without an experienced companion and a compass, the scene ahead of me was pretty much what they were talking about. I knew that visibility would only reduce as I climbed, and the already somewhat nebulous paths would become less defined still. You couldn't even call the moisture whipping diagonal lines across my face rain any more; I was walking through the middle of that occult cloud I'd seen earlier. It turned out it was even more occult when you were inside it. In three miles I had not yet seen another human, but ahead of me I spotted two black dogs near a dead tree. Before I got closer and made them out for what they actually were – sheep – my heart skipped a beat; not because I believed they were the Devil's wisht hounds of Dartmoor legend, but because since the attack on Roscoe the sight of any dog had triggered a new unease in me. I could easily have brought Billy out with me today but had chosen not to. With every step of the way I felt more helpless, more angry towards the owner of the dog who'd mauled Roscoe, whose guilt – unless his conscience got the better of him – I would never be able to prove. I hated to think of Roscoe alone, in pain, not knowing why she was where she was. As I pressed on through the mist I was gripped by the conviction that I was walking purely for her. Yes, it might be safer for me to turn back in view of the weather, but this was not about me.

TV's ALF

With each step the cloud around me was getting thicker. Another even more indomitable wisht hound moved across the path ahead of me: a horse this time. That's if it *was* still the path? At this stage I had only the trickle of water running down it as a guide. I was aiming for Squirrel Cross, surely one of the most sarcastic names on the moor, since there could be few less squirrely places in rural Britain than this. I gave thanks for the compass my parents had bought me last Christmas to aid my moorland walks. That brilliant useful compass, sitting back on my desk at home. The cross loomed out of the gloom like an alien totem: half a cross, really, at best, with a worn stone face that reminded me partly of Zardoz, partly,

incongruously, of TV's ALF. Four paths diverged from the cross and I took the first left-hand one, at a slight diagonal. After less than a minute the path vanished. For the next mile I used some kind of path instinct that's probably very primal but also tied to a trust that had perhaps grown out of seven years of completing at least one rural walk per week. I could not have definitively said what I was on was 'footpath', only said that what surrounded it was fairly definitively 'not footpath'. Prehistoric bird shapes swooped in the gloom ahead and a medium gale shrieked its character assassination in my ear.

I'd seen the Beacon scowling at me so many times, dominating the landscape and the A38 between South Brent and Ivybridge, but I'd never imagined it could be this otherworldly and ominous on top, like that one planet people talk about in a sci-fi film which nobody actually goes to because it's nearly devoid of life. The path began to go downhill, a sign that I would be out of here soon. I was surprised to feel a marginal tickle of relief. Earlier I'd had the passing, accepting thought that it wouldn't be such a bad place to die, Ugborough Beacon. But in this lower-altitude spot the mist cleared and the turf around me widened out into what looked oddly like a golf fairway. This was because what I was on was a golf fairway. I knew the golf course. I planned to play it in a couple of months, in another bout of self-punishment. I was almost back. I still had not seen another human.

I drove home, opened my front door, instantly peeled off most of my sodden clothes. Other clothes – clean, warm – hung on radiators, still unvandalised. The phone rang. It was Dermot. Roscoe had woken up from her anaesthetic. He'd done his best for her and she seemed reasonably bright, but there was a long way to go and only the coming days, again, would reveal if the operation had truly been a success. I had been on walks of at least four miles every day since her accident. I remembered the toothache and backache I'd been suffering from for the last fortnight – mysteriously absent for just a few hours but now back with interest. I ran a hot bath, thinking that it was time to rest for a day or two, and also of all the work I had been postponing.

Early the next morning though I set off again, through long narrow crevices in the hills a few miles from my house: red earth paths and water lanes where you could be quiet and alone. Places where silence has a different kind of depth. I knew where I was going, which was to the village of Stoke Gabriel, but it was only when I got to the churchyard in the centre of the village that I realised why I had truly gone there.

Beside the lychgate at the entrance to the churchyard stands a yew tree estimated to be a thousand years old. Its gnarly limbs, some of them held up by wooden struts, twist down around and on top of gravestones, attempting to re-root, as yews tend to, given enough time. In the places where the exterior bark has flaked off, the underlayer is the colour of dried blood. It's a tree of glorious, wise chaos, associated, like all yews, in folklore with everlasting life or at least longevity. I had a couple of much much younger yews in my garden beneath which my oldest cat, The Bear, loved to sleep. The Bear was approaching twenty-one now and almost entirely deaf. I'd become properly aware of the severity of his impaired hearing the previous August when I was sorting myself some cheese on toast and set my kitchen smoke alarm off, causing the other three cats to scatter but The Bear to merely sit at my feet, looking up at me in a way that seemed to say, 'Hello! Erm, did someone call?' I'd felt he was slowing down before my move to Devon, becoming more of an indoor cat, but since being here he'd loved to be outdoors again, and our two years here so far had seemed like a miraculous extension of his long life, during which rain, clear air and sun appeared to be performing a natural spa treatment on his brittle old body. Beneath the yew, he fell into inordinately deep sleeps and woke from them wide-eyed, as if freshly amazed at the grass and trees and hilltop air. I sometimes told myself the yews had a hand in the fact that he was still with me. They'd been associated with all sorts of magic in the past after all, some of it unexplained, some of it debunked. Until the 1800s their branches were laid in coffins and graves for good luck. In the churchyard at Painswick in Gloucestershire during the first half of the twentieth century nobody could understand why there were always ninety-nine small, clipped yews, and any time a hundredth was planted, it would die, until in the 1960s it was revealed that a local scientist was sneaking into the graveyard and repeatedly poisioning the hundredth yew after it was planted. Fanciful non-pragmatic people like me like to think that the reasons yews are often found in churchyards might relate to some kind of earlier pagan,

Druidic activity, but there is no historical evidence to substantiate this. Of course the contradiction of yews is that their sap is extremely poisonous; they are killers who double as dark green saints of life.

Local legend states that if you walk backwards around the yew in Stoke Gabriel churchyard seven times without stumbling 'one true wish will come to thee'. It's the kind of thing I might not have done alone when I was younger, for fear of looking silly in front of a potential passing stranger, but I cared less about looking silly these days, and about who saw me doing it. With the ground bumpy and the late-afternoon, end-of-year light gloopy, the avoiding-the-stumbling bit was surprisingly tricky – especially if, like me, you'd swiftly downed a pint of ale immediately beforehand, at the Church House Inn next door, which was built in 1183, and in whose walls during renovations a few years ago a three-century-old mummified cat was discovered. After I'd completed the seven circuits I decided not to speak or think my wish, being of the opinion that the yew tree, or its supernatural guardian, would be wise and intuitive enough to know, and would feel patronised by having it spelled out in neon. I walked the seven miles home frontway around, aching, with night chasing me all the way. I called Dermot the vet again when I arrived. Roscoe was eating well, her temperature down a little. She was still very sore and weak, but with luck she might be home by Christmas, which was now just six days away.

In a way a vet giving you an estimate on rebuilding part of your cat is a little bit like a builder giving you a quote on renovating your house. A vet can have a good look around your cat, let you know a rough idea of how much your cat might cost to repair, but the vet can never be definite and can't really predict how costs might escalate when the structural composition of your cat is properly investigated. Roscoe's intestines had already been threaded back inside her body and large amounts of muscle tissue cut away. In the second operation more muscle tissue still was cut away. 'There isn't a lot left to work with if we have to operate again,' Dermot's colleague Trevor admitted to me. I had been hesitant about saying anything about Roscoe on the Internet, but I did decide to write something, as she had been a big part of my last two books, and I was aware that lots of my readers felt like they knew her and would want to know how she was faring. Soon after I uploaded my piece I received a message from a stranger who told me that, if Roscoe was to recover, she should on no account be permitted to go outside again. I wondered if the stranger had a rabbit who had got ill from eating cheese and whether I should write to the stranger, at her postal address in the middle of America, with a written warning that I would not allow her rabbit to eat cheese again. But at the same time a miraculous gesture of love occurred: an example of the way the Internet can unnerve you by being dark and weird then instantly show the astonishing kindness of people. Unprompted, several of my readers clubbed together to create a fund for Roscoe's surgery. More readers of the two books featuring Roscoe found out about it and the fund grew. Without it the following few months would undoubtedly have been very difficult for me to survive financially.

As a teenager, the people I most admired were first professional sportsmen, then, as I hit my twenties, they were replaced by musicians and comedians and novelists. Nowadays, the people I most admire tend to work in the medical professions, often for pitifully little money. This feeling was reinforced following the attack on Roscoe. I was aware not all veterinary clinics were as conscientious and kind as my local one and felt blessed to live near it. Another good thing about the clinic was that it was based in the same building as a local brewery, which had a pop-up bar. I did not quite turn to drink during my visits to check on my sick cat, but it was comforting to know the option was available close at hand.

In the fortnight that Roscoe spent in this warm and caring cat hospital the vets and nurses got to know her stubborn yet affectionate character, and became a little more attached to her than they did to the cats who passed through the place more briefly. They became familiar with her passionate headbutts and the special low rumble she made from her nose when she was being especially stubborn. Steph the nurse admitted that, after their works Christmas drinks get-together on the 22nd, a group of the surgery's employees had sneaked off back to the surgery purely to say hello to Roscoe. She had always been by far the most independent of my cats, and I had often taken the view that she was 'usually off happily doing her own thing', but I was surprised how keenly I felt her absence in the house: the little spaces she occupied so resolutely. The way, despite being barely more than half his size, she would smack Shipley in the face with a karate paw when he stepped out of line, and quite often when he didn't. Her low-key love affair with The Bear, which was sometimes expressed on her part by sleeping on his back. Her tendency to walk on her hind legs when she was particularly elated or hungry and wave her paws around as if celebrating a strike in a tiny cat bowling alley. Her unfathomable obsession with damp towels. Her habit of burrowing into my side as I slept, then, when I moved away to try to get more comfortable, doggedly pursuing me to the other side of the bed and burrowing into my side even more forcefully – once even to the extent that I fell off the mattress. I missed all this keenly and clung to the hope offered by her headbutts when I visited her: the hope that it would all happen again.

37 Boobs

On Christmas Eve Dermot the vet called and said Roscoe could come home for a trial period. I had not expected such a privilege yet. Dermot said that although the infection seemed to be clear and the surgical drains in Roscoe's skin had now been removed, there had been a major breakdown of tissue around one of her bigger wounds. I was warned by both him and the nurse who handed Roscoe over that with the stitches out the wound looked 'very gory and gruesome', but they assured me they were happy with the way it was healing. It was not until I got home with Roscoe that I properly had the chance to inspect it, and I was instantly convinced that she had sustained an extra, life-threatening injury in the ten minutes we'd been in the car. It was so much worse than I'd expected: a deep, gouging hole into her interior. I was supposed to rub manuka honey and gel into this hole several times a day. Surely, if I did, I would injure her further? On Boxing Day, when I took Roscoe back to see Trevor, he said he was pleased with the way she was healing. She was healing? The last time I saw something like this, I had been watching a Wes Craven film.

Here, then, was my festive period, 2015: finding stealthy ways to con Roscoe into taking four antibiotics a day, squirting a carefully measured quantity of painkiller over her meals, rubbing ointment into her wounds, getting out – but not for very long – for walks, sitting in her room (which had previously been my office) and watching her wobble over to me – a little more steadily each day – look into my eyes and let out a piercing, bargaining meow. Taking pity on her, I let her sleep on my bed, even though the wound left unsightly stains on the duvet cover. I watched as she stretched herself along the bottom of the radiator and pressed the wound against it, and I worried she would glue herself to it with her own blood. When she moved, the wound made a wet, unpleasant noise. As if in sympathy, I burned myself, sustaining a painful wound of my own – though no doubt not half as painful as Roscoe's – and got ill in a couple of other minor ways. This wasn't ideal, but at least it imbued our time of incarceration together with an extra feeling of solidarity. We went through another honeymoon period: she looked at me in a different way to how she had done before her accident, chatted to me more, appeared to want me for more than my cooked chicken slices and damp towels.

She returned to the vet's, again, three more times, and they told me the wound had shrunk, but I could not quite convince myself it was true. As other cats in the waiting room let out their eclectic meows – stuttering meows, guttural meows, yob meows, spoilt-boarding-school meows, meows that sounded like Morrissey might, if Morrissey meowed – Roscoe remained silent and newly philosophical. *Shush your whining*, her cartoon button eyes, viewed from between the bars of her wicker prison, seemed to say. *You don't know what hardship is. I freakin' live here.* On her final visit she was shown off by Dermot to the whole team, like a rosette that, while technically only attached to one individual, was ultimately for everyone. By this point she had already been showing a new brightness: tumbling across the living-room floor after a catnip mouse, dancing out of my office on her hind legs when I opened the door in the morning, ready to greet the day head on. But it was only a few days after she'd been signed off by Dermot for the final time, antibiotic-free, that I looked at the main wound and let myself believe how much it had healed. I had permitted myself to believe before, when I thought Roscoe's first operation had been a success, then been crushed by the news of reinfection, so I'd wanted to keep my psychological guard double-solid. Now, though, the evidence was incontrovertible: the wound had scabbed over. Her skin had done the last part of this more or less all on its own. *Isn't skin amazing?* I kept thinking. The fur on her bad side would not grow back properly until the spring. For now it was a patchwork of bare skin, stubble, black tufts and scars which, viewed from a distance, gave her an odd look: part Holstein, part cat. But Roscoe had never been vain; she'd always been far too focused on her career.

That nine lives folklore about cats that everyone has heard about doesn't come from nowhere, but I did wonder if a particular single-minded feistiness in Roscoe had been responsible for her recovery. Our honeymoon period of closeness could not last. A new all-indoor Roscoe was not the future. She was a free-spirited cat who thrived on fresh air, grass, hedgerows, small rodents and giving Shipley comprehensive and regular arse-kickings. Roscoe – steel-willed inside and favouring laconic dialogue – was the chalk to Shipley's cheese. A soft-hearted potty mouth from kittenhood, he had got more profane and chatty with age, to the extent that anyone who knew him soon got into the habit of transposing his yob meows into human swearwords. He'd experienced an easy ride recently, not suffering any repercussions for his cussing sessions, but now, back in the garden, back on business and entirely unselfconscious about her new undercut hairstyle, Roscoe zoned in on him and began to make up for lost time.

'Lick my bellstick!' said Shipley.

'Mewew,' said Roscoe, punching him in the face.

'Sweaty furbollocks!' said Shipley.

'Mewew,' said Roscoe, chasing him across the garden until he cowered under a salix bush.

'I kissed a squirrel while it was pissing and I liked it,' said Shipley.

'Mewew,' said Roscoe, knocking him sideways into

one of the yew trees, in the process waking The Bear, who as always looked startled to still be alive.

Shipley was easily the most doglike of the four cats: he was yappy, liked to rush up to new people who arrived at my house and greet them, followed me around a lot and was oddly happy on his back, gently air-flailing his paws like a spaniel I'd seen at the vet while I waited for one of Roscoe's appointments. But in other ways he could never be doglike. If you tried to discipline Shipley, he'd just tell you in no uncertain terms to make love and travel, or begin insouciantly cleaning his bottom. I could craft an argument that he was all the dog I needed in my life. I had never craved a relationship with a pet based

on you being so stroppy to the pet that the pet learned to respect you and not act up around you. But that was dogs all over. Like horses, they also had an innate sense of when somebody was feeling especially unstroppy and tended to like to take advantage of it. While walking in the immediate post-dusk light not far from home around the time Roscoe started going outside again I met an Irish wolfhound called Ted who provided a good example of this. Ted – who I didn't know was called Ted at the time and who seemed more formidable for this fact – had seen me across a field and bounded ahead of his owner, cornering me gruffly by a kissing gate. As he barked and growled at my face, I got the very definite impression that kissing wasn't on his agenda. 'I'm sorry!' said Ted's owner, jogging breathlessly up just in time to stop Ted biting both my legs off cleanly at the knee. 'Don't worry. Honestly, he's a big softie usually.' He introduced himself as Ollie and we got chatting. I told him about Roscoe. Ollie told me that Ted too had recently undergone a large and costly surgical procedure, after swallowing a large stick which tore open the lining of his stomach. 'I've got to be careful now in case he does it again,' said Ollie. 'We can't go through woodland any more, which makes our walks quite difficult.' Ted was now looking up at me in a far more friendly way, and with my new knowledge of his proclivities, I tried to put his earlier threatening behaviour down to a simple case of mistaken identity, prompted by the dark, my largely brown attire and the fact that I am quite thin. But on another level, I knew that Ted *knew*. He had sensed it from a hundred yards away, across a nocturnal field: I was a person who was nervous around dogs.

But I had a dog in my life who liked me, whose small twangy presence I missed and who I'd been neglecting for quite a long time. It had now been over two months since I'd walked Billy. I'd had my reasons, and I knew Susie understood them. I was also sure Billy's canine radar would pick up on my newly raw nerve endings. But by continuing not to walk my part-time black dog I would surely be doing myself a disservice: performing a version on myself of what I'd have been doing to Roscoe had I kept her indoors forever after her operation. At the beginning of March I arranged for Susie to drop Billy off at my house and plotted a new walking route on my OS map: an ambitious one which would take us all the way to Dartmoor from my front door, before turning back a couple of miles to the south-west, where I'd deliver Billy back to Susie's cottage. I could hear Billy's excited yips from many yards away, and I hurried out to check Roscoe wasn't around and to warn Shipley of the poodle's arrival.

'Get back inside, Shipley,' I said.

'Thirty-seven boobs!' said Shipley.

'Come on, or you're going to regret this,' I said. 'You know the two of you tend to clash.'

'I'm giving up wanking!' said Shipley.

'Go on!' I said. 'Quick!'

'Total eclipse of my arse,' said Shipley, skulking off.

Humid Glass Palaces of Dreams
I met Billy and Susie by the gate, and in time-honoured

fashion Billy instantly began to pogo up and down almost the entire length of me. 'I'm sorry, he smells slightly of lamb,' said Susie. 'He stole some yesterday.' I appraised my estranged woollen companion. He was still Billy, and I was still the person he followed eagerly up hills and along cliff tops without a hint of intellectual enquiry as to why it was happening. We said goodbye to Susie and headed out through little copses, newly intoxicating with the first little flush of wild garlic, then along a narrow logging road where all the trees looked like they'd been in a war, before entering soft patchwork farmland where pylons marched in intimidating robot lines towards the coast. A disturbing dystopian hum in the sky battled with a soundless utopian one in the earth. The hedgerows on the paths and lanes were filling up with primrose, yarrow and lady's smock. I made a quick stop at a small, hidden nursery, in whose greenhouses cheeky blackbirds whizzed through the air, expertly negotiating Australian tree ferns and hanging baskets stuffed with crocus and tulip bulbs. The huge greenhouses in this unassuming place which you'd not guess was there from the road save for its sign sent me into rapture each time I entered them, gave me wild and unrealistic fantasies of my green-fingered destiny. Humid glass palaces of dreams. Lofty unthinkable expansions of the greenhouses of the young, horticulturally ambitious grandparents of the 1960s.

We continued towards Buckfastleigh, where the moor sort of starts, but doesn't. Gates seemed stiff with winter's neglect. One of last autumn's hay bales lay wedged in the fence to the left of one: a downhill runaway yet to be rescued. The fence was strong and had succeeded in halting its descent but splintered and bent in the process. I spent hours leaping from and on hay bales as a kid. One summer my dad worked on a farm and stacked them. Unless they've been in close contact with them people underestimate their staggering heft. In 2012 one rolled down a hill a few lanes away from here and crushed the passing van of the former cellist from the band ELO, killing him instantly.

You wouldn't know this in-between land exists, looking up towards the moor from a few miles south on the top of the hill above my house: small routes that don't lead anywhere commercial, where nature smells busy. Because it's always there, hovering at the edge of your vision, and its character continues to define the ground beneath it for miles, Dartmoor seems closer to where I live than it is. It's in fact around twelve miles to get to a part that's high and tussocky and rough enough to call moor. My aim today was simply to reach that bit, nothing more; merely to touch it in the way you touch the end wall of a swimming pool before turning to do the next length.

Knowing Billy's penchant for winding up creatures from other species, including me, I'd learned not to let him off the lead if there was even the slightest possibilty that some livestock might be around, but as we left a field via a sheep-rubbed stile to join a steep rocky holloway, I set him free. Almost instantly he spotted two pheasants and shot off at a fair, scrappy clip. I gave chase then slipped on the steep sharp rocks beneath my feet, bumping down the hill on my back a few yards and scraping a chunk of skin off the region on and around my elbow. I walk so much these days that I tend to average two or three falls a year. Being philosophical, I reasoned that it had been about time I'd got one of them out the way.

The hills here, on either side of the A38, are less hills, more imperious, bolshie organic emerald walls. At the bottom of the holloway I reattached Billy to his lead and we joined a lane then crossed the dual carriageway and climbed the steep path to the ruin of Buckfastleigh church, which can be seen from the main road poking its head up out of the trees atop a steep bluff, as if watching avidly for trouble. The gradient from the main road below is so steep that it made the conflagration that engulfed the church in 1992 absolute hell to put out, the fire engines having to pump water uphill in a vain attempt to save it. This was the second fire allegedly started by Devil worshippers to wreck the church, following another in 1849, and it finished the place off, leaving its open-air vestry a haven for crows, bats and ghosts. The most ominous crows and bats are generally not recognised as individuals, but the most infamous of the ghosts is Richard Cabell, an evil seventeenth-century squire who is supposed to leave his tomb every year on the anniversary of his death and ride across the moor with his pack of Devil hounds. At other times the hounds circle his grave, shrieking in a blood-curdling fashion, and it's said that if you walk around the tomb seven times backwards, Cabell – or worse, even his master the Devil himself – will bite your fingers: more or less the opposite of the alleged effect of doing the same around the yew at Stoke Gabriel. It was hearing the story of Cabell in 1901 that prompted Arthur Conan Doyle to exclaim, 'I am totally having that!' or words to that effect, then proceed to write *The Hound of the Baskervilles*. An electrician called Max told me about the caves under here, which stretch for almost three miles beneath the A38 and contain a freak stalagmite-stalactite which resembles a figure in seventeenth-century clothes and is known locally as the Little Man. Arguably even more unsettling than any of this is the pagoda-like building on top of Cabell's tomb, which was erected by locals to 'trap in' Cabell's evil spirit. Its concrete heaviness and incongruity are scary in a mundane way. A bat might reject the structure on the grounds that it found it too chillingly bland. If you were being kind, you might compare it to one of the less imaginative small-town toilet blocks of the 1960s. I realise its purpose is purely supernatural-functional, but I do wonder if someone could not have gone to the effort to add a couple of nice picture windows or a bit of wisteria?

In scary patches of countryside such as this, which were frequent on our walks, Billy performed a useful function, having a not dissimilar effect to the one a song from the *Saturday Night Fever* soundtrack might have on a night alone in a haunted manor house. *There are an inordinate number of crows gathering here, and I don't like that mortsafe on that grave over there*, you found yourself thinking, then, *Oh! It's all OK! Look! Billy is here, bouncing up and down like a small haberdashery Space Hopper with teeth!* As a black dog, he was a let-down to the mythology of his tribe. You'd be hard pushed to see the church in more frivolous circumstances than at lunchtime on a bright spring afternoon like this one, directly after rain, accompanied by an animal like him. All the same, I still got an inner chill from the place. I did not want to stay around it for too long.

The gradient increased severely on the last part of our hike, and I was conscious of the skin missing from my arm after my fall in the holloway, but I couldn't stop now. I had set out to touch the moor and that is what I was going to do. On the lane near Wallaford Down, Billy found a good stick, one of the crumbly lichen-pimpled ones you get on the tarmac on and near the moor after a storm. As he grinned up at me with it in his mouth he could easily have been saying, 'I am so high right now, man, *on being a dog.*' But I was about to be his buzzkill. At the standing stone below Gripper's Hill, near a similarly ancient-looking standing sheep, we turned for Susie's cottage at Deancombe, a place with its own black dog legend, concerning a seventeenth-century weaver called Thomas Knowles, whose workaholic ghost terrorised his sons until the local vicar threw churchyard earth in his face and turned him into a canine. Thirty minutes later, when I dropped Billy off, he looked genuinely hurt, and even after almost fourteen miles I was left feeling like I'd wussed out. I did genuinely wuss out not long after that, walking into the centre of Buckfastleigh and doing something I'd never done before during a walk: I asked a taxi to take me home. I was looking forward to seeing Roscoe and feeling the contrast of her grudging, hard-earned respect after the unconditional sort I'd been receiving from Billy for the last few hours, but she wasn't around when I got in.

I reminded myself that this was a good thing and ran a bath. I glanced at myself in the bathroom mirror: I appeared tired but had an outdoor brightness around my eyes. A long walk could so often be a strange, exhausting form of rest. I enjoyed lowering my aching muscles into the hot water, though. Afterwards, with considerable relish, I went to retrieve the pair of fresh pyjama bottoms I'd left to warm on a radiator at the start of the day. I located them on the floor, flecked with tiny black and white hairs, a couple of tiny leaves and some dried mud. But that was OK. There would always be other pyjama bottoms. The world was positively overrun with them.

10

DAWN OF THE DAD

My late paternal granddad Ted was an almost constantly grinning man with a moustache, glasses and a large scar which ran across most of the entirely bald dome of his head. Right from when I was very small I'd known that he'd been injured in the Second World War, but it wasn't until later that I asked about the scar's exact origin. 'NO, HE DIDN'T GET IT WHILE HE WAS FIGHTING,' my dad told me. 'TED DIDN'T DO ANY FIGHTING. HE WAS MENDING A PLANE AND WAS IN THE WAY WHEN THE PROPELLER STARTED GOING AND IT CLONKED HIM ONE.'

Maybe there was a point when my dad addressed his dad as 'Dad' but I only ever heard him call him 'TED' or 'TEDWARD'. To me this says as much about Ted's extreme Tedness as it does about the jocular relationship the two of them shared. In my memory Ted is preserved as a human teddy bear: cuddly, circle-faced, dopey, entirely guileless and often found in the woods. But teddy bears are not built to survive alone. In my grandma Joyce my granddad found his complementary opposite: stern and fearful, a woman who once called the police on her own son for putting pennies on a train track close to their house. Joyce's role was to reduce Ted's head injuries to a minimum, remind him not to post his house keys in the letter box at the end of the road or leave loaves of bread on the roof of the car prior to journeys, and, during visits to heavily mirrored buildings, stop him from spending too much time apologising profusely to other moustachioed men with scarred bald heads for blocking their path. Ted's – arguably more significant – role was to shake Joyce out of her naturally pessimistic state of mind with a succession of dancing classes, neighbourhood bonfires, fancy-dress balls, caravan holidays and walking expeditions to the Peak District.

The council house where Joyce and Ted lived for almost their entire married life was on the western edge of Nottinghamshire, close to the Derbyshire border, where a large portion of my family have resided for the best part of the last century and where our lives have been flavoured by a bucolic yearning for our taller, more attractive neighbouring county. My grandparents were part of a new generation of ramblers who went to the Derbyshire part of the Peak District in the 1950s and 1960s as a weekend escape from their factory jobs, freed by the greater access to the countryside opened by the Kinder Scout Trespass in 1932. 'MARVELLOUS!' my granddad would say upon rounding a corner and getting a view of Dovedale or Milldale or Chatsworth. 'JUST MARVELLOUS.' Ted was one of that last tribe of men who managed to make driving through Britain at weekends a hobby without being a speed junkie or petrolhead. When Shell and their contemporaries put together countryside guidebooks aimed at touring motorists after the Second World War, my grandparents were the kind of people they were thinking of. But when my dad was a kid the area where they lived was still fairly rural itself too – enough to be a fertile foraging ground to satisfy my granddad's wood obsession. One day in the mid-fifties word spread around the neighbourhood that the big oak tree at Tommy Thompson's farm had come down in the storm, and my granddad and his dad – also named Ted – immediately grabbed a two-man crosscut saw and headed up there. The bus stop you waited at to get the number 32 into town was beside a pen containing a neighbouring farm's large and angry bull. The high-rise flats at Balloon Woods, a quarter of a mile away, had yet to be built, and my dad and his gang, led by his older cousin Flob, made dens and fires in the woods and put coins on the train track, hiding nearby and cheering as trains wooshed by and squished the bronze flat. Venturing further into the wilderness in the direction of Trowell, he and another kid from the same council estate, Jim Spurgeon, found what they thought was an abandoned house but which, when they entered it, contained a Gypsy family dressed in rags. 'I WAS REALLY SCARED, BUT I SHOWED THEM MY KNIFE AND THEY WERE REALLY IMPRESSED,' my dad told me.

On a summer's day early in the second decade of this century, many years since I'd last visited this area, I met my dad in the Co-op car park around a mile from my grandparents' old house. 'I'M NOT WALKING WITH YOU IF YOU WEAR THAT,' my dad said, pointing to the straw hat on my head, a prized item of headwear I'd purchased from a car boot sale in Lincolnshire for three pounds. After that we said hello and began to walk south in the direction of Wollaton Park. My dad pointed to a 1980s housing estate on our left named after a famous ice-skating duo where, for a very brief time more than twenty years ago, my parents rented a two-bed semi. 'THAT WAS ALL WASTE GROUND OVER THERE IN THE FIFTIES AND SIXTIES,' he said as we turned into the estate. He pointed to some houses on our right. 'THE CANAL USED TO BE THERE, BUT IF I WENT AND PLAYED NEAR IT I COULDN'T TELL YOUR GRANDMA BECAUSE SHE SAID I'D GET POLIO. WHEN THEY DRAINED IT THE O'DOHERTYS TOOK LOADS OF TENCH, BREAM AND PERCH HOME AND PUT THEM IN THEIR BATH. SEE THAT MANHOLE COVER? THEY WOULD HAVE HAD THAT OFF IN SECONDS JUST TO SEE WHAT WAS UNDERNEATH. WHY DO PEOPLE HAVE PERSONALISED REGISTRATION PLATES? WHEN THEY DRIVE PAST ME I ALWAYS WAVE AT THEM SO THEY KNOW I RECOGNISE THEIR IMPORTANCE AS PEOPLE. JIM SPURGEON WAS VERY ADVANCED FOR HIS AGE. AT OUR SCHOOL WE DIDN'T HAVE SEX EDUCATION. WE HAD HIM INSTEAD. HE TOLD ME HAVING

AN ORGASM WAS LIKE HAVING A HUNDRED CHRISTMASES AT ONCE.'

When my dad starts talking about his childhood, all you can do is quickly hitch your trailer to the back of the juggernaut and hope that some of it – maybe, say, a wheel and the number plate – is still in one piece by the end. Except, technically, there is no end. When my mum or I ask my dad to stop telling a story we generally do so not because we aren't interested in the story but because we know that if we don't, the story will just segue into another story, and another, and eventually the whole history of the universe will be told through the prism of Jeff Spurgeon, the O'Dohertys, Joyce, Ted, the less salubrious end of Wollaton and the Bilborough estate. My mum likens the way he talks to the way a man with two brains might talk, or someone acting as a translator for his own words, but translating in an odd, rarely sensical way that in fact creates a mild form of oral abstract art. I grew up with the tendency to speak in the slightly hushed, reticent voice of my mum's side of the family, which constituted a genetic development against the odds, since both sides of my dad's family were unusually loud. When my mum and dad first got together in the 1960s and they and Joyce and Ted drove to Derbyshire for a weekend walk, the noise would frequently get too much for my mum, and she would have to tell them she had a headache and needed to be silent for a while in the hope that they might be too. During Christmas 1985 Joyce talked at my nan so much that my nan had to excuse herself to visit the toilet, where she quietly vomited. At Ted's funeral my dad chose not to employ a vicar and took charge of the ceremony himself. Had he not been told it was time to stop, I got the sense the eulogy could have gone on indefinitely and might still even be taking place right now, fifteen entire years later. During my dad's speech, which praised Ted's boundless good nature, gardening skills and enthusiasm, my grandma shouted, 'I can't hear you!' at my dad, which, in its way, felt just as fitting an addition to the day as the decision to play Bing Crosby's 'Accentuate the Positive' when the coffin disappeared. I have no recollection of my granddad saying a negative word against anyone during the entire twenty-seven years that I knew him. I'm sure he wouldn't have had any criticism of my dad's eulogy and would have thought the length and volume of it just marvellous.

My grandma and granddad's council house, which they moved into at the beginning of the 1950s and vacated in the mid-1990s, appeared unchanged when my dad and I wandered past it on our way back towards Balloon Woods from the Co-op. After walking through the new estate and the old site of Wollaton Colliery, we'd hooked around the other side of Bilborough, where women in their forties used to shout, 'Sod off back to your end!' from their doorsteps at my dad and his gang if they ever strayed there. My dad stopped to point out the exact spot in his old road once occupied by a squashed frog that he'd told the other kids on the road was a monkey, charging them a halfpenny each to have a look at it. He then pointed to a spot on the pavement where Terrence O'Doherty had writhed in a violent ball with a greaser from a rival neighbourhood until my grandma

broke the ruckus up by striding over to them, eyeing them flintily and asking if they were 'making love'. Across the road the allotment where my granddad grew his vegetables had now been concreted over. Next to the garages that had replaced it was the O'Dohertys' old place, where my dad once lifted up a sofa cushion and found a writhing nest of pink mice. Eric, the one of the nine O'Dohertys with whom my dad was friendliest, was enlisted to help my granddad mend his Wolseley and my dad was jealous. At a similar time, around his seventh birthday, my dad was challenged to a fight by the oldest O'Doherty, Elizabeth, who was thirteen and in my dad's words 'FOOKIN' ENORMOUS'. He was soundly beaten. 'THE WHOLE AVENUE CAME OUT TO WATCH. IT WAS BECAUSE THERE WAS NO TELLY IN THOSE DAYS.' Remembering this and looking at his old front door, my dad was quiet for no more than a fraction of a second but enough for it to be noticeable and for the air to turn wistful. 'DID I TELL YOU THAT WHEN I STARTED SCHOOL YOUR GRANDMA BOUGHT ME THIS ABSOLUTELY MASSIVE SCHOOL UNIFORM SO IT WOULD LAST ME THE WHOLE FIVE YEARS I WAS THERE?' he asked me. 'FOR THE FIRST TWO YEARS I LOOKED LIKE DAVID FOOKIN' BYRNE IN THAT TALKING HEADS VIDEO.'

When I used to arrive at my grandparents' house, the first object to greet me was an imposing grandfather clock dating from the mid-1800s. My granddad bought the clock for next to nothing in Nottingham in the late 1940s. Not yet being a driver, he somehow managed to lug the clock, with the sole help of his brother Ken and a wheelbarrow, all the way up the steep slope of Sherwood Rise, on the edge of the city, back to the house where he and Joyce lived before this one: a distance of over two miles. At my primary school, in assembly, we often sang Henry Clay Work's 'My Grandfather's Clock'. Its opening line, about the clock being too large for the shelf, always confused me. Only a fool – a fool much much more foolish than even the kind of person who'd choose a wheelbarrow to cart a clock two miles home – would have attempted to put a gigantic bastard such as this on a shelf. Then there was the bit in the song about the clock being taller by half than the old man himself but weighing not a pennyweight more. My granddad was only of average height and his clock had a few inches on him, but he'd have to have been a remarkably short, overweight grandfather with a very tall clock – one you'd be even less likely to try to put on a shelf – for the maths to make sense. Not far from my granddad's grandfather clock there were some notches on a doorway made where he and my grandma had periodically recorded my height: these moved more slowly than I'd have liked them to then remained static at around 5 feet 6 inches, not because I stopped growing at 5 feet 6 inches but because, like most adolescents, during the period when I rapidly gained height I was too truculent to wish to have such progress recorded for posterity on an architrave. I often wondered if I'd end up as tall as the grandfather clock, but I didn't quite make it, as I can verify by standing next to it in its current home, my parents' hall. One shiftless afternoon when my dad was in his early teens, he reached up to the top of the clock and found a set of explicit playing cards hidden there, which ultimately led to his sexual awakening and that of several other boys in the neighbourhood. When my parents inherited the clock, they did not inherit the playing cards, whose whereabouts remain unknown.

If you strolled straight on past the grandfather clock further into my grandparents' house – without being distracted by the playing cards – you'd end up in the kitchen: a culinarily austere room which always smelled of pepper and in whose adjoining larder my grandparents always kept a can or two of what they called 'pop' – usually ginger beer or lemonade or, in later years, shandy from the Co-op, in cans that, though still in date, had mysteriously already acquired a faint patina of age – waiting for me. My mum remembers entering the kitchen on her first ever visit to the house and discovering my granddad wearing a party hat while washing the dishes. Since it was not Christmas and hadn't been anyone's birthday, she thought this slightly odd. My dad later explained that making Ted wear the hat was Joyce's scheme to curb his habit of leaving the immersion heater on for long and financially injurious periods of time. If Ted glanced in a mirror and noticed he was wearing the hat or reached up to his head and found the hat there, he'd know the immersion was still on.

If you continued through the kitchen into the backyard, past a small veg patch additional to those on Ted's allotment, whose soil was always rich and evenly hoed, you reached Ted's shed. In here was every tool imaginable, all meticulously organised: drawers and shelves of screws and nails, ordered by size: hardware for every emergency – a collection devoted to the art of mending rather than making. My granddad knew precisely where every bradawl, spanner, socket wrench, trowel and ratchet was in his shed, yet somehow never got quite accustomed enough to the location of the upper shelves not to repeatedly bang his head on them.

My own most memorable first-hand encounters with my granddad's legendary doziness include the time he caddied for me on the local golf course and, arriving on the second tee and reaching for my driver, I found the flag from the first green sticking unceremoniously out of my bag. This occurred during the same year that he sent a Christmas card to my parents reading, 'To Joyce and Ted. Happy Christmas! Love from Joyce and Ted.'

My granddad didn't play golf but was very enthusiastic about my decision to take it up, as he was about all the numerous sporting activities of my early teens. Seconds after I'd watched the tiny, unconventional Ian Woosnam – more terrier than sportsman – sink the putt to secure his unlikely victory in the 1991 US Masters tournament, my parents' phone began to ring. I picked up, wondering who it could be at this time, past midnight, when my mum and dad were in bed. I said a nervous, quiet hello in the voice of the women on my mum's side of the family. 'DID YOU SEE THAT?' my granddad said. 'BLOOMIN' MARVELLOUS. AMAZING. MARVELLOUS. WHAT A MAN!'

My dad and I crossed a couple of roads and headed towards Balloon Woods, where a large estate of bungalows stood and there were small paths – jitties and twitchells, as I grew up calling them, and still do, much to the bewilderment of anyone from south of Burton upon Trent – with a profusion of signs asking people to clean up after their dogs. 'NOBODY USED TO WALK THEIR DOGS IN OUR ROAD IN THE FIFTIES,' my dad said. 'THEY JUST LET THEM OUT TO RUN AROUND THE STREETS FOR A BIT INSTEAD.' I have a memory of walking up here as an eight- or nine-year-old, when the high-rise flats were still up, and coming across a playground with broken swings, a leaning roundabout that looked like it had been hot-wired by joyriders and crashed, and shattered glass all over the tarmac: a dystopian vision I shied away from even as a child with a nagging need to climb any new structure that looked even vaguely fit for the purpose. My dad and I looped around the identikit one-storey houses now standing on the site of the playground, passing a woman in a garden arguing into her mobile phone with a man called John who she accused of not doing his share, and climbed onto a footbridge over the railway. My dad looked down the track and remembered the time my grandma had jumped up and down on another footbridge not far from here, part of the old Black Path, now demolished: a tiny figure pogoing in rage a couple of hundred yards from where he and Jeff Spurgeon stood in readiness for a train with their coins, shouting to them that she knew what they were doing and was going home to call the police. Jeff Spurgeon's dad died that year, along with two of the other dads on the avenue. 'I SPENT THE NEXT YEAR

TERRIFIED THAT MY DAD WOULD DIE, EVEN THOUGH HE SEEMED PERFECTLY HEALTHY,' my dad said. I noticed that exactly next to where he stood 'mick' had serendipitously been scrawled on the bridge in blue paint by a graffiti artist. My dad was christened Michael, but Mick is the name he prefers and the name by which friends and family know him. When my dad meets posh people he has noticed that they often don't wish to call him Mick even though that is what he has introduced himself as; they opt, without his permission, to call him Michael or Mike instead. But in my mind Michael and Mick are very different people, and Mike is

somewhere way off in a different name galaxy, doing his own thing in tinted spectacles and a leather jacket with rolled up sleeves. My dad is Mick. My granddad called my dad Mick, but my grandma tended towards Michael, especially when she was angry or telling him not to do something, which was often. My grandma was not posh, but her voice had a memorable eloquence and authority to it, like it was always coming at you through a speaker or down a brass tunnel, almost like an East Midlands version of the voices you heard on old news broadcasts. A voice that is now extinct.

A place name that comes up repeatedly in my dad's stories of his childhood is Jacko's Oller. When he spoke of it while I was growing up it formed in my mind as many different things: a deep hole of magical Lewis Carroll properties, a grassy warren teeming with feral Brylcreemed children, a shout of such volume and force that it had stayed suspended in the air above the edgelands of west Nottinghamshire since 1956. What it actually constituted was a large depression in the land formed of the remains of ancient bell pits, clay pits and small open-cast mines. The 'Jacko' referred to an early patriarch of the Jacksons, a family of farmers and coal merchants who thrived in the 1920s but had died out by the early 1960s. My dad remembers that within minutes of the hearse carrying the last of the Jacksons from the farm, local Teddy boys descended on the place and began illegally disassembling its roof. When my dad clashed with my grandma, Jacko's Oller was where he escaped to run around with his Davy Crockett rifle and re-enact the Winning of the West. A few years later he and his mates played cards with the area's Gypsies, who always took their money, and he and Flob made fires and dens. Fires were everywhere: under the tripods and vanners where the gypsies cooked their meals, in the farmland, near the dens, even on the canal when it iced over in 1963, the coldest winter of the twentieth century. Woodsmoke as ubiquitous as air. Sometimes the gang ventured bravely further west, across the Wild Frontier into Derbyshire, and attended the fair in Ilkeston. 'CAN YOU IMAGINE IT?' my dad asked, still staring down the railway line in that direction. 'BEING FOURTEEN. WITH FLOB AND HIS GANG, IN THEIR TED JACKETS AND DRAINPIPES. HANGING OUT WITH GIRLS AND HEARING ROY ORBISON FOR THE FIRST TIME. IT WAS INTOXICATING.'

I try to remember instances when I have witnessed my dad being quiet for several continuous minutes, apart from when he has been asleep, and it takes some effort to do so, but something does spring to mind: the times in my teens and later when he and I visited my grandma and granddad. 'WE CAN'T STOP FOR LONG,' my dad would say as we arrived, sometimes because we couldn't but also to pre-emptively put a time limit on my grandma's stories. We would turn right at the grandfather clock and sit in Joyce and Ted's living room and listen as Joyce, with Ted as her backing vocalist, updated us on stuff that had happened to people we had never met in rooms we had never set foot in: the 'crumpet' my granddad flirted with every month at the over-sixties dance in Sandiacre, Agnes and Roy's caravan at Rutland, the teenage singer they'd seen at the pub in Stapleford in the talent competition who I really should write about for one of my music magazines, the escape and return of Irene's tortoise. My dad, being a man with two brains, was able to take it all in even when he looked like he wasn't, but I could feel his unease at my grandma's domineering conversational manner, the way it took him back uncomfortably, as well as comfortably, to places in his past. He was the same as his parents in that he was loud and liked the countryside and went to the library a lot, but he was different to them in many other ways: he'd decided, not unlike many young working-class people in the mid-1960s, that he wanted a bit more out of life. Unlike Ted, who was frequently known to salute when visiting his GP, he did not retain a huge amount of respect for authority figures. He had ideas above his station, which again was very unlike Ted, who if he had developed an idea above his station would no doubt have asked around to see if anyone more middle class than him would like to use it. By the time my dad was fifteen he was doing three different jobs, travelling to Europe alone, hitchhiking to Brighton to watch mods and rockers fight, learning the trumpet and going out with a girl six years his senior. 'I DECIDED I DIDN'T WANT TO BE A SKINNY LAD OFF A COUNCIL ESTATE; I WANTED TO BE A BLACK MUSLIM JAZZ DRUMMER,' he told me. He failed to fulfil this ambition but, alongside my mum, who he met at seventeen, fulfilled another, which in the context of his relatives was outlandish enough: he became a teacher. The two of them then did what Ted and Joyce had never considered doing even at that point later in life when they finally could: they purchased their own house. As if that wasn't enough, they cooked moussaka and wore Afghan coats and saved up to buy prints of art featuring naked European women. But my parents, just like their parents before them, faced barriers against what they wanted to achieve: of income, of self-belief, of class, and, like anyone, of luck. Barriers they've made a huge effort to stop me from facing too, but which a wider appreciation of society has since made me realise I have faced, if on a smaller scale. Sometimes the barriers are always there; they just diminish a little with every generation.

With their greater ambitions, my parents got closer to Derbyshire than their parents, but they didn't quite make it all the way. It remained the place where you walked at weekends but could never actually live: the impenetrable Fairytale Hill Kingdom. My dad returned from their walks and painted intricate watercolours of its dales and stone barns and ash copses and ruffian sheep. Three times we moved to houses which teetered tantalisingly on the wrong side of the border. Around the most southerly of these, in fields less than an hour's walk from Jacko's Oller that looked not dissimilar to how my dad's old stamping ground had looked twenty-five years earlier when the developers were yet to move in, I began to live an early adolescence not all that dissimilar to his: I joined a gang, loitered a lot, spat on pavements unnecessarily. Although I'd spent the first decade of my life in the countryside, I'd arrived there from a brief spell in suburban south Nottinghamshire and the children in the village seemed simultaneously unsophisticated and dangerous. They sniffed glue and had fist fights, but many of them also sang in the church and baled hay at weekends. Some of them stole valuable items from houses and schoolrooms but they also invited me to scrump and play knock-a-door run with them. We scrumped less inventively than my dad and his gang, who, inspired by a Bash Street Kids caper from the *Beano*, had eaten the apples where they hung, leaving dozens of cores dangling surreally from the trees. My grandma only ever allowed my dad to see the *Beano* after it had been read by his uncle Frank, who at the time was in his early forties.

Ted liked to visit us in the village because we were geographically much closer to him and Joyce than we'd been before and because a lot of horses were ridden on the lanes nearby and he could stop his car behind them, get his shovel out of the boot and load up with their manure for his allotment. A tall, broad girl – the sister of one of my classmates – who rode one of the horses was known to everyone as Dosser. It wasn't until three years later, shortly before I left the village, that I found out her name was Charlotte. About eight of us, including Charlotte, regularly played a game called churchy, which was exactly the same as dobby or tag, save for the fact that it took place in the churchyard. Down by the canal and in the woods there were always torn-up pages of porn magazines. Who left them there? Nobody knew, but the phenomenon was so common that nobody posed the question. A stray boob in a tree or half a bellend in some bulrushes was commonplace, and after a while slightly anaesthetising, like our own early outdoor version of going online. Looking to broaden their horizons, a few of the lads in the village rode their bikes a couple of miles to the M1 services at Trowell and played the fruit machines or looked longingly at exotic teenage girls from Watford and Selby and Market Harborough and Pontefract who were in the midst of bisecting the country with their families.

I loved football at this time and, inspired by the 1986 World Cup in Mexico, played a lot of it with the other kids in the village, but I also had whooping cough, so my main contribution to matches was the meagre, sluggish one of a donkey with surprisingly deft footwork. I laughed along with everyone else as they poked fun at my painful comedy honks, periodically decamping to the side of our makeshift pitch to throw up. One week in 1988, when the road through the village was closed so Ken Russell could film his BBC adaptation of D. H. Lawrence's *The Rainbow*, we moved our pitch to the tarmac, then, when we tired of Maradona scissor-kick re-enactments, staged running races along it: our own village Olympics. I won one of the sprints, ee-awing absurdly away as I crossed the makeshift finish line, which Dosser had fashioned from some baler twine. Then I threw up. Lee had heard that a sex scene in *The Rainbow* was going to be filmed in the village hall and told me and Rocker that Imogen Stubbs, the actress playing Lawrence's heroine Ursula Brangwen, had outstanding jugs, so the three of us sneaked up to the back window of the hall and Rocker climbed on some crates but he slipped and we heard one of the ADs or grips emerge from the front door to see what the commotion was. One of us, I can't remember who, shouted, 'Run!' and we did, but later, after I'd thrown up again, Rocker said the window had been blacked out so we wouldn't have seen any pretend television sex even if we hadn't been rumbled.

'Anyway, jugs aren't that important. They're not the best part of a woman. They're what you like when you're younger and you're not a proper man yet. You two will understand soon,' said Lee, who was almost two years older than us and just approaching his fifteenth birthday.

For the next few years the ghost of Lawrence – the laureate of Nottingham–Derby border struggles – seemed to stalk my parents and me. The last of my mum and dad's three Nottinghamshire–Derbyshire border houses – the only one not ruinously beset by structural issues relating to a nearby mine – could not have been situated more squarely in the middle of Lawrence's quintessential landscape, overlooking the ruined abbey from his short story *A Fragment of Stained Glass* and only a stone's throw from the star-crossed reservoir from *Women in Love*. Lawrence – whose real name was David Herbert Richards – grew up a couple of miles down the road, in the town of Eastwood, where joyriders often hot-wired the cars that they later set fire to in our lane. Not long after Christmas 1993, after my mum and dad had signed the tenancy contract on the house but not yet moved in, my dad excitedly drove there through the snow, alone, with a canvas and a selection of paints, then sat in an unheated bedroom and painted the freshly whitened valley which rolled down from the house then rose to the woods: a scene by far the most Almost Derbyshire one he had ever lived amid. After years as a supply teacher he had just got a permanent job teaching at Greasley Beauvale Primary School, where Lawrence had once been a pupil. One lunchtime not long after that, my dad came out to the school car park and found the janitor taking the back off a huge, sturdy Victorian cupboard. He asked what the janitor planned to do with the cupboard. 'It's going to t' tip, me duck,' said the janitor. Built beautifully from pitch pine, with a pleasing liquorice quality to its grain, the cupboard had previously resided in Lawrence's old classroom. Later that week I helped my dad carry the cupboard into a borrowed van then into our house. The cupboard moved again in 1999, to my mum and dad's next house in the north-east of the county, and has been in their living room ever since. It is known as Dave's Cupboard. Shortly after Dave's Cupboard was acquired, my dad wrote a children's story, submitted it to a national prize committee and won, subsequently signing with the literary agents Pollinger, who were best known for handling Lawrence's estate. This eventually helped to pay his and my mum's rent, which went to the Barber family, who for centuries had owned the local mines, and whose dynasty appeared in not vastly disguised form in Lawrence's novels.

When my dad visited my grandma and granddad and announced that, after two and a half decades of trying and failing to do so, he was going to have his work published, Joyce's immediate reaction was to open her purse and produce a sheet of Basildon Bond writing paper on which was scrawled a few lines of verse. '*I've* written something too,' she announced, handing the poem to my dad. Ted said he thought the fact that my dad had been published was marvellous.

I've listened to a fair bit of Lawrence on audiobook in recent years and discovered that this is a useful hobby to take up if you regularly wish to sink into a deep trough of despondency on long car journeys. I find him much more depressing than Thomas Hardy, perhaps because Hardy's books don't take place in intellectual and topographical terrain that is so palpably an echo of where I lived. I got about halfway through Lawrence's 1913 novel *Sons and Lovers* while driving from Devon to Nottinghamshire in early 2016 but had to break off from it just to remind myself that life contained a flicker of hope. I want to read more of his writing though, as the north-west Nottinghamshire pit country he describes is incontrovertibly a part of me, and helps me understand some of the geographical factors that make me who I am. I recognise an earlier version of a very particular Nottinghamshire world view and way of speaking in his books: a geographical nearliness, a rigid knowing of your station, a tone that can come across as grudging even when it isn't. Back when I lived in East Anglia I met the nature writer Ronald Blythe for not much more than an hour and didn't tell him where I was from, but clearly he picked up on my Almost Derbyshire aura. 'Tom is tall, dark and thin and looks like he has escaped the denouement of a D. H. Lawrence story,' he wrote later in his column for the *Church Times*.

After abandoning my Lawrence audiobook and arriving at my parents' current house, hanging my coat in the hall opposite Ted's grandfather clock and drinking tea overlooked by Dave's Cupboard, I went to bed, knocking my glass of water all over my clothes and mobile phone as I switched off the bedside lamp. The following day my dad and I set off on another walk along the wrong side of the Derbyshire border, in the countryside around Eastwood, Greasley and Moorgreen. Before we left, my mum, who, along with my auntie Mal and uncle Chris, had decided to join us, sat down with me to discuss the route. My dad went upstairs, returning a couple of minutes later with a pile of watercolour paintings. He handed me the top one.

'What's this?' I asked. The painting depicted two well-loved children's book characters walking through a dark

underpass hand in hand while three grotesque, hatchet-faced men in trenchcoats loitered on the other side.

'IT'S WINNIE THE POOH AND PIGLET ABOUT TO BE ASSASSINATED,' my dad said.

'Is it one of yours?'

'YEAH.'

He handed me the remainder of the paintings and I browsed through them. There were about a dozen in total: all works in progress, mostly of a madcap or macabre nature. One featured a bearded man on a wooden cross with a not-displeased expression on his face, surrounded by people in tunics wielding sticks with feathers attached.

'Does this one have a name?' I asked.

'YEAH,' he said. 'THAT'S *THE TICKLING TO DEATH OF JESUS*.'

My dad went outside to fetch some wood and I continued to look through his art. He'd always painted, as far back as I can remember, but he'd been working particularly hard since being semi-retired, and his style had developed a new freedom. This was very different material to the Derbyshire landscapes he had painted when I was a child. Here were disco dog walkers, nightmare medieval murder scenes in complex mirrored formations, Spiderman handing spare change to a busker, a bank of feline gods staring down in judgement at the grotesque figures presiding over a pedigree cat show. I was so mesmerised that time must have briefly frozen, and when I looked out the window after what I thought was four seconds, my dad was 200 yards away, wrestling a log near the small river that runs behind his and my mum's house. Seemingly another four seconds later, he

was back inside, one hand full of kindling, the other full of chocolate. When my dad was young, Ted would regularly take him and eight or nine other boys over to Balloon Woods and Jacko's Oller to forage for logs, then bring the wood back with one boy on the end of each log. Almost sixty years later the only things that had changed were the location and that my dad generally worked alone.

'He's always got a load of wood in his hands,' my mum said. 'I ask him to wash them but he forgets. There are black marks all over the walls and banister. The chocolate is worse. I saw a big smear of it in the middle of the novel he's reading. He said it's his bookmark.'

I pictured a different abode, in a parallel dimension, where my dad lived in solitude, unmarried: a remote, dirt-floored shepherd's hut strewn with spilt paint, rabbit carcasses and Yorkie Bar wrappers. The embers of a small fire burned outside, arcane pieces of masonry scattered around it.

The phone rang, and my mum picked up. It was my auntie Mal, wanting to know what the plan was for the walk. My mum handed the phone to me, and Mal and I agreed on a basic five-mile route, with a four-mile epilogue just in case we felt ambitious. 'Then those who feel like going all the way can,' said Mal.

'OOH MISSUS!' said my dad, who'd clandestinely picked up the other receiver and been listening in.

Clandestinely picking up the other receiver and listening to conversations has long been a habit of my dad's. One time my mum was telling me about a life-drawing class she'd attended at which their village postman turned out to be the model. Just as my mum reached the story's climax, my dad, via the other receiver, chipped in: 'EVERYONE RECOGNISED HIM BY HIS SACK.'

Unlike the Peak District, the area around Eastwood

has never been renowned Walking Country, and unsurprisingly we passed no other ramblers on our route, but on the outskirts of Kimberley we were joined by a few men in tracksuits with dogs. We took a short cut across a small park, and a black Labrador barely out of puppyhood gleefully nudged a red ball along beside us. 'LOOK OUT FOR THIS BASTARD,' my dad advised us. 'IT WILL HAVE YOUR FACE OFF.'

Mal and I suggested that my dad was perhaps being unnecessarily negative.

At Greasley church my mum, Mal and Chris and I stopped to look at the churchyard's burgeoning snowdrops and ancient yew tree, and at the gravestone of Millicent Shaw, who was crushed to death in the middle of a populist crowd frenziedly rushing to attend a local hanging in 1844. My dad pointed to the adjacent lay-by. 'WE HAD OUR HUBCAPS NICKED HERE IN 1995,' he said. Outside the church stood a faded tourist information board featuring a photograph of Lawrence. 'LOOK AT HIM. DOESN'T HE LOOK A STUCK-UP TWAT? DO YOU HAVE THAT FLUORESCENT JACKET I GAVE YOU IN YOUR CAR FOR IF YOU BREAK DOWN ON YOUR JOURNEY BACK TO DEVON TOMORROW?'

Once every month my dad would walk a mile through the woods not far from here and deliver our very reasonable rent to Lady Barber by hand at Lamb Close House. He knew the two main rules: 1) Know your station in life, and 2) Don't mention D. H. Lawrence. More than half a century after Lawrence's death the Barber family still nursed a grudge about the thinly veiled, none-too-flattering versions of their relatives in his novels. Researching a Lawrence piece for the *Spectator* magazine to coincide with the centenary of the novelist's birth in 1985, the journalist Richard West was told upon visiting the area that Lady Barber's husband, Sir William, would on no account talk to him about the subject. When Sir William was still alive, early in my mum and dad's tenancy, he once played the piano for my dad and invited him to play a game of Name That Tune. Later Lady Barber permitted him to compile her a jazz mix tape, which she confessed caused her to gyrate slightly. Once, as my dad left after delivering our rent, she pointed to her dog's bed and announced with a cackle, 'There's your blanket, Mr Cox!' to my dad, who did not own the blanket in question and did not own a dog but whom Lady Barber clearly viewed as occupying a position in society not dissimilar to one. On another day, in a more generous mood she gave him a tour of the grounds, which took in a nursery full of Victorian toys, garages housing a collection of top-of-the-range 1920s cars and a huge greenhouse containing a lump of coal which, in my dad's words, was 'THE SIZE OF A TRANSIT VAN': a touching memento of when the Barber family first realised they could make money off the sweat, toil and blood of the poor.

We headed in the direction of Bog End, an ominously named place, particularly in a county where 'bog' is not most commonly used to denote marshy or muddy ground. It was not until I left Nottinghamshire and moved south that I realised that most people did not think 'I'm going to the bog' was a normal, or even acceptable, way to announce your intention to visit the nearest toilet. But Bog End in fact contains an exquisite wildflower meadow, whose sun-dappled spring state I have had recurring hazy William Morris dreams about. I often have relaxing dreams about the belt of countryside from here to the Peak District in which the more stark and unsightly elements of the landscape – the chippies, the headstocks, the spoil heaps – are always conveniently edited out. I have not thus far inherited my dad and granddad's knack for having dream premonitions. Many years ago my dad dreamt about a woman who was in a phone box hit by a careening car. Not long afterwards in central Nottingham an out-of-control Vauxhall Viva obliterated a phone box containing my parents' friend Jean, an incident from which Jean stepped away miraculously unhurt. My dad also dreamt about a new gate on the lane beside the house we rented from the Barbers a few days before someone unexpectedly built a new gate in the exact same spot. When recovering from a heart attack in the mid-eighties Ted dreamt about his sister-in-law Irene beckoning to him on the night she died, even though he didn't know she'd died or even that she'd been ill at the time. The other member of the family noted for his premonitions was my granddad's uncle Harry, a practising spiritualist who, using only the power of his mind, once pinpointed the exact place on his shelf where my granddad had stored an issue of *Reader's Digest* that Harry wanted to borrow.

Bog End was not at its best today, under a dishwater February sky, but my dad assured me that my dreams of its wildflower meadow were grounded in the solid fact of several childhood picnics. As we climbed out of the small Not Quite Derbyshire valley below it, he went into what I have come to recognise as his jazz fusion nostalgia mode. 'I PUT AN EASEL UP THERE IN 1982 AND PAINTED IT THEN GOT BITTEN BY A HORSEFLY. DID YOU KNOW D. H. LAWRENCE SMASHED A 78 RPM BESSIE SMITH ALBUM OVER HIS WIFE'S HEAD? HE DIDN'T LIKE HER PLAYING BESSIE SMITH ALL THE TIME. I LOVE BESSIE SMITH. WOMEN IN JAPAN IN OFFICES PAY YOUNG MEN TO COME AND MAKE THEM CRY THEN DAB THEIR TEARS AWAY. I READ ABOUT IT. THEY'RE CALLED SOMETHING BOYS.' He adjusted his new hat, which fell slightly over his ears. 'I CAN'T HEAR MYSELF.'

'You're lucky,' said Mal.

We reminisced about a letter of complaint Mal and her colleague Dave had received while working for Derbyshire County Council, regarding some speed bumps that had been installed on a road in a town half an hour south of here. 'My mate bost his sump,' the letter, which came from someone called or representing an organisation

DEAR DAVE
                    I LIVE ON ~~Ho~~
THORNE ST IF YOU THINK I AM NOT
GOING TO DRIVE DOWN SOUTH ST FROM
BUTT LANE YOU CAN FUCK OFF AND
ITS ABOUT TIME YOU SORTED THE
FUCKER OUT ITS A BASTARD SHAMBLES
(MY MATE BOST HIS SUMP) SO
DON'T YOU START COMING THE BOLLOCKS
WITH ME

              GET FUCKED YOU TWAT

         Thorne st blook

called Thorne St Blook, had raged, before signing off with the firm instruction 'Don't you start coming the bolloks with me.' Mal and I wondered aloud where the letter was now. I recalled that the version I had at home was just a photocopy, not the original.

'I'VE GOT IT IN A FOLDER IN MY OFFICE,' said my dad, who was now several yards ahead of us, striding purposefully towards the outskirts of Watnall.

I was in my late teens when my parents moved to the house near here: a point in my life when my love of the countryside was drowned out by an intangible inner restlessness that I now recognise as the standard need of an overambitious, quarter-moulded young yokel to go somewhere else and find out who he was. I dragged the phone into my bedroom and conducted interviews with motormouthed musicians in California and Texas and Georgia then bashed the conversations into a semblance of shape for my own self-edited fanzine then, later, proper music magazines and newspapers based in London. I included our home phone number in the fanzine. My dad and I competed excitably to get to the phone first when it rang as, for the first time in our lives, it had become something we associated with good news. He usually won. Away from the Legoland estates we'd lived on previously and supply teaching jobs in inner-city Nottingham, he'd shaken off a bout of depression and was happier than I'd seen him in years. 'THAT BLOKE OFF THE RADIO CALLED EARLIER,' he told me one day when I returned home from my girlfriend's house. 'JOHN PEEL. I DIDN'T TAKE A NUMBER BUT HE SAID HE'D CALL BACK.'

He never did. The softest most flawless Jersey calves made eyes at me from the field opposite, our gang of bantam chickens did circuit after circuit of the garden digging for grubs, and a gentle, elderly German shepherd named Tina from two doors away came in each afternoon to ask politely for a biscuit then leave. Ray Manzarek called and speculated about Marianne Faithfull's role in Jim Morrison's death, while Frank from next door prowled about in the twitchell with a shotgun, looking for the fox that had got some of his partridges.

My means of escape from all this stifling surreal beauty was the 1977 Toyota Corona that my granddad passed on jointly to my dad and me. The winter before he passed the Toyota on to us, he and Joyce drove to see us. Snow fell hard during their visit, and a small drift formed around the car, meaning that to get the vehicle back onto the road a passing group of hardy cyclists had to be enlisted to push it, a task that, even bearing in mind the snow, necessitated an unusually high level of grunting. It was only later, when the cyclists were almost finished, that it dawned on Ted that he'd forgotten to take the handbrake off. He weighed up mentioning this to them and decided it was best to leave it. On other occasions he had been known to park the Toyota in the dead centre of the lane, blocking all traffic from both directions, and regularly left a small paraffin stove burning inside the car's footwell to keep the interior from getting frosted up. I remember him running a couple of red lights around this point in the mid-nineties, and that the donation of the car was at least partly due to a concern that it might be time for him to stop driving, but he purchased another car soon after and in fact stayed on the road until not long before his death, in 2002. Ted had a history of bad luck buying cars, including a couple that broke down during maiden journeys from the point of purchase. It never appeared to bother him: he still rhapsodised about what 'good blokes' the men who'd sold them to him had been, and he had the skill to fix the problems himself. When my parents' Morris Minor broke down in the mid-seventies, he loaned them his Triumph Herald to drive to work and spent the morning cycling around Nottingham scrapyards until he found the replacement part he needed to fix the problem. The smell of engine oil is indelibly associated with him in my mind. Right from that first Wolseley, all his cars were kept in immaculate condition, but by the time my dad and I had had custody of the Toyota for a year lines of moss rose from the wheel arches across its door panels like eco-friendly go-faster stripes. In a young bozo's attempt to save petrol by trundling the last mile home down the lane with the engine off, I crashed the car into a hedge at low speed when the steering lock clicked on and sent me sideways. I moved away from home, to York, for a while, then moved back. As a twenty-year-old living in the sticks with his parents, two miles away from the nearest bus stop and four times that far from the nearest train station, I relied crucially on the car to connect me to what I told myself was civilisation but I treated the Toyota with scant respect. Now of course I see it as the best car I ever had, and not just because I have reached an age when, as a man, I am contractually obliged to have a car from my past that I refer to as 'the best car I ever had', but at the time I was myopic regarding its plus points, just as I was myopic regarding the plus points of the valley where we lived.

Despite my blindness to much of my immediate surroundings, I remember walking into the thick woods separating the house from the M1 during those antsy summers of urban yearning and experiencing great moments of birdsong peace. I wonder if, on the second or third day of hiding out in these woods, as the police helicopters circled above, the armed robbers who escaped into them in 1995 began to relax and experience a similar form of peace. I sometimes mentally combine these armed robbers with the other armed robbers who tied our neighbours to chairs, beat them with baseball bats and sprayed mace in their pet greyhound's eyes, but this is incorrect: they were definitely different armed robbers. The neighbours who suffered the attack lived at the farm at the end of the track which our house fronted, looked after retired racehorses and had an enormous damp barn full of over a century of damp equestrian literature, which my dad helped them to coerce into some kind of order. The barn, long since under different ownership, is now a less damp tea room, serving a selection of D. H. Lawrence-themed lunches, including a dish called Lady Chatterley's Platter whose exact contents I declined to investigate when I went there, being in one of my more conservative moods at the time. Our old house and our neighbours' now boast big fences, nearly-as-big dogs and KEEP OUT signs, which is depressing but should perhaps not be viewed too reactionarily as a sign of changing times, since my parents were burgled twice during their five and a half years living there.

'THREE TIMES,' said my dad as we walked across the ridge heading away from the direction of Derbyshire, not quite in view of the house, with IKEA just visible in the distance.

'Two,' said my mum.

'NO. YOU'RE FORGETTING ABOUT THE SHED.'

'Oh yes. You're right.'

In the pub after our walk, not far from my old school, my mum, my dad, Mal, Chris and I ate some chips while two men on the table opposite discussed their favourite motorways. They agreed that the M62 was their least favourite but did not reach a consensus on the number-one spot. 'What's Sinbad up to today?' one asked. 'He's gone to Cleethorpes on a fanny hunt,' replied his friend. My dad removed his mobile phone from his coat pocket: an inexpensive clamshell around a decade old that displayed an alert for 144 unread messages.

'I'VE NEVER LOOKED AT ANY OF THEM,' he told me. 'I DON'T KNOW HOW.'

I had one unread message on my own phone. It was from the lady who, with a slight sense of class betrayal, I paid to clean my house for two hours every week. She wanted to know if she could adjust her hours for next week and also wondered if I realised I'd locked her in the house when I set off yesterday. I didn't, just as I hadn't the other time I'd absent-mindedly done it three weeks earlier. She said it was OK, since she'd managed to find the key to the French windows and let herself out that way.

Nobody can remember the exact moment my granddad's scatterbrain gene kicked in, but a poll of those who knew him puts it at around the age of thirty-six, four years before he set fire to a stranger's coat by putting his still-lit pipe in his pocket during a coach trip from Ilkeston to Mablethorpe. I was always closer to my nan than I was to Ted and Joyce, and have often been told that my looks, as well as my character, are closer to hers and those of her husband Tom. But in recent years, as my hair on my head has become slightly less thick and the hair on my face slightly thicker, I've started to see a hint of Ted in the mirror. This effect will no doubt become more extreme if I finally start wearing my glasses as often as I should. It has also got me thinking about my genetic destiny, especially on days when I put the coffee beans straight into the mug, lock my cleaner in the house or place a bottle of unused shampoo directly into my brown recycling bin.

I kidded myself for a few years that my increased doziness might be down to a mind overstuffed with nonsense or the pace of modern life, but I'm now facing up to the fact that my Ted gene is fully operational. I suppose a big signpost was the moment in 2013 when I got a bit too involved in a folk album I'd just bought, forgot to check on my bonfire and accidentally set a fairly large portion of my next-door neighbour's garden alight. Increasingly, friends and strangers chase after me as I exit pubs and shops, waving my clothes and valuables in the air. But that's OK. Ageing is often about facing up to your flaws. Admitting your mistakes is something everyone has to do at some point. One day last year I put my wallet in the fridge, for example, and I now realise that was a mistake.

I mentioned some of these incidents to my dad a few years ago, seeking reassurance, following a couple of occasions when I'd come perilously close to recycling my car keys in bottle banks. I felt confident that he at least hadn't inherited the doofus gene: he was always double-checking that he'd switched appliances off and, for all his excitability and turbulence, was a rigorously organised person. He sat me down and said in what was for him an unusually hushed voice, 'Why do you think I'm so neurotic? It's not just because I got it from your grandma. I have to be like that or I'd walk around doing stupid things all the time.' He too had first experienced the phenomenon during his mid-thirties, he said, during a holiday when he broke an up-and-over garage door off its hinges by pulling it the wrong way. 'IT'S A LATENT COX TRAIT. I WAS GOING TO WARN YOU ABOUT IT THE OTHER SUMMER WHEN YOU DROVE INTO THAT PARKING BARRIER AND SNAPPED IT, BUT I THOUGHT I'D GIVE IT A WHILE JUST TO MAKE SURE.'

I felt a little hard done by. My dad had had great fun playing practical jokes on his dad – I am thinking here particularly of the time he convinced Ted that he'd received a call from my grandma on an unattached analogue telephone many yards from any building – but because of his pesky compensating for his own condition I'd been robbed of the chance to do the same thing with him. Instead I had been doomed to a life of being told 'REMEMBER TO PUT YOUR HEADLIGHTS ON' and 'DON'T SAW INTO YOUR ARM WHILE YOU'RE CUTTING THAT WOOD.' Now my illness had been confirmed, I could no longer even claim he was fussing unduly. Then there is the worry about how my doziness might become more of a liability as it escalates, due to my habit of sometimes having ideas above my station. Never getting ideas above his station perhaps made Ted's doziness easier to manage. Not long before he died, my parents took him – with Joyce, who was by then suffering from dementia – on a visit to a country house with a garden open to the public. Not a mansion, but a big place – seven or eight bedrooms, half a dozen acres of land. 'Ah. If I could do it all over again and got luckier, who knows...' Ted sighed. My mum and dad smiled, thinking that in a fantasy parallel life this would indeed be a lovely place to live. 'I could have been the gardener here,' continued Ted.

Back in my mum and dad's living room after our Bog End walk, I went through some old photos from Joyce and Ted's collection: my granddad and my dad's uncle Ken pretending to be rally drivers in an abandoned wreck of a car they'd found on a walk; my grandparents immaculately attired at work parties; the two of them and Ken dressing up, often in very androgynous fashion; my granddad grinning in photo after photo; my grandma's older brother Les in what for all the world looked like the promo shot for a 1940s heart-throb starring as a Los Angeles gumshoe. 'PEOPLE LOOKED LIKE FILM

STARS AT THAT POINT BECAUSE THEY COULDN'T AFFORD TO EAT PROPERLY,' my dad said. 'BEING FAT WAS A SIGN OF WEALTH. NOW IT'S THE RICH PEOPLE WHO ARE SKINNY.' My granddad's side of the family all grew their own veg. By the time they were twenty each of them had killed at least one chicken with their bare hands. In a time before unemployment benefit they found coal for their fires by waiting along the railway line for the chunks that would drop off trains. 'MY AUNTIE IRENE USED TO PUSH A PRAM AROUND PRETENDING SHE HAD A BABY AND USE IT TO STEAL COAL FROM THE OPEN-CAST MINE IN BRAMCOTE. SHE GOT ARRESTED FOR IT.' He passed me another photo: my granddad in a suit and tie, grinning as usual, surrounded by beer bottles and seven people I'd never seen before. 'LOOK AT THIS,' he said. 'YOU CAN TELL IT WAS AN INNOCENT ERA. PRE-INTERNET, PRE-DOGGING.' Joyce's family, though not well off, did not suffer the same poverty as Ted's did in the twenties and thirties: her mum, Ethel – a woman even more fearsome than her – ran a haberdashery shop and lived in a house full of buttons. Joyce went on to work in a shoe shop and for a library supply company.

I couldn't help returning to that photo of Joyce's brother Les, a dashing debonair figure who a stranger might be forgiven for not at first guessing was a Nottingham-based dental technician with a sideline in hypnotism. After Joyce first met my mum, she told my dad that she had good teeth, describing them as 'like celery roots'. 'I remember looking in the mirror afterwards to check if they had ridges on them,' my mum said. Perhaps influenced by her inside knowledge of the dental trade, Joyce advised me that it might be worth thinking about having my own teeth out early in life, as it would save a lot of hassle as I got older. I was approaching my seventeenth birthday at the time. Much of her life appeared to be about sensibly preparing for her years as an old age pensioner. By the time she and my granddad turned forty – when they were both very healthy and active – she already had their names on a list for a retirement bungalow. In her defence it should be pointed out that when their retirement years did arrive they seemed to spend a lot of them having a very good time, which they told us about in great detail in what became a reversal of more traditional family meet-ups, where the old people listen to the young people tell them about all the fun, energetic stuff they've been doing.

Joyce was the only close family member I was frightened of when I was a child. But maybe that was useful: all my other close relatives apart from my daredevil uncle Tony were big softies, and one Victorian influence wasn't such a bad thing for me. High-spirited behaviour was not tolerated in Joyce's presence, which might go some way to explaining why my dad indulges in so much of it now. My memory of her relationships with those close to her reminds me of something the novelist Richard Russo's grandfather once said about his grandmother: 'With your grandmother, you always have a choice. You can do things her way or you can wish you had.' The general line of thinking is that she and Ted did argue early in their relationship but not later on, after Ted realised that to let her have her way 100 per cent of the time led to a simpler, easier life.

As I continued to flick through the photos, I could hear my mum and dad in the kitchen preparing the evening meal. My dad then announced that he was going upstairs to the loft. My mum asked why he was doing that, and he said he wanted to fetch the electric heater for her to use during the life-drawing class she had organised for tomorrow. I heard the fridge start to beep, as it did when somebody hadn't shut the door properly and it felt the need to warn them.

'You don't need to do that now,' my mum said. 'Do it in the morning. Dinner will be ready in a minute, and I've put some nibbles out in the other room.'

'NO, I'M GOING TO GET IT DONE NOW,' said my dad. 'I DON'T WANT YOUR LIFE MODEL TO BE COLD. DON'T USE THAT WORD, NIBBLES. I'VE BANNED IT. IT MAKES ME CRINGE. IS THAT FRIDGE REVERSING?'

'Did you know you bent the potato masher?'

'NO, I DIDN'T. I APOLOGISE PROFUSELY.'

A recurring line of my dad's is that his dad was dozy and happy-go-lucky and his mum was intelligent and neurotic, and he drew the short straw by ending up dozy and neurotic. 'I'M GLAD YOU GOT YOUR MUM'S PERSONALITY, NOT MINE,' he has told me. He's being unfair to himself here and not wholly accurate, but I can see another combination of Ted and Joyce in him: a thundering lust for life combined with the ability to create obstacles out of nothing in a future that doesn't exist, a sometimes exhausting ego combined with a generosity that on occasions has run to the self-damaging, a negative outlook underpinned by an essential softness and good nature. No human is just one thing. That said, Ted perhaps came a bit closer than some of us. Towards the end of my granddad's life my dad asked him if he'd ever done anything horrible. Ted pondered the question for almost a full minute then said there was one thing he had often regretted which he felt was unfair and hurtful, and that was the times during 1936 when he and a gang of his mates would go into the chip shop in Stapleford five minutes before it closed and ask, 'Have you got any fritters left, missus?' to the woman serving there, and if she said, 'Yeah,' they would shout, 'Well, you fried too many of them, didn't you, missus!' and run away.

Ted could be bawdy, in a fluffy unthreatening sort of way. Pretty much as soon as I reached puberty he started asking me if I was getting any 'crumpet'. Before my adolescence he often referred to me as 'KILLER', which became 'LADYKILLER' as I got older. I was sorry to disappoint him by remaining in a long-term committed relationship with the same girl from my late teens to the middle of my twenties. In view of this side of his nature it was somewhat apt that he spent most of his adult life working in a factory that made women's underwear. My great-granddad, Ted senior, also worked in a women's underwear factory. The legend is that during the 1930s Ted senior designed the part of a knitting machine that made women's stockings fit more snugly around the heel then made the mistake of telling his boss, who immediately patented the idea. Apparently the boss was always sure to send Ted senior a turkey every Christmas though, and Ted senior was content with that.

Before his teaching days my dad also worked in a women's underwear factory for a while. In fact, I am the first of a century of men on Ted's side of the family never to have worked in a women's underwear factory. I feel I am somehow letting the side down here, but I'm still not all that old, and publishing is a very uncertain industry to work in during the early part of the twenty-first century, so I suppose there's still time and anything could happen. When my dad was a kid Ted's ability to mend the knitting machines that made ladies' undergarments was so prized that he worked for a time in a Belgian factory which was having trouble with its machines. The Belgians were so impressed with his work that they offered him a permanent position at a far better wage than he'd ever had, but Joyce did not want to move to Belgium because she thought they had weird toilets. 'WHILE HE WORKED THERE HE LIVED WITH A BELGIAN FAMILY AND WALKED THROUGH A FRENCH WINDOW IN THEIR HOUSE,' my dad told me. 'WELL, I SUPPOSE IT WAS A BELGIAN WINDOW. DO YOU KNOW WILLIAM LEE? HE WAS FROM CALVERTON AND HE INVENTED THE FRAMEWORK KNITTING MACHINE. KNITTING HAS ALWAYS BEEN MASSIVE IN NOTTINGHAM. ALL THE HOUSES IN RUDDINGTON USED TO HAVE THREE FLOORS. THAT'S BECAUSE THE TOP FLOOR WAS FOR KNITTING. EVERYONE WAS KNITTING LIKE FOOK. AND THAT'S WHY HOSIERY WAS SO BIG IN NOTTINGHAM, AND WHY YOUR GREAT GRANDDAD AND YOUR GRANDDAD GOT JOBS IN HOSIERY FACTORIES. I DIDN'T KNOW ANY OF THIS UNTIL I WENT TO LEICESTER TO BUY DRUGS AND HAD A STAND-OFF WITH A MOD THERE. WE BECAME MATES FOR A BIT AFTERWARDS. HE WORKED IN HOSIERY.'

When my granddad was away, my dad and Joyce tended to clash without a teddy bear to soften the atmosphere in the house. When my dad's shoes fell to bits Joyce sent him to school in some of her own. She gave him charcoal tablets to combat what she called his bilious attacks. My dad wasn't aware that he had bilious attacks and didn't even know what they were, but she assured him that he did and that they needed to be combated. Meanwhile, a co-worker of Ted's in Brussels named Kurt became obsessed with Ted and began to follow him everywhere he went. Ted had to gently explain to Kurt that he was married and not on the market. Kurt told Ted he was the most finely dressed man he had ever seen.

Clothes were always important to Ted. If he dressed up, he really dressed up. If he didn't, he really didn't. His tendency to look a little dandyish or extremely scruffy and rarely anything in between is one that both I and my dad have inherited. Around the turn of the last decade, when my dad finally had the income to buy the clothes he hankered after, I accompanied him to a tailor in the town of Holt in Norfolk, where he spent so much time trying on suits and asking the proprietor her opinion that three hours later when we finally left she announced that she was going to have to go upstairs to have a lie-down and some ginger nuts. Just before we sat down for our meal the night before our walk to Bog End my mum asked my dad if he knew he had a large stain on the front of his T-shirt, at which my dad hurriedly pulled the T-shirt over his head and put it back on, inside out. 'Ta-da!' he said. 'Gone.'

A Sunday ritual in my grandparents' house was that while the roast was cooking all leather footwear in the house – whether it belonged to Ted, Joyce or a visitor – was buffed by Ted to a high, mirror-like sheen. Before walks in the Peak District it was mandatory for walking boots to be thoroughly cleaned and dubbined. I don't clean my own walking boots since my staunch belief is that they'll only get dirty again very soon afterwards. As for dubbining, I have never even entertained the idea. Also, I live in south Devon, where there is invariably a puddle or creek somewhere nearby if you get desperate. I did feel a bit bad in March 2015 when my parents and I visited Wolfscotedale, where Joyce and Ted's ashes are scattered, and I looked down at all the dry cakey West Country mud I'd carried up there with me. It was one day when I perhaps should have made more effort.

Before that afternoon it had been many years since I'd visited the Peak District, and seeing the curtain in the land that marks the entrance to it from the south knocked me for six. As I passed towards Ambergate along the A610, Crich Stand, the lone ring at the top of the curtain, rose out of the mist ahead, and a concomitant geyser of memories rose out of some mist inside me. My dad racing home further down the valley to get me back in time to see that night's episode of *The Incredible Hulk*, overtaking, unthinkably, a Ford Capri, and me realising properly for the first time that overtaking was something a person could legally do and becoming excited by the future personal implications of that. The spectre of the ruined Wingfield Manor, one of the venues on the ghost of Mary Queen of Scots' haunting tour of the UK, appearing in fading foggy light in the valley below our Morris Marina's headlights then staying in the corner of my mind's vision for days afterwards. Getting the cable car up the Heights of Abraham to see my cousin Fay working at the cafe at the top: the ambience of roller disco created by the decor and staff uniform. A raft race at Matlock Bath, Ted wrapped up against the cold in layer after layer, looking even more teddy bearish than ever. Our old, deceased weekend life. This curtain in the land is much more significant than the actual Nottinghamshire–Derbyshire border a few miles behind you. The change is negligible as you travel from Eastwood, the last town in Nottinghamshire, to the spoil-heap-shadowed Langley Mill, where I once saw an empty shop with the heartbreaking handwritten sign which read, 'Rob me if you like: I've been burgled so many times I've got nothing left' in its window, or Ripley, where I contracted food poisoning from a transport cafe ham sandwich in 1987, or Codnor, from whose Codnor Pets and Aquatics my parents purchased my first goldfish. I noted as I waited at the traffic lights beside the latter establishment that it now sold air rifles, pistols, crossbows and knives as well as aquatics. I found it hard to imagine anyone wanting to buy a gun and a goldfish at the same time. If they sold barrels too it might have made a bit more sense.

The change, by contrast, as you continue west to Ambergate with Crich Stand looking down its nose at you and turn right towards Whatstandwell, is like the change that occurs when you meet a venerable witch at the edge of a wasteland who takes you by the hand and says, 'It's OK. I know where the good place is with the enchanted stone and the wise sheep who speak,' and leads you directly to it. It is not the fault of Ripley and Langley Mill and Alfreton and Codnor that they got the tyre stacks, chippies and bleak-looking pubs. Tyre stacks, chippies and bleak-looking pubs have to go somewhere, and not even the most rampant environmental charlatan would want to scatter them over the other side of the Crich divide: it would be like fly-tipping in Middle Earth.

For a year, maybe more, before I drove through the Peak District to Wolfscote Dale, in my dreams I'd been seeing a tower looming over a giant rock face not quite a cliff but very reminiscent of one. It always felt like a calming place, but where was it? I couldn't work it out. It seemed like it should be in Devon, somewhere near the sea, but it didn't match up to anywhere in Devon I had so far visited. It reminded me a little bit of the Daymark, an octagonal nineteenth-century shipping tower on the south Devon coast near Kingswear that I had often walked to, sometimes in atmospheric fog, but that wasn't it; the Daymark is a little too brutalist, sci-fi in a starker way. As soon as I saw Crich Stand – built in 1923, the year of Ted's birth, on the site of at least two apparently more gloomy and ominous previous towers, in remembrance of the members of the Sherwood Foresters regiment who had died in the First World War – loom up ahead, I knew immediately that that was what I had been dreaming about.

The Stand continued to watch me for several miles as I made my way in the direction of Matlock, parallel to the Derwent, and I had to tell myself to stop looking at it after veering into roadside gravel not far from the turning to Wirksworth. 'Kimberley Ales', announced big painted letters on the side of a pub. A benevolent gesture: an area as magnificent as this, stooping to import ales from the less magnificent area where I grew up. The brewery was now defunct, but still. The road here keeps following the river

and gives the impression Derbyshire is one long valley, a deep, green avenue to the Proper North. I turned left at Cromford and climbed for the Peak through remorseless rain, reluctantly leaving behind Scarthin Books, Britain's best second-hand bookshop: a warren of maps and local history and excellent home-made soup, whose owner gets about on a tandem, just like Ted and Joyce did for a lot of the 1940s and fifties. I stopped for a wee by a stone wall, and the wind blew my wee over the wall and into the adjacent field. I don't know where my wee ended up. In fact, several hours later it seemed entirely possible that my wee could still be airborne, making its way steadily towards Glossop. Despite the cold, I was getting warnings from my car that it was overheating. My car is fairly modern so vocalises its anxieties about its health quite openly. It even beeps at me when it's worried about running out of petrol. I miss the old attitude to petrol from cars – the 'Oops. All gone. Oh well!' attitude of the mossy Toyota. But in this case my car's panic was justified. The engine's coolant filter was broken. If I had been Ted I'd have been straight under the bonnet, sorting that out in no time. But I am not Ted, only parts of Ted, and not the most useful parts, so instead I splashed a load more coolant into the engine and resolved to take it to a garage at the earliest opportunity.

In the village of Alstonefield I parked and met my mum and dad, and we began to walk in the direction of the River Dove, passing rainfucked barns, a farmhouse with a ram skull proudly displayed in its window and a herd of Belted Galloway cattle. We paused to admire the cattle through the soupy downpour.

'THEY WERE MY FAVOURITE AS A KID,' my dad remarked. 'THEY'RE HALF PANDA, HALF COW. THE BULLS KILL YOU. FOOK! I WANT TO PAINT THEM!'

'You've got shortcrust pastry crumbs down the front of your coat,' my mum said to me, and she was not incorrect.

My dad's mood became a little more sober as we reached the hillside where Joyce and Ted's ashes were scattered. 'FOOKIN' HELL,' he said. 'IT'S GOT STEEPER SINCE 2002. I'M GOING TO SLIDE DOWN ON MY SIDE.' As I helped my mum down the ravine towards the Dove and my dad slid behind us, two professional-looking hikers coming from the opposite direction kindly stood aside for us.

'MY DAD'S JUST UP THERE,' my dad said to the hikers, gesturing over a craggy knob in the drenched hillside behind us, beyond which a distant tumulus looked like a jelly pudding stubbornly drawn in HB pencil through the defiant moisture.

'Oh, there's one more of you to come, is there?' asked one of the hikers, continuing to stand aside.

'NO. I MEAN HIS ASHES. HE'S BEEN DEAD ALMOST THIRTEEN YEARS.'

I wondered where my grandma and granddad's ashes had ended up after my mum and dad had scattered them at the top of the hill respectively thirteen and twelve years earlier. It rains a lot here, so runnels of lightly mudded water probably washed them down the slope. Some ashes perhaps eventually made it into the Dove. Maybe some didn't. Everything returns to the earth in the end and is remade, so in a sense what was technically happening at present was that my dad was sliding down Ted and Joyce. My dad continued to slide down Ted and Joyce, almost all the way to the bottom. It was an activity that Joyce would no doubt have disapproved of, viewing it as high-spirited. 'Michael!' she would have called my dad, but of course a Michael would have been far less likely to do something like that. It was the act of a Mick.

Near the bottom of the slope my dad got himself upright again, picked up his pace and nipped ahead of my mum and me, across the river. By the time we reached the foot of the ravine, he was talking to a party of teenagers on the other side of the footbridge. 'Oh God,' said my mum, as we admired some bracket fungus. 'I bet he's telling them about Cottesmore.' Cottesmore was the inner-city Nottingham secondary school where my dad taught in the 1970s. It had remained one of his favourite conversation topics to the present day, but I was amazed that my mum could tell from a distance of over a hundred yards that this was what he was talking about until it hit me that close to five decades of marriage can endow people with many particular skills.

'Were you telling them about Cottesmore?' my mum asked my dad when we caught him up.

'YEAH. WHAT'S WRONG WITH THAT? I TOLD THEM ABOUT THE TIME I BROUGHT MY CLASS HERE ON A SCHOOL TRIP IN 1974 AND THEY CHARGED SOME CATTLE AND ALMOST GOT SOME PICNICKERS TRAMPLED TO DEATH. BARRY LASKOWSKI WAS THE RINGLEADER. AND VINCENT BROWN...HE WENT ON TO WIN

MR UNIVERSE.'

'Were they interested?' I asked.

'THEY PRETENDED TO BE BUT I THINK THEY WERE BEING SARCASTIC. I TOLD ONE OF THEM OFF FOR SMOKING BUT IT TURNED OUT HE JUST HAD A PEN IN HIS MOUTH.'

With that my dad was off again, telling me the story about the time in 1976 when two pupils burgled one of his colleague's houses – a teacher who had moved into the same neighbourhood as the children as a socialist gesture – and sprayed graffiti on its living-room wall, then, when they found out the house belonged to the teacher, who was their favourite, voluntarily returned all the stolen goods. Then, after that, the story about a boy named Mark who used to sit quietly in the library and read Just William books but went on to put a petrol bomb in Hyson Green police station. My dad brought his Cottesmore pupils to Derbyshire on a few occasions, and they were always high-spirited: the most city of city kids, many of whom had never seen proper countryside before. Upon spotting expert climbers working their way up the rock face at Froggatt Edge, many of the boys, including Lenford Marquis and Lloyd Clockton, ran over to join in. 'THIS WAS NOT LONG AFTER LLOYD GOT LOCKED IN A CUPBOARD,' remembered my dad. 'I TOOK THEM ALL THROUGH SOMEONE'S GARDEN BY MISTAKE ON THE SAME WALK. YOU SHOULD HAVE SEEN THE FACES OF THE PEOPLE IT BELONGED TO. I DON'T THINK THEY'D SEEN LAIRY SIX-FOOT JAMAICAN TEENAGERS BEFORE.'

If the Peak District is a mounted painting, the nearby cities are situated like hastily placed drawing pins at the edges of the mount. Because of the foot traffic, the path along the Dove – the first river I ever swam in – is rarely totally quiet in daytime, even in thick end-of-winter rain like today's. Complaints about the Peak District becoming besmirched by crowds are nothing new. In J. B. Firth's *Highways and Byways in Derbyshire* of 1905 he laments the vulgarisation of the Derwent Valley: its litter and its transformation into a 'tripper's Paradise' populated by hordes of 'callous rowdies' from the conurbations that distantly surround it. Devon is a place much more synonymous with holidaymakers, but its central walking country remains emptier than this, even in high season. That's because it only has drawing pins in one direction from the edge of its mount. If you tried to attach a drawing pin in any other direction the drawing pin would be swept away by some large waves. But in this rainy, high-altitude terrain I rediscovered much to remind me of my current home. As we pushed towards Milldale, skirting the Staffordshire border, and the rain soup cleared to mere consommé, the scenery looked like Devon in a different jacket. It was hard to conceive that there was no coastline just over the horizon, let alone within sixty miles. I understood why Derbyshire had been nagging at my subconscious lately: this bleak, craggy, up-and-down terrain and damp climate was a deep, ingrained part of me. By moving to south Devon I'd finally made myself aware of it. The top of Lustleigh Cleave on Dartmoor was my Froggatt Edge, the Teign and Dart were my

Dove and Derwent (the original meaning of both 'Dart' and 'Derwent' is roughly 'river valley thick with oaks'). Devon was not just somewhere I'd moved to because of two love affairs – one, destined not to last, with a woman and one, still burgeoning, with a landscape. It also kept me connected to Ted. And maybe during his lifetime Derbyshire had kept Ted – whose mum had grown up on Dartmoor – connected to Devon, whether he knew it or not.

We arrived at Milldale, whose stone footbridge and matching surrounding cottages my dad had painted in intricate detail when I was young and we were living in the first of our Almost Derbyshire houses. I recall moaning on walks around here as a nine- or ten-year-old, but my mum remembers a weird stamina I had a few years prior to that: an ability to keep going on ambitious routes around Chatsworth and Eyam and Padley and Wirksworth

that belied my age and tiny legs and which, if she was honest, she found just a bit unsettling. My parents were tired now, on the bridge at Milldale, and I realised with a pang that the ten-mile-plus walks in which I now liked to indulge at least once a week were never going to be within their reach again. The final stretch of the walk, up the hill towards the George pub at Alstonefield, was hard going. While they caught their breath I stopped to say hello to a farmer rebuilding a stone wall, for a few minutes admiring his craftsmanship and the slow satisfaction of mending. A miracle structure made from local material that withstood the elements purely due to weight distribution, ventilation and mortarless adhesion, being repaired with care and unhurried love. I barely suppressed the urge to join in. About half an hour earlier a slow, tentative sun had finally called off the rain. As its light fell through the branches and we passed along the Dove where the river nips below the high bank of Lode Lane my dad had pointed to a spot where, for many years, an abandoned Wolseley had hung suspended in the foliage: a car like Ted's that had been driven too hastily or faced a problematic obstacle in its path, or perhaps both, then, unclaimed, had seemed more of an embedded natural part of the landscape with each passing season until one day it was gone.

ACKNOWLEDGEMENTS

21st-Century Yokel is the result of my stubborn conviction that something that a lot of people told me for many years wouldn't be 'marketable' enough to work would be a much better book than the marketable stuff they recommended that I did instead, but it also only exists because, as it began to take form, a few other people *did* believe in it: in particular, my editor Simon Spanton and my agent Ed Wilson, who have offered support of the kind you hope you will get from editors and agents in optimistic, childlike dreams but rarely would be so bold as to hope for in realistic wakefulness. I am very lucky to have you both on my side. I'd also like to thank the rest of the Unbound team for giving me the springboard to launch this book in a non-conventional way and my astoundingly loyal and lovely readers for helping to get the project off the ground in a manner that would not have been possible in the publishing industry climate of six or seven years ago. The Bear's Army: you rock, as ever. I don't write for newspapers any more and all my non-book writing goes on my website, some of which turns into book writing, and for which the unsolicited, unpaid proofreading skills of Dave Holwill, Lesley Bourke, Becca Broad, Amanda Corp and Miranda Whiting have been invaluable. Thank you for your eagle eyes. I sometimes think writing is just the sum of your disappointments and hopes in life plus all the books you have read but that's not quite true. This selection you're holding is also indelibly flavoured by the nature lovers I have spent time around in the last couple of years whose positive worldview and excitement about wildlife has been so infectious: bee goddesses Hayley Anderson and Emily Reed, butterfly overlord John Walters, beaver tracker Stephen Hussey, moorland rootsman Michael Nendick, arboreal mastermind David Prout, eco sextons Ru and Claire Callender, caterpillar guru Jenny Porrett. I must also in this category count my parents Jo and Mick, who were helping to get me excited about buzzards, moss, newts and bees long before I even realised it. But I have much more to thank them for – particularly my mum, whose linoprints feature in this book and have been an inspiration to me during its creation. A few of these stories came together a little more cohesively during spoken word shows in 2015 and 2016. Thanks to everyone who booked me for one of those – especially Chris Woodley-Stewart and Samantha Holland and to Chris Booth and Lucinda Guy for letting me ramble about my rambling on Soundart Radio once a month. Cheers also to the Dominick Tyler for teaching me the terms Cornubian Batholith and Witches' Knickers. Check out his book *Uncommon Ground*: it's really great. And finally a big salute to brilliant comedy actress and fellow Pentangle nut Alice Lowe for giving me the title to this book. She says she can't remember ever doing so, but she definitely did, and I have documented proof. After reading one of my old columns for the *Guardian* in spring 2012, not long after I was first attempting to write about life in the countryside in a digressive way that brought in folklore, music and family, as well as landscape and wildlife, Alice asked 'Have you ever thought of calling yourself the 21st-Century Yokel?' So I did.

SUPPORTERS

Unbound is a new kind of publishing house. Our books are funded directly by readers. This was a very popular idea during the late eighteenth and early nineteenth centuries. Now we have revived it for the internet age. It allows authors to write the books they really want to write and readers to support the books they would most like to see published.

The names listed below are of readers who have pledged their support and made this book happen. If you'd like to join them, visit www.unbound.com.

Alison Adams
Julie Adams
Trish Adams
Kathleen Ahearn
Adrian Ainsworth
Elisa Aitchison
Ann Aitken
Jenny Al-Timimi
Becky Alcock
Andrew Aldridge
Christina Alexander
Jane Allardyce
Jenny Allcock
Judy Allen
Kelly Allen
Nicola Allen
Sarah Allen
L Allen-Jones
Kathy Allso
Clare Altham
Denise Altoff
Caroline Anderson
Charlotte Anderson

Jan Anderson
Sara Anderson
Gillian Andrew
Tamsin Andrews
Chelle Andronicos
Emma Anger
Misha Ankwell
Jenny Anslow
Guillermo Aprile
Sandra Armor
Rita Armstrong
Mark Arnold
Kay Arthur
Sue Arthur
Donna Asher
Dawn Ashford
Lindsay Ashford
Louise Ashton
Dawn Atherton
Auchentoshan and Laphroaig
Rose Auerbach
Nick Avery
Janna Avon

SUPPORTERS

Ali Awcock
Clare Axton
Terri Babbitt
Beverley Back
Carole Backler
Donna Baff
Nancy Bailey
Ed Baines
Emma Baines
Debby Baker
Fran Baker
Trevor Baker
Emma Ball
Phil Ball
Jan Ballantyne
Ali Balmond
Lyssa Barber
Renée Baris
Ian Barnard
Rosemary Barnes
Ellen Barnett
Rosie Barnett
Jenny Barragan
Sara Barratt
Sue Barry
Yvonne Benney Basque
Kate Batchelor
Laura Baughman
Leslie Bausback
Gisele Baxter
Michelle Bayley
Beachofdreams Beachofdreams
Kirsty Beagley
Ally Beal
Grumpy Bear
Jane Beardshaw
Naomi Beaumont
Kate Beazley
Ella Bedrock
Alison Beezer
Gloria Belcher

Kay Belk
Donna Bell
Sharon Bell
Gareth Bellamy
Jane Bembridge
Alison Bendall
Linda Bennett
Anita Benson
Sue Bentley
Stacy Paul Berglund
Rosemary Berry
Tracie Bettenhausen
Mary Bettuchy
Bijould Bijould
Charlotte Bilby
Heather Binsch
Maggie Birchall
Chuck B. Bird
Helga Björnsdóttir
Rhian Blackmore
Gabrielle M Blake
Amy Louise Blaney
John Blythe
Elspeth Body
Vickie Boggio
Megan Boing
Jane Bolinger
Bollux
Gemma Bolt
Gilly Bolton
Steven Bond
Alice Bondi
Christen Boniface
Alex Booer
Fiona Booth
Jeannie Borsch
Sarah Boswell
Chloe Botting
Lesley Bourke
Lynn Bourne
Jan-Joost Bouwman

SUPPORTERS

Lindsey Bowden
Niki Bowden
Judith Bowers
Catherine Bowles
Lucy Bowyer
Elizabeth Bradley
Karen Bradley
Vanessa Bray
Caroline Bray and Flannel
Gill Brennand
Gemma Bridges
Jules Bristow
Charlotte Broadhead
Alexander Brook
Eleanor Brooke-Peat
Aimi Brookes
Jon Brooks
Lisa Brooks
Ann Brown
Emma Brown
Katharine Brown
Kathleen Brown
Richard Brown
Sally Browning
Sarah Browning
Gill Bruce
Leslie Buck
Elaine Buckley
Miss Bulloch
Rebecca Bullock
Janet Bunker
Sri Bunnik
Rachel Burch
D Beth Burchard
Amanda Burden
Rachel Burgess
Julie Burling
Donna-Marie Burnell
Christina C Burns
Jane Burns
Joanne Burrows

Jo Burt
Heather Bury
Brandi Butler
Stef Butler
Helen Button
Heather Byram
Anne Byrne
Gemma Byrne
Ann Yergin Byrne & Ross Byrne
Vivian Cafarella
Judi Calow
Avril Cambray
Lisa Cameron
Donatella Campbell
Kate Campbell
Lynn Campbell
Liz Campbell-Taylor
Lara Canfield
Allison Carey
Catherine Cargill
Caroline
Caroline Carpenter
Liz Carr
Lorrie Carse-Wilen
Philippa Carter
Kelly Cartwright
Deni Case
Fleur Cass
Tricia Catford
Susan Catley
Stephanie Cave
Rachel Cawthorne
NJ Cesar
Justin Cetinich
Kathryn Chabarek
Tamasine Chamberlain
Katie Chambers
Mary-Kate Chambers
Liz Chantler
Patricia Chaplin
Samantha Chapman

SUPPORTERS

Zoe Chapman
Heather Chappelle
Ailsa Charlton
Gill Chedgey
Susan Chedgey
Gareth Cheesman
Nigel Denise Chichester
Joan Childs
Rachel Chilton
Charli Chmylowskyj
Kirsten Christiansen
Valerie Christie
Amy Ciclaire
Lisa Claire
Adrian Clark
Dee Clark
Lily Clarke
Alison Cleeve
Julie Clemett
Gill Clifford
Dael Climo
Freyalyn Close-Hainsworth
Waving Cloud
Suzy Coates
Aimee Coelho
Michael Collard
Carolyn Collé
Susan Collicott
Catherine Collins
Natalie Collins
Sally Collins
Isabelle Conneely
Brida Connolly
Trisha Connolly
Annemarie Connory
David Conrad
Michelle Conroy
Susanne Convery
Jeff Cook
Judith Cooke
Lesley Cookman

Philip Coombes
Fi, Nick & Alex Cooper
Collette Coote
Margaret Cooze
Hillary Corbett
Sue Corden
Rosie Corlett
Íde Corley
Rachael Corn
Adrian Cornell
Ellie Cornell
Amanda Corp
Andrew Cosgriff
Katy Costello
Anne Costigan
Kati Cowen
Carol Cowles
Jo Cox
Ann Crabbe
Kathryn Craddock
Duncan Craig
Julie Craine
Suzi Crockford
Rachel Cronin
Nancy Crosby
Rachel Cross
Lynn Crossley
Cat Croxford
Carolyn Culbertson
Mary Cullina
Lisa Cullingworth
Lezley Cunningham-Wood
Jane Cureton
Cush
Lindsay Cuthill
Victoria D'Arcy
Nicole D'hondt
Eduardo da Costa
Beth Dallam
Patricia Daloni
Jackie Daly

SUPPORTERS

Claire Daniells
Polly Daniels
Nick Darlow
Caroline Davidson
Claire Davidson
Karen Davidson
Alison Davies
Jim Davies
Lisa Davies
Lizzy Davies
Meryl Davies
Rob Davies
Sandra Davies
Catherine Davis
Donna Davis
Jeanette Davis
Lisa Davis
Michael Davis
Sandra Davis
Jeannie Davison
Mark Davison
Alexandra Dawe
Liz Dawson
Rebecca Dawson
Søstrene Pihl de Yngre
Joanne Deacon
Karen Deakin
Alison Deane
Elizabeth DeBold
Michael DeCataldo
Joanne Deeming
Vicky Deighton
Jamie Dempster
Kelly Dempster
Lucy Dennison
Abigail Dent
Albert Depetrillo
Hannah Rose Deverell
Martin Dixon
Mike Dixon
Catherine Donald

Graeme Donaldson
Kirsty Doole
Sarah Dorman
Marina Dorward
Alexia Drew
Kate Dreyer
K Driver for Dad
Kathryn Drumm
Tim Ducker
Angela Dunavant
Heather Dunn
Julie Dunne
Sue Dunne
Vivienne Dunstan
Charlotte Durkin
Pene Durston
Michael E
Naomi Early
Rachel Easom
Christopher Easterbrook
Sarah Eden
Claire Edgley
Katie Edmonds
James Edmonston
Elizabeth Edwards
Patricia Edwards
Eirlys Edwards-Behi
Tom Ellett
Jamie Elliott
John Elliott
Ember
Valerie Emery
Alice Anne English
Raelene Ernst
Jeanette Esau
Esta
Alan Estes
Anne Evans
Isobel Evans
Karen Evans
Kate Evans

Rachel Evans
Rhiannon Evans
Dee Ewing
Rachael Ewing
Joe Fairbairn
Jeffrey Falconer
Paula Fancini-Hooper
Alison Faraday
Tina Farquharson
Clare Farrar
Charlotte Featherstone
Helen Fedchak
Mark Feldon
Welsh Felix
Alison Felstead
Verity Ferguson
Peter Fermoy
Kathryn Ferranti
Susannah Field
Suzy Fieldhouse
Charlotte Finch
Erika Finch
Fiona Finch
Hayley Finch
Jane Finnan
Dave Fisher
Liz Fisher
Fiona Fitzsimmons
Nick Fitzsimons
Nicola Flack
Fiona Floyd
Jen Foley
Aurora Fonseca-Lloyd
Jack Fontana
Jonathan Ford
Caleb Foreman
Shelley Forrester
Anna Forss
Jenny Fortnam
Alison Foster
Anna Foster

Fiona Fowkes
Catherine Fowler
Becky Fox
Lily Fox
Anne Fox-Smythe
Philippa Francis
Tiffany Francis
Dan Franklin
Fay Franklin
Nancy Franklin
Mary Freer
Karen French
Rebecca Frost
Sally Fulham
Steve Fuller
Sharon Gabriele
Renée S. Gagnon
Lynn Gale
Majda Gama
Mel Gambier-Taylor
Elizabeth Gannon
Heather Gaona
Saffron Gardenchild
Ian Gardiner
Emma Gardner
Zoe Garnett
Deborah Gatty
Elaine Gauthier
Sam Gawith
Sarah Gay
Clare Gee
E Gee
Stephanie Gee
Jane Gelleburn
Sarah Gent
Josie George
Kirsten Gibbs
Claire Gibney
Justin Gilbert
Andrea Gilbey
Amber Gill

Andrene Gill
Laura Gill
Joanne Gillam
Tracy and Grace Gillard
Zofia Gilroy
Sharon Glosser
Sue Glynn
Dave Goddard
Maria Godebska
Jennifer Godman
Sophie Goldsworthy
Susan Goodfellow
Helena Goodman
Tristan Gooley
Mandy Gordon
Wrigley Juniper Gordon
Rachel Goswell
Susan Gottlieb
Kate Goulding
Sarah Goulding
Natalie Graeff
Emma Graham
Jayne Graham
Lyndsey Graham
Sue Grannon
Flick Grant
Rebecca Grave
Rebecca Greer
Amy Gregson
Dee Greig-Dunn
Jo Griffin
Mary Elizabeth Griffin
Louise Griffiths
Mike Griffiths
Rachel Griffiths
Lisa Grimm
Sharon Grimshaw
Helen Grimster
Michelle Grose
Rebecca Groves
Juliana Grundy

Robbie Guillory
Martin Gunnarsson
Rebecca Jobes Gurney
Sherril Gurney
Laura Guy
Kate Habberley
Terri Hackler
Julie Hadley
Michelle Hajder
Anna Hales
April Hall
Katie Hall
Laura Hall
Matt Hall
Jenny Hallett
Lisa Hallett Howard
Marie Halova
Lynne Hamel
Bryan Hamilton
Nicola Fox Hamilton
Sharon Hammond
Stephen Hampshire
Imogen Hampton
Margaret Hand
Samantha Handebo
Kate Hannaby
Cathy Hanson
Amanda Hanusch-Moore
Joan Haran
Mark Harbers
Emma Harcourt
Lisa Hardi
Emma Hardy
Hilary Harley
Candy Harman
Rebecca Harper
Rachel Harrington
Christine Harris
Laura Harris
Lisa Harris
Stephanie Harris

SUPPORTERS

Gale Hartel
Nicky Hartle
Nona Hartman
Kirsty Hartsiotis
E Ruth Harvey
Kay Harvey
Matt Harvey
John Harvie
Lynne Hastie
Anya Hastwell
Luke Hatton
Marianne Hauger
Kate Hawes
Emily Hawkins
Jerry Hawkins
Rebecca Hays
Denise Hayward
Sharon Hayward
Kate Haywood
Alexandra Hazanov
Trefor Hazlewood-Jones
Elspeth Head
Bethan Healey
Emma Heasman-Hunt
Anne-Marie Heighway
Lynne Henderson
Heather Henry
Elizabeth Henwood
Amanda Herbert
Shannon Hermes
Gill Hesketh – adored partner,
  beautiful friend
Amanda Heslegrave
Anneka Hess
Alice Hewitt
Jo Hewitt
Steph Heywood
Anne Hiatt
Jan Hicks
Carlien Hillebrink
Jo Hinde

Sharon Hinde
Bendy Hippy
Beth Hiscock
Kahana Ho
Jackie Hobbs
Emily Hodder
Martina Holbach
Jason Holdcroft
Rocki Holder
Samantha Holland
Katharine Holliday
Beth Hollins
Kim Holmes
Lynne Holt
Barbara Holten
Robyn Hopcroft
Pamela Hopkins
Sharon Hopkinson
Clare Horne
Sandra Horner
Philippa Hornsby
Catherine Horsley
Bill Horsman
Andy Horton
Peter Hoskin
Belinda Hosking
Caroline Howard
Jacki Howard
Nat Hudson
Sally Huggins
Clare Isobel Hughes
Dave Hughes
Jennifer Hughes
Linda Hughes
Michael Hughes
Robin Hughes
Yvette Huijsman
Daniel Hull
Sandy Humby
Vashti Humphrey
Rona Hunnisett

Leah, Rob, Riley and Oscar Hunt
Darcy Hurford
Marian Hurley
Claire Hutchinson
Jayne Hyde
Sophie Hylands
Alison Iliff
Bethany Ingles
Dagny Ingram
Hazel Ireland
Marie Irshad
Anna Jackson
Judith Jackson
Sherridon Jackson
Lindsey Jackson-Kay
Pamela Jacobs
Sandra James
Julie Jamison
Isobel Jarvis
Henry & Misti Jeffreys
Christine Jenner
Niki Jennings
Stinne Jensdotter
Marianne Brøndlund Jensen
Lisa Jepson
Wendy Jervis
Jo Jex
Kate Johns
Andrea Johnson
Vicki Johnson
Helen Johnston
Pauline Johnstone
Beverley Jones
Kate Jones
Laurel Jones
Lesley Jones
Meghan Jones
Myra Jones
Sue Jones
Susan Jones
Suzi Jones

Sally Jordan
Alice Jorgensen
Lise Jörgensen
Sara Joseph
Karen Jung
Vickie Kakia
Lura Kaplan
Matilda Karlsson
Lori Kasenter
Joanne Kaye
Nicola Keareyq
Maryrose Keenan
Frances Keeton
Michele Kelly
Christina Kennedy
Emily Kern
Debbie, Graeme, Rigby, Charlie
 & Dudley Kerr
Mary Kersey
Helen Kershaw
Audrey Keszek
Rosie Keszek
Vicky Kett
Jennifer Keynton & Lyra Triggs
Dan Kieran
Jill Kieran
Peta Kilbane
Talis Kimberley-Fairbourn
Denise Andrea King
Janet T King
Louise King
Jon Kiphart
Miranda Kirby
Claire Knight
Mel Knott
Patricia Knott
Rudy & Elmo Knott
Rick Koehler
Laurie Koerber
Teppo Koivula
Melanie Koorevaar

Christy Kotowski
Helen Kramer
Krystalwand Krystalwand
Laurie Kutoroff
Jenni Kylan-Mcleod
Samantha Laabs
Kevin Lack
Susan L Lacy
Stephanie Lahey
Anna Lambert
Agnès Landa
Peter Landers
Manda Pepper Langlinais
Karen Lankester
Alexandra LaPerruque
Joelle Lardi
Ash and Rowan Large
Izzie Latham
Terry Lavender
Jessica Law
Laurie Lawhorn
Judith Lawless
Stephanie Lay
Alison Layland
Linda Layland
Catherine Layne
Vianney le Masne
Katherine Leaf
Gill Leal
Capucine Lebreton
Diane Lee
Suzie Leighton
Naomi Leite
W. David LeMarble
Denne LePage-Ahlefeld
Kimberly Lepovsky
Barb Lerch
Catherine Lester
Mary Lester
Jane and Cliff Lethbridge
Jill Lethbridge

Amy Leung
Beth Lewis
Cath Lewis
Darlene Lewis
Katherine J. Lewis
Marian Lewis
Pam Lewis
Susan Leyland
Liiiiiiiiiiiiiiis Liiiiiiiiiiiiiiis
Bonnie Lilienfeld
Jill Lincoln
Susan Lindon-Hall
Diane Lindsay
Jonathan Ling
Steve Livingston
Lou Lloyd & Jan Robertson
Victoria Lloyd-Hughes
Louise Locock
Ellen Logstein
Anne Long
Kirrily Long
The Long Kitties of Boone, Iowa
Sheila Severs Loveland
Jennifer Lowe
Katherine Lowe
Jude Lucas-Mould
Helen Luker
Luna
Kara Luscombe
Amy Lynch
Michael Lynskey
Gill Lyon
Zoe Macdonald
Filipa Machado
Laura Machicao
Helen Mackenzie-Burrows
Emmalene Magill
Molly Mahoney
Catherine Makin
Jennifer Malise
Annemaree Maloney

Lynn Mancuso
Claire Mander
Christy Chanslor Mangini
Alice Mannering
Laura Manners
Michele Mantynen
Sheryl Mardlin
Judi Marie
Sharon Marks
Anne-Marie Marshall
Elissa Marshall
Wayne Marshall
Charlie Martin
Emma Rachel Martin
Lesley Kathryn Martin
Joanna Martins
Catherine Maslen
Catherine Mason
Inês Matos
Suzanne Matrosov-Vruggink
Olly Matthews
Vicky Maull
Jane Mawson
Hayley Maye
Cat McCabe
Mercedes McCarthy
Siobhan McClelland
Gill McColgan
Claire McConnell
Jennifer McConnell
Kate McCormack
Megan McCormick
Terri McCoy
Joel McCracken
Stuart McCulloch
Gayle McDonald
K McDonald-Johnson
Anna Gallen McDonough
Helen McElwee
Angela McGhin
Campbell McGill

Clare Mcglone
John A C McGowan
Ann McGregor
Alison McIntyre
Allan McKay
Colleen McKenna
Vanessa McLaughlin
Cate Mclaurin
Mandy McLernon
Rawnie McManus
Jason McMaster
Catherine McNamara
Leanna McPherson
Leanne McQuillan
Denise McSpadden
Dorothy Mead
Ffranses Medland
Francine Meek
Ben Mellor
Laura Mellor
Morag Melvin
Belinda Merchant
Stacy Merrick
Nicola Messenger
Kat Metcalf
Ali Middle
Elgiva Middleton
Beth Milford
Madz Millar
Jackie Miller
Libby Miller
Michelle Miller
Scott Millington
Chris Mills
Sara Mills
Kay Minchington
Adele Mitchell
Andrea Mitchell
Jacqueline Mitchell
Tina Mitchell
John Mitchinson

SUPPORTERS

Amber Moggie
Rowan Molyneux
Lani Momeyer
Bonnie Monroe
Slug Monroe
Natalie Moore
Janet Moorhouse
Sarah Mooring
Liz Moran
Sarah Moran
Elizabeth Morant
Dave Morgan
Jenny Morgan
Trish Morgan
Rhosyn Morgan-Davies
Charlie Morley
Katie Moroski
Mercy Morris
Sandra Morris
Suzie Morris
Katrina Moseley
Rachel Mosses
Sarah Mottershead
Juls Moulden
Sue Mowbray
Philippa Moxon
Florentina Mudshark
Linda Muller
Graham Mummery
Doreen Munden
Wendy Murguia
Claire Murphy
Lesley Murphy
Claire Murray
Clive Murray
Jane Alice Murray
Meg Murrell-Peloquin
Mel Mutter
Hugh N
Laura & Jason Nadler &
    their cats

Kirsten Naegele
Debbie Nairn
Sheila Nasea
Carlo Navato
Gemma Nelson
Sophie Nelson
Jane Nethercott
Tim Neville
Caroline Newell
Stephanie Newell
Sarah Newton-Scott
Ducky Nguyen
Laura Niall
Nicholasdouglass
Nicholasdouglass
Claire Nicholson
Liz Nicolson
Jacqueline Niehaus
Sue Nieland
Kate Noble
Cathy Nock
Holly Noe
Julie Noonan
Artur Nowrot
Adele Nozedar
Lynn Nugent
Rebecca O'Dwyer
Mark O'Neill
Hannah O'Regan
Andrew Oates
Sarah Oates
Sandra Oberbroeckling
Helen OHanlon
Gregory Olver
Linda Oostmeyer
Emily Oram
Caroline Ost
Bárbara Otero
Alison Owen
Deborah Owen
Emily, Jon and Axl Owen

Sue P
Scott Pack
Maria Padley
Earnie Painter
Jo Palfrey
Juliet Palfrey
Claire Palmer
Jane Palmer
Pam Palmer
Imogen Paradise
Lev Parikian
Lisa Parker
Catherine Parkin
Luke Parks
Sophia Passmore
70s Pat
Karen Paton
Trish Paton
Gill Patterson
Carolyn Paul
Cara Payne
Emma Payne
Noreen Pazderski
Rachel Pearce
Ann Peet
Rachel Pellowe
Karie Penhaligon
Heather Pennington
Pam Penzey
Ryan Perry & Lisa Perryman
Dave Peterson
Leslie Phelps
Joel Phillips
Sandra Piche
Maria Pickering
Alvis Piksons
Kelsey Pilkington
Awkward Pisswhiskers
Julia Pitcher
Terri Platas
Hannah Platts
Jo Plumridge

Lucy Plunkett
Justin Pollard
Frances Pook
Jackie Poole
Jennifer Porrett
Naomi Porter
Selina Postgate
Nicola Poulter
Gill Powell
Lindsay Powell
Kate Power
Brooke Pownceby
Catherine Prendergast
Virginia Preston
Emma Prew
Jo Price
Susan E. Priller
Christina Pullman
Kate Pyle
Lisa Quattromini
Kate Quayle
Melissa Quinn
Rachel and Sherlock
Agnieszka Raczek
Sue Radford
Helen Rainbow
Lucy Raine
Laura E. Ramos
Ann Rance
Peter Randall
Tina Rashid
David Ratcliffe
Karl Ravenstone
Anne Rawnsley
Angela Rayson
Caroline Read
Kerie Receveur
Victoria Reed
Alison Rees
Ian Rees
Sue Reid
Vivienne Reid-Brown

Nuala Reilly
Peg Reilly
A. A. Pancho Reyes
Marie Reyes
Debra Rhodes
Lesley Rhodes
Maureen Rice
Elizabeth Richards
Julie Richards
Melissa Richards
Judith Riches
Ruth Richmond
Henry Ridgwell
Lisa Riffe
Joseph Riley
Meryl Rimmer
Nicola Rimmer
Vicky Rimmington
Gina Rinehart
Kerry Rini
Diane Ritter
Susanna Roberts
Amanda Robertson
Anna Robertson
Marie Robertson
Matthew Robertson
Leanne Robins
Lesley Robinson
Louise Robinson
Rachael Robinson
Julie Robison
Rachel Robison
Kathryn Rochard
Patricia Rockwell
Mike Rodriguez
Jane Roe
Valerie Roebuck
Beastie Cat & Cassie Cat Rogers
Breony Rogers
Jeanette Rogers
Josie Rogers

Anne Gleeson Ronan
Donna Rooney
Vikki Rose
Catherine Rosevear
Elizabeth Rothwell
Nanette Rudge
Sue Rupp
Gillian S. Russell
Michael Russell
Tony Russell
Nicola Ruth
Angela Rutter
Julie Rutter
Nick Rutter
Sioban Ryan-Togni
Marie S
Katelin Safford
Puskas Salts
Marie Sandland
Callum Saunders
John Saunders
Adrian Savage
Christine Savage
Sarah Savage
Sherri Savage
Diane Schmidt
Samantha Schofield
Wag Schofield
Anne-Marie Scott
Carolyn Scott
Sarah Scott
Betsy Scroggs
Alison Scruton
Rose Seabury
Jane Seager
Rachel Marie Seale
Amy Seales
Andrew Seaman
Peter and Angela Seary
Carly Seddon
Yvette Sedgley

SUPPORTERS

Emma Selwood
Elena Senra
Katherine Setchell
Mariese Shallard
Christine Shanks
Katie Shanks
Lori Shannon
Iola Shaw
Jane-Anne Shaw
Jon Shaw
Matt Shaw
Lloyd Shepherd
Emmajane Sheppard
Jo Sherwood
Josephine Sherwood
Helen Shiner
Neil Shipman
Karen Shipway
Rachel Shirley
Jo Short
Laura Sibra
Jenn Siegel
Isabelle Sikora
Nicola Simpson
Melissa Sims
Susanna Basso Sinagra
Ruth Sinclair
Ruth Singer
SisterRainbow
Caroline Skelton
Debbie Slater
Jane Slavin
Jenny Slide
Toby Sligo
Zoe Slocombe
Smalls
Smidgen of The Far Pavilion
Alice Smith
Carolyn Smith
Charlotte Smith
Christina Smith

Daniel Smith
Hannah Smith
Julian Smith
Kate Smith
Lan-Lan Smith
Liz Smith
Maggie Smith
MTA Smith
Nicola Smith
Rosemary Smith
Sarah Smith
Sheila Smith
Therese Smout
Susan Smyth
Lynnae Sniker
Ingrid Solberg
Yve Solbrekken
Roberta Solmundson
Kristy Sorensen
Caroline Sparks
Gregory Spawton
Lyn Speakman
Gem Spear
Lisa Burton Spears
Maureen Kincaid Speller
Rosslyn Spokes
Rosemary Spragg
Kathy Springer
Luke Spry
Helene Stafleu
Andy Stainsby
Pam Stanier
Arwen Stanton
Debbie Stark
Hannah Stark
Inger Bjurnemark Stark
Rory Steabler
Cheryl Steckel
Ros Stern
Kirsty Stevenson
Damian Stewart

SUPPORTERS

Sticky-Sounds Zine
Mary Stoicoiu
Shelagh Stoicoiu
Bob Stone
Carmen Stone
Emma Jane Stone
Samantha Storey
Stephanie Strahan
Jennifer Strait
Angela Stratford
Duncan Strickland
Jess Stroud
Amanda Sturt
Carol Styles
Richard Sulley
Sioned Summers-Taylor
Helen E Sunderland
Adam Sussman
Laurel Sutton
Sophie Swainger
Nick Sweeney
Catherine Sweet
Toni Swiffen
Russell Swindle
Kirsty Syder
Angela Sykes
SarahLouise Tallack
Gipsi Tana
Rebecca Tanner
Alison Taylor
Beverley Taylor
Brigid Taylor
Dave Taylor
James Taylor
Shereen Taylor
Tracy Taylor
Peter Taylor & Kim Jarvis
Caitlin Tefft
Jennifer R Teichmann
Gareth Tennant
Courtney Tetreault

Sue Tett
Kim Thain
Will Thames
Janis Thomas
Mary Law Thomas
Andrea Thompson
Claire Thompson
Dena Thompson
Fern Thompson
Helen Thompson
Mary Ann Thompson
Kylie, Donna, Shelley &
  Lynne Thomson
Mark Thornton
Donna Tickner
Lynne Tidmarsh
Eloise Tierney
Adam Tinworth
Joanne Todd
Delyth Toghill
Stacy Tomaszewski
Crystal Tompkins
Deborah Toner
Costanza Torrebruno
Angela Townsend
Ryan Trainor
Karen Trethewey
Katherine Trill
Katie Truax
Noah True-Daniels
Kate Tudor
Jill Tulasiewicz
Mason Turner
Nicola Turner
Russell Turner
Ruth Turner
Dom Tyler
Mark Tyler
Mike Vallano
Eva van der Leen
Elisabeth Van Every

SUPPORTERS

Robin Van Sant
Anne Vasey
Hannah Velten
Colette Verdun
Alexander Verkooijen
Tamy Vermande
Kellie Vernon
Vikki, Fay and Matilda
Sally Vince
Vivian Vincek
Rosalind Vincent
Lisa Vine
Alice Violett
Kate Viscardi
Clarisse Visch
Louise Vlach
Nicole Vlach
Ann TeethingBeastie Voelkel
Mary Beth Vono
Katherine Wadbrook
Frey Waddams
Leslie Wainger
Laura Wainwright
Tim Wakeham
Sarah Wakes
Karen Waldron
Charlotte Walker
Joni Walker
Mand Walker
Mike Walker
Paul Walker
Pip Walker
Robin M. Walker
Robsa Walker
Heather Wallace
Karen Wallace
Alison Waller
Dr Alison Waller
Linda Wallis
Declan Walsh
Matthew Walton

Jamie Ward
Joolz Ward
Toni Warmuth
Alice Watkins
Laura Watkins
Susie Watson
James Watt
Catherine Watts
Cathrine Watz
Stewart Waudby
Tracey Waudby
Lesley Wealleans
Nina and Roy Weaver
Weaverbird
Linda Webb
M. F. Webb
Lisa Webster
Daniel Weir
Aletta Welensky
Dawn Welham
Jane Werry
Casey West
Elizabeth West
Lyn West
Lucy Weston
Fiona Whalley
Sara Wharton
David Wheatley
Katy Wheatley
Hannah Whelan
Kate White
Rebecca White
Mark Whitehead
Robert Whitelock
Miranda Whiting
Annalise Whittaker
Laura Wilce
Badger Wild
Peter Wilde
Annette Wilkinson
Wendy Wilkinson

Lorna Will
Jeff Willans
Linda Willars
Caroline Williams
Karl Williams
Becca Williamson
Claire Willis
Laura Willis
Corrine Willson
Joan Wilson
Kirsten Wilson
Laura Wilson
Oliver Wilton
Kim Winspear
Anna Wittmann
Sally Woller
Becky Wood
John Wood
Judith Wood
Laura Wood
Laura Woods
Cate Woodward
Nick Wookey
Alison Woolcock

Brenda Wordsworth
Vanessa Worrall
David Wrennall
Beth Wright
Elizabeth Wright
Melanie Wright
Melissa Wright
Rachel Wright
Susan Bakalar Wright
Diana and Alun Wyburn-
  Arseneau-Powell
Jeremiah Wyke
Jo Wynell-Mayow
Neil Yeaman
Amanda Yeardsley
Jo Yeates
Jennifer Yocum
Julie Hazel Young
Lindsay Zaborowski
Ellen Zahl
Marcin Zajko
Birgit Zimmermann-Nowak
Jen Zvirgzdins